山形県の教員採用試験過去問シリーズ⑤

2025年度版

山形県の 英語科

過去問

協同教育研究会 編

協同出版

本書には，山形県の教員採用試験の過去問題を収録しています。各問題ごとに，以下のように5段階表記で，難易度，頻出度を示しています。

難易度

非常に難しい	☆☆☆☆☆
やや難しい	☆☆☆☆
普通の難易度	☆☆☆
やや易しい	☆☆
非常に易しい	☆

頻出度

◎	ほとんど出題されない
◎◎	あまり出題されない
◎◎◎	普通の頻出度
◎◎◎◎	よく出題される
◎◎◎◎◎	非常によく出題される

※本書の過去問題における資料，法令文等の取り扱いについて

本書の過去問題で使用されている資料や法令文の表記や基準は，出題された当時の内容に準拠しているため，解答・解説も当時のものを使用しています。ご了承ください。

はじめに～「過去問」シリーズ利用に際して～

教育を取り巻く環境は変化しつつあり，日本の公教育そのものも，教員免許更新制の廃止やGIGAスクール構想の実現などの改革が進められています。また，現行の学習指導要領では「主体的・対話的で深い学び」を実現するため，指導方法や指導体制の工夫改善により，「個に応じた指導」の充実を図るとともに，コンピュータや情報通信ネットワーク等の情報手段を活用するために必要な環境を整えることが示されています。

一方で，いじめや体罰，不登校，暴力行為など，教育現場の問題もあいかわらず取り沙汰されており，教員に求められるスキルは，今後さらに高いものになっていくことが予想されます。

本書の基本構成としては，出題傾向と対策，過去5年間の出題傾向分析表，過去問題，解答および解説を掲載しています。各自治体や教科によって掲載年数をはじめ，「チェックテスト」や「問題演習」を掲載するなど，内容が異なります。

また原則的には一般受験を対象としております。特別選考等については対応していない場合があります。なお，実際に配布された問題の順番や構成を，編集の都合上，変更している場合があります。あらかじめご了承ください。

最後に，この「過去問」シリーズは，「参考書」シリーズとの併用を前提に編集されております。参考書で要点整理を行い，過去問で実力試しを行う，セットでの活用をおすすめいたします。

みなさまが，この書籍を徹底的に活用し，教員採用試験の合格を勝ち取って，教壇に立っていただければ，それはわたくしたちにとって最上の喜びです。

協同教育研究会

C O N T E N T S

第１部

山形県の
英語科
出題傾向分析

山形県の英語科　傾向と対策

2024年度では，これまでと異なり中学校，高等学校の区別なく共通問題となっている。

リスニング問題，文法・語法問題，読解問題，和文英訳問題などが出題されている点は変わらない。2023年度と比べて，出題傾向，大問ごとの配点に大きな変動は見られない。

リスニング問題は，対話や英文を聞いて，その内容についての質問に対する適切な答えを選ぶ選択肢の問題や，ディクテーション形式などで構成されている。放送が一度しか流れない問題もあるが，問題のレベルとして特に難解なものはない。全体の所要時間は約15分，問題量としてはやや多めなので，実用英語検定準1級程度の教材で一定時間リスニング問題に取り組む感覚をつかんでおくとよいだろう。短文ディクテーション形式も継続して出題されることが予想されるので，苦手な人は，リスニング問題のナレーションを利用し英文1文を書き取るなどして，対策をとっておきたい。

文法・語法問題は，2024年度も主として文法知識および語彙力を問う空所補充問題のみ出題されている。設問は15問と多いが，難易度は大学入試レベルでさほど難問ではない。過去問題を解くほか，大学入試レベルの文法問題集を1冊仕上げておくことで対処可能であろう。

読解問題は，2024年度では長文読解総合問題が中高共通2題，2023年度では中高共通問題1題，中学校選択問題1題であったため，ここは大きく変更になった点である。英文量は共に700語から800語程度で多少長くなり，難易度は大学入試上級レベルと考えてよい。設問は選択式の空所補充，英問英答，内容に関する記述問題などバラエティーに富んでいる。設問は語義や内容に関する選択式問題もあるが，英語，日本語，両方による記述式問題の割合が大きい。記述問題では，本文に即して正確に訳出することが求められている。過去問題を解くほか，同レベルの長文問題集で読解力をつけておくとよい。

2024年度の長文の内容は火星や言語学習をテーマにした科学記事であった。例年教育や言語に関するテーマが多かったが，関連の情報には日頃からできるだけ目を通しつつ，他の分野についても英語の雑誌や記事などで多読しておくことが望ましい。

上記のほか，和文英訳が1題と学習指導要領を踏まえて授業案を提示する100語程度の英作文が1題出題されている。和文英訳は，問題文が比較的短く，特にひねった問題ではないが，ひとつの文にひとつの正解があるわけではないので，より多くの慣用表現や文法事項・構文を学習し，間違いのない英訳を心がけることが必要である。

英作文では，学習指導要領の内容を理解したうえで，設問の趣旨を汲み取った実践的な指導やその効果，留意点などを書くよう求められている。日頃から学習指導要領に目を通し，実際に現場で行われている授業の指導法なども把握しておくことを勧める。

2023年度はICT機器をどのように指導に取り入れるかというテーマが出題されていたが，2024年度はネイティブスピーカーや英語が堪能な地域人材の活用についてであった。平均的に1文で20語～25語程度と考えると4～5文を目安にすればよいことがわかる。100語程度の語数制限の下，自分の考えをまとめられるよう書き慣れておこう。また自分の考えを英語で表現できるよう語彙や表現のストックを持っておくとよい。

過去5年間の出題傾向分析

中学＝●　高校＝▲　中高共通＝◎

分類	設問形式	2020年度	2021年度	2022年度	2023年度	2024年度
リスニング	内容把握	◎	◎	◎	◎	◎
発音・アクセント	発音					
	アクセント					
	文強勢					
文法・語法	空所補充	◎	◎	◎	◎	◎
	正誤判断					
	一致語句					
	連立完成					
	その他					
会話文	短文会話					
	長文会話					
文章読解	空所補充	◎		◎▲	◎▲	◎
	内容一致文	●▲	●▲	◎●▲	◎●▲	◎
	内容一致語句	◎▲	▲	◎	◎●▲	◎
	内容記述	◎●▲	●▲	◎●▲	◎●▲	◎
	英文和訳					
	英問英答	◎●▲	●▲	●▲	●▲	◎
	その他			◎●	◎●▲	
英作文	整序					
	和文英訳	●▲	●▲	●▲	●▲	◎
	自由英作	●▲	●▲	●▲	●▲	◎
	その他					
学習指導要領		●▲	●▲			

第２部

山形県の
教員採用試験
実施問題

2024年度　実施問題

【中高共通】

【１】(放送による問題)これはリスニング・テストです。放送の指示に従って答えなさい。

ただいまから，リスニング・テストを行います。問題は，1，2，3，4の四つです。聞いている間にメモを取っても構いません。

1　では，1の問題から始めます。問題は，No. 1とNo. 2の2問です。

これから読まれる英文に対する応答として最もふさわしいものを，続いで読まれるa，b，cの中から一つ選び，記号で答えなさい。答えは，大文字，小文字どちらでも構いません。なお，英文と応答は1度しか読まれません。

では，始めます。

No. 1　I heard you have a sweet tooth.

a. Yes. I can't resist eating sweets.

b. Yes. I will sweep the floor.

c. Yes. You can have the one.

No. 2　I wonder why my smartphone doesn't have good reception now.

a. You must be smart enough to memorize the number.

b. Maybe because we're out of range here in the basement.

c. Did you leave your smartphone at reception yesterday?

2　次に，2の問題に移ります。問題は，No. 1からNo. 3までの3問です。

これから，短い対話文を読みます。そのあとでクエスチョンと言っ

て質問します。その答えとして最もふさわしいものを，続いて読まれるa，b，c，dの中から一つ選び，記号で答えなさい。答えは，大文字，小文字どちらでも構いません。なお，対話文・質問・答えの選択肢は1度しか読まれません。

では，始めます。

No. 1 M: Excuse me, do you have a smaller microwave oven around this price?

W: We are out of stock now, but well have some in a few weeks.

M: Well, I'd really like to get one sooner.

W: I see. Our other stores in this area might have some, so could you give me some time to check? If you give me your e-mail address, I'll tell you which store can help you.

Question: What does the clerk need to know?

a. The price of a microwave oven.

b. The address of a store in another area.

c. The customer's contact information.

d. The time the customer will call the clerk.

No. 2 M: The radio is too loud. I can't concentrate on my studies. Who turned it on?

W: I did. You know I always do the housework listening to music. It helps me finish the household chores quickly.

M: Mom, I am trying hard to complete all of my weekend homework assignments today, since my cousin is visiting us tomorrow. We want to enjoy our time with him, don't we?

W: All right, you win.

Question: What will the mother most likely do right after this conversation?

a. She will most likely help her son complete the housework.

b. She will most likely assign another chore to the cousin.

c. She will most likely go and see the cousin with her son.

d. She will most likely turn the radio down or turn it off.

No. 3　W: Hey, Kevin, did you get the cat you were talking about?

M: I've been thinking about whether to get it or not, but I can't make up my mind yet.

W: Are you concerned about the cost?

M: It's not that, and my house has enough space to keep a pet. It's that I'm away on business a lot, and I can't leave a cat alone.

W: Don't you know that we have a machine to feed cats automatically and a webcam to monitor them?

M: Really? I didn't know that. Thank you for your advice.

Question: Why is Kevin hesitating about owning a cat?

a. Because he usually leaves for work late.

b. Because he travels frequently on business.

c. Because he has no room for it in his house.

d. Because he thinks it would cost too much.

3　次に3の問題に移ります。問題は，No. 1からNo. 3までの3問です。

これから，あるまとまりのある英文を読みます。そのあとで，クエスチョンズと言って，その英文について三つの質問をします。その答えとして最もふさわしいものを，質問に続いて読まれるa，b，c，dの中から一つ選び，記号で答えなさい。答えは，大文字，小文字どちらでも構いません。なお，英文・質問・答えの選択肢は全体を通して2回読まれます。

では，始めます。

The internet's first personal data collectors were websites and applications. By tracking users' activities online, marketers could deliver targeted advertising and content. More recently, intelligent technology in physical products has allowed companies in many industries to collect new types of information, including users' locations and behavior. The personalization this data allows, such as constant adaptation to users' preferences, has become central to the product experience.

The rich new streams of data have also made it possible to tackle complex challenges in fields such as health care, environmental protection, and urban planning. Take Medtronic's digital blood-glucose meter. It alerts patients and health care providers that blood-glucose levels are nearing troubling thresholds, allowing preemptive treatments. And the car service Uber has recently agreed to share ride-pattern data with Boston officials so that the city can improve transportation planning and prioritize road maintenance. These and countless other applications are increasing the power — and value — of personal data.

Of course, this flood of data presents enormous opportunities for abuse. Large-scale security breaches, such as the recent theft of the credit card information of 56 million Home Depot customers, expose consumers' vulnerability to malicious agents. But revelations about companies' covert activities also make consumers nervous. Target, an American retailer, famously aroused alarm when it was revealed that they used data mining to identify shoppers who were likely to be pregnant — in some cases before they'd told anyone.

Questions

No. 1 What has become central to the product experience?

a. Locating users online constantly has.

b. Finding users' behavioral patterns has.

c. Protecting users' personal information has.

d. Adapting to users' tastes continuously has.

No. 2 What can Boston officials do by making use of the rich new streams of data?

a. They can improve transportation planning for their city.
b. They can prioritize the needs of vehicle service companies.
c. They can request Uber to repair and maintain the roadways.
d. They can help the citizens develop smartphone applications.

No. 3 What is true about the passage?

a. The internet's first personal data collectors monitored users' activities online but failed to deliver targeted content.
b. Medtronic's digital blood-glucose meter alerts users only when blood-glucose levels pass troubling thresholds.
c. When security breaches occur on a large scale, they leave consumers open to attack from malicious agents.
d. Consumers never know the fact that data mining has been conducted to identify a specific group of people secretly.

4　次に4の問題に移ります。問題は，No. 1とNo. 2の2問です。
これから，英語による対話文を読みます。(　　)のところに入る英語を聞き取り，書きなさい。対話文はそれぞれ2回読まれます。
では，始めます。

No. 1　M: I think we should start planning our upcoming vacation.
W: Well, (　　　　　　　　　　)?

No. 2　W: Dad, I'm going out to play tennis with my friends.
M: OK, but don't (　　　　　　　　　　).

これで，リスニング・テストを終わります。次の問題に移ってください。

(☆☆☆☆◎◎◎)

【2】次の英文や対話文の中の(　　)に最も適するものを，以下のア～エの中からそれぞれ一つずつ選び，記号で答えなさい。

1　As she had a bad stomachache, she was made (　　) the bitter medicine against her will.

ア　take　　イ　to take　　ウ　be taken　　エ　taking

2　If I had followed all the good advice that was given to me when I was a child, I (　　) a better person now.

ア　was　　イ　will be　　ウ　would have been　　エ　would be

3　My colleagues objected (　　) backcountry skiing alone.

ア　to my going　　イ　me of going　　ウ　me to going

エ　on me to go

4　Lisa and Meg are still on the waiting list, and until they get confirmed flight reservations their travel plans are (　　).

ア　up in arms　　イ　up to date　　ウ　up and about

エ　up in the air

5　All things (　　), I think we made a successful presentation.

ア　consideration　　イ　considering　　ウ　considered

エ　to consider

6　Only on a few occasions (　　) think to wear that luxurious dress.

ア　never she would　　イ　would she ever　　ウ　she did not

エ　she would

7　Gas, coal, and nuclear power account for 37 percent, 32 percent, and 6 percent (　　) of the energy supply.

ア　immensely　　イ　eminently　　ウ　respectively

エ　collaboratively

8　As Andy was young, he was (　　). He was so concerned about his appearance that he spent nearly all his salary on suits, shoes, and ties.

ア　profound　　イ　inopportune　　ウ　consecutive　　エ　vain

9　A few days ago I (　　) while working outside. When I woke up, I was being carried to the hospital by ambulance.

ア　diluted　　イ　fainted　　ウ　collected　　エ　persisted

10　The new recruit in our section (　　) his lack of experience by working hard.

ア　compared with　　イ　combined against　　ウ　compensated for

エ　competed with

11　Most of the fans got so (　　) with the pop star's performance that they started screaming.

ア　carried away　　イ　dolled up　　ウ　mixed up

エ　picked off

12　The surgeon's office building is (　　) to the hospital building, so it is very easy for him to visit his recovering patients.

ア　intrepid　　イ　errant　　ウ　flawless　　エ　adjacent

13　A: Bob, how is your diet going?

B: Not so good. Yesterday I (　　) to temptation and had a second helping of ice cream.

ア　succumbed　　イ　tarnished　　ウ　swaggered　　エ　hassled

14　The trek across the mountains turned out to be more (　　) than the aid workers had expected. By the time they reached the refugee camp, most of them were worn out.

ア　laconic　　イ　shattered　　ウ　arduous　　エ　contingent

15　Many cheeses produced in this region are well known for their (　　) aromas, but if you are a cheese enthusiast, you will not mind their smells at all.

ア　incumbent　　イ　pungent　　ウ　nimble　　エ　gullible

(☆☆☆☆◎◎◎)

【3】次の英文を読んで，以下の問いに答えなさい。

Re-creating Mars as it was four billion years ago using climate and terrain models, researchers concluded methane-producing microbes could once have thrived mere centimeters below much of the Red Planet's surface, consuming atmospheric hydrogen and carbon dioxide while protected by overlying sediment. But that buried biosphere would have ultimately retreated deeper into the planet, driven by freezing temperatures of its own making — perhaps to its ①<u>doom</u>. Their study, published in *Nature Astronomy*, proposes that the interchange among hydrogen, carbon dioxide and methane (all heat-trapping greenhouse gases) would have triggered global cooling that covered most of Mars's surface with inhospitable ice.

"Basically what we say is that life, when it appears on the planet and in the right condition, might be self-destructive," says study lead author Boris Sauterey, a postdoctoral fellow at Sorbonne University. "It's that self-destructive tendency which might be limiting the ability of life to emerge widely in the universe."

In 1965 the late chemist and ecologist James Lovelock — then a researcher at NASA's Jet Propulsion Laboratory — argued that certain chemical compounds in an atmosphere act as biosignatures indicating life's presence on another world. On Earth, for instance, the coexistence of methane (from methane-producing bacteria, called methanogens) with oxygen (from photosynthetic organisms) constitutes a potent biosignature: each gas eradicates the other in ambient conditions, so the persistence of both indicates a steady replenishment most easily explained by biological sources. Lovelock's work forms the basis of today's scientific search for alien life. It also informs the Gaia hypothesis, which he codified with biologist Lynn Margulis during the 1970s. This hypothesis, named after a "Mother Earth" deity from Greek mythology, suggests that life is *self-regulating:* Earth's organisms collectively interact with their surroundings in a way that maintains environmental habitability. For instance, higher global temperatures from excess atmospheric carbon dioxide also (X) plant growth, which in turn siphons more of the greenhouse gas from the air, eventually returning the planet to a cooler state.

In 2009 University of Washington paleontologist Peter Ward put forward a less optimistic view. At planetary scales, Ward argued, life is more self-destructive than self-regulating and eventually wipes itself out. In contrast to the Gaia hypothesis, he named his idea after another figure from Greek mythology: Medea, a mother who kills her own children. To support (1)his *Medea hypothesis*, Ward cited several past mass extinction events on Earth that suggest life has an inherently self-destructive nature. During the Great Oxidation Event more than two billion years ago, for instance, photosynthetic cyanobacteria pumped huge amounts of the gas into Earth's oxygen-starved atmosphere. This eradicated the earlier dominant life-forms: methanogens and other anaerobic organisms for which oxygen was toxic. "You just look back at Earth's history, and you see periods where life was its own worst enemy," says Ward, who was not involved in the new study. "And I think this certainly could've been the case on Mars."

On Earth, though, the flood of oxygen also proved crucial for biological diversification and the eventual emergence of our biosphere's multicellular ancestors — showing that (Y). Until life is found on other worlds, however, we are left to examine the question through theoretical studies such as Sauterey's.

Kaveh Pahlevan, a research scientist at the SETI Institute, who was not involved in the study, says that the work "does broaden the way we think about the effects that biospheres can have on habitability." But he notes that it considers only the planet-altering effects of one metabolism type. The study would not capture the intricacy of something akin to the Great Oxidation Event, which ②hinged on the conflicting influences of methanogens and cyanobacteria. Sauterey acknowledges this limitation: "You can imagine that a more complex, more diversified [Martian] biosphere would not have had the negative effect on planet habitability that just methanogens would have had," he says. The study highlights how a complex ecosystem, like that of early Earth, may be essential to recovery from otherwise catastrophic environmental change.

Beyond life's potential fate, the study suggests a way to find it: Although the researchers did not explore the possibility of present-day methanogens lurking deep within Mars's subsurface, they did pinpoint places untouched by ice for large swaths of the planet's history where such microbes could have once thrived closer to the surface. One spot is Jezero Crater, the current target of the *Perseverance rover's search for biosignature-bearing materials. But (2)<u>it</u> is possible that fossil evidence of early methane-producing microbes would be under too much sediment for Perseverance to reach.

(注) *Perseverance：パーシビアランス(米国の火星探査車)

(Allison Gasparini, "Mars's Downfall" , *SCIENTIFIC AMERICAN*, February 2023による。ただし，設問の都合で一部省略及び改変している。)

1 下線部①，②を別の語で言い換えたとき，最も意味の近いものを，次のア～エの中からそれぞれ一つずつ選び，記号で答えなさい。

① ア dignity　イ diagnosis　ウ deterrent　エ death

② ア stayed　イ depended　ウ passed　エ seized

2 本文中の空欄(X), (Y)に入る英語として最も適切なものを，次のア～エの中からそれぞれ一つずつ選び，記号で答えなさい。

X ア vomit　イ convince　ウ boost　エ evaporate

Y ア defining a situation as Gaian or Medean might be a matter of perspective

イ Ward has also supported the Gaian point of view as a coauthor of the study

ウ this dramatic increase in the amount of oxygen subsequently devastated Mars

エ it is only a question of time before Lovelock discovers more evidence of it

3　下線部(1)の中でWardが主張したことを，本文に即して日本語で書きなさい。

4　下線部(2)が指す内容を，本文に即して日本語で書きなさい。

5　本文の内容に即して，次の問いに英語で答えなさい。

(1)　According to Sauterey and his members, what could methanogens have consumed on Mars?

(2)　Under the Gaia hypothesis, how does the collective interplay of living things with their surroundings occur on Earth?

6　本文の内容に最も合うものを，次のア～オの中から一つ選び，記号で答えなさい。

ア　Sauterey says that life's self-destructive nature allows more life-forms to appear in the universe.

イ　More than two gases are necessary to show a biosignature on any planet.

ウ　Cyanobacteria absorbed a huge amount of oxygen during the Great Oxidation Event.

エ　Pahlevan points out that the study led by Sauterey has a certain limitation.

オ　Sauterey and others found places to examine the possibility of microbes still living on Mars.

(☆☆☆☆☆◎◎◎)

【４】次の英文を読んで，以下の問いに答えなさい。

For proficient speakers, choosing words, pronouncing them, and stringing them together with the appropriate grammatical markers is essentially automatic. Furthermore, much of what these speakers say is drawn from predictable patterns of language that are at least partly formulaic. That is, fluent speakers do not create new sentences by choosing one word at a time but rather by using strings of words that typically occur together. This use of patterns applies not only to idiomatic expressions, but also to much conversational language and written language in a specific genre (Ellis, Simp son -Vlach, and Maynard 2008).

Another aspect of automaticity in language processing is the retrieval of word meanings. When proficient listeners hear a familiar word, even for a split second, they cannot help but understand it. Such automatic responses do not use up the kind of resources needed for processing new information. Thus, proficient language users can give their full attention to the overall meaning of a text or conversation, whereas less proficient learners use more of their attention on processing the meaning of individual words and the relationships between them. The lack of automatic access to meaning helps to explain why second language readers need more time to understand a text, even if they eventually do fully comprehend it. $_{(1)}$The information processing model suggests that there is a limit to the amount of focused mental activity we can engage in at one time.

Information processing approaches to second language acquisition have been explored by many researchers. Drawing on J. R. Anderson's (1995) work, Robert DeKeyser (1998, 2001, 2007) and others have investigated second language acquisition as 'skill learning'. They suggest that most learning, including language learning, starts with declarative knowledge, that is, knowledge that we are aware of having, for example, a grammar rule. The hypothesis is that, through practice, declarative knowledge may become procedural knowledge, or the ability to use the knowledge. With continued practice, the procedural knowledge can become automatized and the learner may forget having learned it first as declarative knowledge.

According to this perspective, once skills become automatized, thinking about the declarative knowledge while trying to perform the skill actually disrupts the smooth performance of it. Think, for example, of trying to drive a car or skate while intentionally thinking about and preparing every move. With enough practice, procedural knowledge eclipses the declarative knowledge, which, in time, may be forgotten. For this reason, fluent speakers may not even realize that they once possessed the declarative knowledge that set the process in (X).

Sometimes changes in language behaviour do not seem to be explainable in terms of a gradual build-up of fluency through practice. These changes have been described in terms of restructuring (McLaughlin 1990). They seem to be based on some qualitative change in the learner's knowledge. Restructuring may account for what appear to be bursts of progress, when learners suddenly seem to 'put it all together', even though they have not had any new instruction or apparently relevant exposure to the language. (Y) For example, when a learner finally masters the use of the regular *-ed* ending to show past tense, irregular verbs that had previously been used correctly may be affected. Thus, after months of saying 'I saw a film', the learner may say 'I seed' or even 'I sawed'. Such overgeneralization errors are not based on practice of those specific items but rather on their integration into a general pattern.

Another concept from psychology offers insight into how learners store and retrieve language. According to transfer-appropriate processing (TAP), (2)<u>information is best retrieved in situations that are similar to those in which it was acquired</u> (Lightbown 2008b). This is because when we learn something our memories also record aspects of the context in which it was learned and even the cognitive processes involved in the way we learned it, for example, by reading or hearing it. To date, most of the research on transfer-appropriate processing has been done in laboratory experiments, for example, comparing the learning of word lists under different conditions. However, the hypothesis seems to offer a (Z) way of explaining a widely observed phenomenon in second language learning: knowledge that is acquired mainly in rule learning or drill activities may be easier to access on tests that resemble the learning activities than in communicative situations. On the other hand, if learners' attention is drawn to grammatical forms during communicative activities in which their cognitive resources are occupied with a focus on meaning, the retrieval of those forms on a grammar test may be more difficult.

(Patsy M. Lightbown and Nina Spada, *How Languages are Learned Fourth edition*による。ただし，設問の都合で一部省略している。)

1　下線部(1)はどのようなことを示唆しているか，本文に即して日本語で書きなさい。

2　本文中の空欄(　X　)～(　Z　)に入る英語として最も適切なものを，次のア～オの中からそれぞれ一つずつ選び，記号で答えなさい。

X　ア　doubt　イ　motion　ウ　haste　エ　parallel
オ　summary

Y　ア　Also, it is more likely that a lower proficiency learner produces fewer self-repairs than a high proficiency learner in a task designed for using a correct tense.

イ　Therefore, learners may extract evidence about their utterances, including whether for the target language the structure they produced was acceptable or not.

ウ　It may also explain apparent backsliding, when a systematic aspect of a learner's language incorporates too much or incorporates the wrong things.

エ　However, a few studies show that learners receiving recasts are outperformed by learners provided with other forms of corrective feedback.

オ　This progress frees up the learners' cognitive resources to notice other aspects of a language and makes their working knowledge of it more sophisticated.

Z　ア　prolific　イ　nomadic　ウ　compulsory　エ　docile
オ　plausible

3　下線部(2)の理由を，本文に即して日本語で書きなさい。

4　本文の内容に即して，次の問いに英語で答えなさい。

(1)　According to the author, what can proficient language users concentrate on when they are retrieving word meanings of a text or conversation automatically?

(2) According to the author, what happens if people try to perform their automatized skill and simultaneously think about the declarative knowledge?

(3) Has most of the research on transfer-appropriate processing been conducted outside a laboratory until now?

5 本文の内容に最も合うものを，次のア～オの中から一つ選び，記号で答えなさい。

ア Proficient speakers don't use predictable patterns of language, but select each word carefully to express themselves.

イ The reading speed of second language learners is unexplainable in terms of how automatic their access to meaning is.

ウ DeKeyser and others studied second language acquisition as 'skill learning', which helped finish Anderson's work in 1995.

エ Restructuring may explain some cases where rapid and noticeable advancements in language proficiency occur.

オ How learners pay attention during communicative activities doesn't influence their performance on a grammar test.

(☆☆☆☆☆◎◎◎)

【５】次の1，2について，指示に従って答えなさい。

1 次の日本語を英語に直しなさい。

全ての従業員が建設的に意見を交わすことができる職場環境をつくることは，全ての人にとって有益だ。

2 「中学校学習指導要領」(平成29年3月告示)及び「高等学校学習指導要領」(平成30年3月告示)には，「指導計画の作成や授業の実施に当たっては，ネイティブ・スピーカーや英語が堪能な地域人材などの協力を得る等，指導体制の充実を図るとともに，指導方法の工夫を

行うこと。」と示されている。ネイティブ・スピーカーや英語が堪能な地域人材などを授業で活用する利点や効果と，具体的な授業での活用場面を，学習指導要領の趣旨を踏まえ，100語程度の英語で書きなさい。ただし，語数には，句読点や符号は含まないものとする。なお，解答の総語数を，(　　)の中に記入すること。

(☆☆☆☆☆◎◎◎)

解答・解説

【中高共通】

【1】1　No. 1　a　No. 2　b　2　No. 1　c　No. 2　d　No. 3　b　3　No. 1　d　No. 2　a　No. 3　c　4　No. 1　(Well,) how about going somewhere tropical with a nice beach　No. 2　(OK, but don't) exert yourself too much in this intense heat

〈解説〉山形県のリスニングテストでは，問題用紙に文字情報が一切ないため，英文，質問文，選択肢を正確に聞き取らなければならない。設問1は適切な応答文を選択する問題。設問2は男女2人による短い対話文，英語による質問文，選択肢を聞いて，適切な選択肢を選ぶ問題。設問3は180語から200語程度の英文，質問文，選択肢を聞いて，適切な選択肢を選ぶ問題。設問4は部分ディクテーション問題で，短い対話文を聞き，解答欄の空所に聞き取った英文を書き取る問題である。設問1と2では放送は1回のみ，設問3と4では放送は2回流れる。内容理解に必要なキーワード，例示された固有名詞の聞き取りスキルが必須である。　1　No.1　a sweet tooth「甘いもの好き」，can't resist～ing「～せずにはいられない」。　No.2　reception「受信。他の意味ではフロント，受付(不可算名詞)」，out of range「圏外で」。　2　No.1　out of stock「品切れ」，clerk「店員」。　No.2　household chore「家事」，most likely「おそらく」，right「ちょうど(副詞)＝just」，turn the radio on／off

「ラジオのスイッチをつける／消す」，turn the radio up／down「ラジオの音量を上げる／下げる」。　No.3　be concerned about「～について心配する」，on business「仕事で」，hesitate「ためらう」，leave for work「出社する」，have no room for～「～の余地がない」。　3　インターネットでの個人情報収集に関する危険性が述べられている英文の聞き取りである。教育環境ではインターネットの活用が不可欠である以上，教員にとってこのようなテーマには慣れていて当然なので理解しやすい問題と言える。　No.1　英文スクリプトの第1段落最終文で，絶えずユーザーの好みに適合させるようなpersonalizationがプロダクト体験の中核となったと述べている。　No.2　英文スクリプトの第2段落4文目で「市が交通計画を改善するため」と述べている。Uber社はボストン当局者と運行パターンデータを共有することに同意したのであって道路修繕工事は請け負っていないのでc は不適切。　No.3　英文スクリプトの第3段落2文目に「大規模なセキュリティ違反は，悪意あるエージェントに対する消費者の脆弱性をさらけ出している」とあるのでcを選択。aでは第1段落2文目に「対象向けコンテンツの配信を行う」とあるのでfailed は不適当。bでは第2段落3文目に「血糖値が危険閾値に近づくと危険アラートを知らせる」と述べているのでpassは不適切。dでは英文スクリプト第3段落最終文に「企業側がデータマイニングを使用したことが明らかになると」とあるのでneverは不適切。
4　No.1　How about～ing?の構文。　No.2　exert oneself「奮闘する，頑張りすぎる」，intense heat「猛暑」。

【2】1　イ　　2　エ　　3　ア　　4　エ　　5　ウ　　6　イ　　7　ウ
8　エ　　9　イ　　10　ウ　　11　ア　　12　エ　　13　ア
14　ウ　　15　イ

〈解説〉1　使役動詞make＋O＋動詞の原形に関する構文に関する受動態の問題。受動態にすると動詞の原形の前にto不定詞が入る。against one's will「～の意に反して」。　2　仮定法過去完了の構文。① If S had過去分詞～, S' would have過去分詞….「もし(過去に)～したら，(過去に)…しただろうに」と，② If S had 過去分詞～, S' would 動詞原形….「もし(過去に)～したら，(現在は)…だろう」の2パターンある。主節にnowがあるので，ここは②で考える。　3　イディオムobject to～ing「～に反対する」に動名詞の意味上の主語を組み合わせた問題。動名詞の意味上の主語は，one's～ing「(人)が～すること」の形で表現できる。「私の同僚は，私が一人でバックカントリースキーに行くのを反対した」。　4　イディオムup in the air「宙に浮いて，未定で」の意。up in arms「腕を組んで，憤慨して」，up to date「最新式の，現代的な」，up and about「床を離れて，元気になって歩き回って」。　5　イディオム化した受動態の独立分詞構文の問題。All things being considered, という分詞構文でbeing が省略されもの。「あれこれ考えてみると，すべてを考慮すると」の意。　6　否定語が文頭に出ると倒置の語順になる。倒置は疑問文の語順にすると覚えておくとよい。Onlyには「～だけしかない」という否定的な意味が含まれている。「彼女がそんな豪華なドレスを着たいと思ったのはほんの数回しかなかった」。
7　account for～「～を占める」，respectively「それぞれ」の意。immensely「非常に，大いに」，eminently「きわめて，優れて」，collaboratively「協力して」。　8　vain「虚栄心の強い，うぬぼれの強い，無駄な，空虚な」。profound「奥深い」，inopportune「時期に適さない，折の悪い」，consecutive「連続した」。　9　faint「気絶する」。dilute「薄める，強度が弱くなる」，collect「収集する」，persist「固執する，言い張る，持続する」。　10　recruit「組織に新たに加わった新人」，compensate for「償う，補償する，補う」。　11　get carried away「～に夢中になる」。get dolled up「おめかしする，メイクとドレスをばっちり決める」，get mixed up「混同する，巻き添えを食う，悪いことに関わり合いになる」，pick off「狙い撃ちされる」。　12　surgeon「外科医」，adjacent to「～に隣接して」。intrepid「勇敢な，大胆な」，errant「道を踏み外した，誤った」，flawless「欠点のない，完璧な」。
13　succumb to「～に屈する」，temptation「誘惑」，second helping「(飲食の)お代わり」。tarnish「変色する，色あせる」，swagger「威張って歩

く」，hassle「悩ませる，口論する」。　14　trek「トレッキング」，aid worker「援助隊員」arduous「根気のいる，困難な」。laconic「口数が少ない，ぶっきらぼうな，簡潔な」，shattered「粉々になった，荒廃した，動転した，くたくたに疲れた」，contingent「偶発的な，不慮の」。
15　be known for「～で知られている」，pungent「鼻にツンとくる，辛い」。incumbent「在職中の，現職の」，nimble「機敏な，理解の速い」，gullible「騙されやすい，信じ込みやすい」。

【3】1　①　エ　②　イ　2　X　ウ　Y　ア　3　惑星規模では，生命は自己調節的であるというよりはむしろ自滅的であり，最終的にはそれ自身を全滅させるものであるということ。　4　メタンを発生させた初期の微生物の化石証拠が，あまりにも大量の堆積物の下にあるために，パーシビアランスには採取できないだろうということ。　5　(1)　They could have consumed atmospheric hydrogen and carbon dioxide.　(2)　It occurs in a way that maintains environmental habitability.　6　エ
〈解説〉1　①　doom「運命，破滅」の意なのでエが正解。dignity「尊厳」，diagnosis「診断」，deterrent「抑止力，妨害物」。　②　hinge on「～に依存する，左右される」の意なのでイが正解。seize「捕まえる」。
2　X　ガイア仮説の説明を念頭に，in turnという表現に注目すると，「地球の気温が上昇すれば植物の成長が進み，その植物の成長のおかげで大気中の温暖化ガスを吸収し，結果的に地球の気温を下げて元の気温に戻す」という文脈になるので，boost「促進する」を選択。vomit「嘔吐する」，convince「納得させる」，evaporate「蒸発する」。
Y　ア「ガイア仮説かメデア仮説として状況を定義するのは観点の問題なのかもしれない」。地球上で酸素量が膨大になった大酸化イベントは大量絶滅を引き起こし自己破壊的なメデア仮説の根拠となったが，生物学的多様性を生み出すきっかけになり多細胞性生物の出現にとって重要でもあったためガイア仮説の自己調節的な側面もあり，結局見方次第ではどちらの仮設も有用となりうるのでアが適切。

イ 「Ward氏もまたその研究の共著者としてガイア仮説的な観点を指示した」。Ward氏はガイア仮説でなくメデア仮説の提唱者であるので不適当。 ウ 「このような酸素の劇的な増加がその後の火星を荒廃させた」。地球では，酸素の増加が生物学的多様性と我々の祖先となる多細胞性生物の出現に重要であることを証明したが，火星が荒廃した環境である理由にはならないので不適切。 エ 「Lovelock氏がそれに関する証拠をより多く発見するのは時間の問題である」。酸素の増大による大量絶滅はWard氏の自己破壊的なメデア仮説の根拠となるものであるが，自己調節的なガイア仮説を提唱したLovelock氏が証拠を発見するという文意はそぐわないので不適切。 3 第4段落2文目を参照して日本語にする。 4 代名詞itは，that節以下を指すので，その内容を書く。too～to (do)構文が使用されているので，あまりにも堆積物が多くて到達できないという否定的な意味合いが込められていることに注意。 5 (1) consumeをキーワードとする。第1段落冒頭文後半に，consuming atmospheric hydrogen and carbon dioxide.とある。(2) 第3段落5文目後半でself-regulatingの説明として，地球の生命体と環境との関係が述べられている。そこからin a way that maintains environmental habitabilityの表現を抜き出してまとめる。

6 ア 「Sauterey氏が言うに，生命の自己破壊的な性質のためにより多くの生命体が宇宙に出現する」。第4段落，第5段落の内容から，Sauterey氏ではなくWard氏の考察から導かれた見解である。

イ 「どの惑星でも生命の痕跡を示すには3種類以上のガスが必要である」。第3段落前半で，地球での生命存在指標となっているものとしてメタンと酸素の2種類のガスを挙げて例示している。 ウ 「大酸化イベントの時期にシアノバクテリアは膨大な量の酸素を吸収した」。第4段落5文目で，酸素が不足した地球の大気に対しシアノバクテリアは光合成により膨大な酸素の発生源となったとあり，酸素を吸収したのではない。 エ 「Pahlevan氏は，Sauterey氏の提唱する研究にはある種の限界があることを指摘した」。第6段落でPahlevan氏はSauterey氏の研究の盲点を指摘しており，それに対しSauterey氏も同様に認めたと述べているので正解。 オ 「Sauterey氏とその研究グループは，火星にはまだ微生物が生息しているという可能性を調べられる場所を見つけた」。第7段落最終文に「初期のメタン生成微生物の化石証拠」と述べており，生きている微生物ではない。

【4】1　人が一度に集中して行うことができる知的活動の量には限界があること。　2　X イ　Y ウ　Z オ　3　何かを学習するとき，人の記憶はそれを学習した状況の側面や，読んだり聞いたりするといった学習する方法にかかわる認知的な過程までも記録するから。　4　(1)　They can concentrate on the overall meaning of the text or conversation.　(2)　They cannot perform the skill smoothly.　(3)　No, it hasn't.　5　エ

〈解説〉1　suggest 以下の節を訳す問題。engage in「～に携わる」，at one time「一度に」。　2　X　set～in motion「～を動かす，引き起こす，働かせる」。流暢になるスキルを習得する際に，まずはそのスキルの宣言的知識が契機となり，十分な練習を行い手続き的知識に変え自動化させていくプロセスの始まりとなる。doubt「疑い」，haste「急ぐこと」，parallel「平行，対応，一致」，summary「要約，まとめ」では意味をなさない。　Y　第5段落の要点に注目する。「言語行動における変化は，すべて練習により徐々に形成されてくるという観点からは説明できない。そこには再構築という概念が必要で，学習者の知識に質的変化が起きている点に注目すべきである」とした上で，空欄Yの前では再構築という概念で学習者の急速な進歩という肯定的な変化を説明できるとし，空欄Yからは逆に過剰般化という否定的な変化を説明している。空欄Yの直後にFor example とあることから言語学習における否定的な現象を述べた英文が入ると考え，ウ「また，再構築という概念であれば，学習者が言語を習得する際に過剰な体系化を引き起こしたり誤った形で覚えてしまったりするという，明らかな後退現象を説明できる」が文脈的に合致する。　Z 「この仮説を使えば第2言語学習で広く散見される現象を説明する手段を提供してくれそうだ」と述

べているが，「転移適切性処理」は心理学の概念であり，言語学習における認知プロセスを説明するのに著者はこの概念を利用して自分の仮説を立てようとしている。そこで，どのような手段なのかを考えると，「まだ断定するには慎重だが説得力のある説明ができそうな手段」と解釈し，オplausibleを選択。prolific「多産な」，nomadic「遊牧の」，compulsory「義務的な」，docile「従順な」，plausible「妥当と思われる，もっともらしい」。　3　下線部(2)に後続する英文が，This is becauseで始まっているので，このbecause節がその解答となる。述語動詞recordの目的語として，aspects of context (in which it was learned) とthe cognitive processes (involved in the way [we learned it, for example, by reading or hearing it])の2つが並列されていることに注意。　4　(1)　第2段落4文目参照。the overall meaning of a text or conversationの句を利用。(2)　第4段落1文目参照。disrupts the smooth performance of itの句から，形容詞smoothを副詞に，名詞performanceを動詞に品詞転換して利用。disrupt「混乱させる」の否定的な意を汲んでcannotで否定文にする。(3)　第6段落4文目参照。「今日まで室内実験で研究してきた」とある。5　ア「上級者は予想可能な言語パターンを使わずに，自分の意見を述べるのに注意して言葉を選ぶ」。第1段落冒頭から3文目まで参照し不一致。　イ「第2言語学習者のリーディング速度は，どれほど意味を自動的に把握しているかという観点からは説明できない」。第2段落5文目を参照し，説明できるとあるので不一致。　ウ「DeKeyser氏とその研究グループは，第2言語習得をスキル学習として研究し，1995年Anderson氏の著作を完成させるのに役立った」。第3段落2文目を参照し，Anderson氏の研究を参考にしたとあるから不一致。　エ「再構築という概念なら言語能力の急速的に目覚ましい上達が起きるケースを説明できるだろう」。第5段落4文目を参照し一致。　オ「学習者がコミュニケーション活動中にどのように意識を働かせるかは，文法テストの成績には影響しない」。第6段落最終文に，「コミュニケーション活動中に文法に注目しても，学生の認知リソースは文法ではなく意味の方に向けられているので，文法テストの時に文法に関する情報想起はより困難になる」とあり，否定的な影響があると述べているので不一致。

【5】1　Creating a workplace environment where all employees can exchange their opinions in a constructive way can benefit everyone.　2　(解答例) Speaking English with others is an effective way to improve English communication skills. Although English used in class is standardized, it may differ from the English spoken in real life. In order for students to learn skills in overcoming communication difficulties due to this difference, I'll suggest occasional extracurricular activities to interview foreign tourists, with a preliminary teaching curriculum of guiding students to interview in a polite manner, both verbally and non-verbally, while being sensitive to foreigners' feelings. Through these activities, students will be aware that foreigners speak English with a variety of accents, which will help them understand that they shouldn't be ashamed of making mistakes when speaking English. Such experiences will inspire confidence in them and keep them highly-motivated to talk with people in English.(127 words)

〈解説〉1　最初に和文の主語，述語を確認しよう。「職場環境をつくること」が主語でCreating a work(place) environment,「有益だ」が述語なのでcan benefit＋人(or is beneficial to／for 人)。次に修飾部を確認し文法的に間違えないようにつなげていく。「全ての従業員が建設的に意見を交わすことができる」では，関係副詞whereかin which を使用。「意見を交わす」はexchange their opinions,「建設的に」は in a constructive wayでもconstructivelyでもよい。「建設的な意見を交わす」と考えてexchange their constructive opinionsでも良いだろう。　2　学習指導要領の内容を踏まえて，授業でネイティブ・スピーカー等を活用する利点とその具体的な活用方法を述べる。押さえておきたいポイントは，標準的な音声に接すること，正確な発音の習得，英語による情報発信や自身の考えの表出，相手の発話の理解，そして，それらの機会創出などと考えられる。また，学習指導要領解説では，人材面についてALT

の活用，地域在住外国人，外国からの訪問者や留学生，外国生活経験者，海外の事情に詳しい人，英語が堪能な帰国生徒などを挙げている。このような語句をベースにして自分の考えを具体的に絞り込んで短くまとめていく。自分が生徒に対して具体的にどのような作業をさせたいかを考え，内容のアウトラインをまとめてから書き出すとよい。文法的な間違いには注意しつつ，ディスコースマーカーを駆使しながら分かりやすくまとめる。解答例では，外国人観光客にインタビューをさせる活動を想定し，クラスの中の英語と異なる実際の英語に触れる経験を通して，生徒が間違いを恐れなくなり，自信をもち，コミュニケーションへの意欲を維持できるという利点を挙げている。

2023年度　実施問題

【中高共通】

【1】(放送による問題)これはリスニング・テストです。放送の指示に従って答えなさい。

ただいまから，リスニング・テストを行います。問題は，1，2，3，4の四つです。聞いている間にメモを取っても構いません。

1　では，1の問題から始めます。問題は，No. 1とNo. 2の2問です。

これから読まれる英文に対する応答として最も ふさわしいものを，続いて読まれるa，b，cの中から一つ選び，記号で答えなさい。答えは，大文字，小文字どちらでも構いません。なお，英文と応答は1度しか読まれません。

では，始めます。

No. 1　Let's call it a day today.

a.　Really? It dates back to the 1960s.

b.　I agree. Let's finish up tomorrow.

c.　It is another name for Thursday.

No. 2　Should I buy new clothes or should I save my money?

a.　Each option has pros and cons.

b.　Whatever you are.

c.　That's very kind of you.

2　次に，2の問題に移ります。問題は，No. 1からNo. 3までの3問です。

これから，短い対話文を読みます。そのあとでクエスチョンと言っ

て質問します。その答えとして最もふさわしいものを，続いて読まれるa，b，c，dの中から一つ選び，記号で答えなさい。答えは，大文字，小文字どちらでも構いません。なお，対話文・質問・答えの選択肢は1度しか読まれません。

では，始めます。

No. 1

M: Oh no! I found a rip in my jacket. I want to wear it at the meeting. Can you sew up the rip?

W: Why can't you do it yourself? You always ask me to do it.

M: I've never been good at sewing.

W: Well, it's time for you to learn.

Question: What advice does the woman give to the man?

a. To make his own jacket.

b. To take the time to learn to sew.

c. To buy a sewing machine.

d. To learn how to wear the jacket.

No. 2

W: Do you remember that the wedding reception for Tom and Jessica will be held next month? What would make a good wedding gift?

M: Isn't it enough to give money?

W: I want to give them something special and personal. Just giving money is boring.

M: Then you should think of something because I have no idea.

Question: What does the man want to do?

a. He wants to make a wedding gift.

b. He wants to give the woman advice.

c. He wants the woman to give the present back.

d. He wants the woman to decide on a present.

No. 3
W: I have to prepare our dinner. Would you go to the cleaner's and pick up the laundry, Jack?
M: I'm busy watching TV.
W: You have been doing that for two hours, though.
M: Well... OK, Mom. I'll pick it up in thirty minutes. How much is there?
W: About three shopping bags full.
M: That sounds like a lot. Then you should come with me.
Question: What will the woman most likely do in thirty minutes?

a. She will most likely pay money for groceries.
b. She will most likely go shopping with her husband.
c. She will most likely pick up the laundry with her son.
d. She will most likely go to the cleaner's by herself.

3 次に3の問題に移ります。問題は，No. 1からNo. 3までの3問です。
これから，あるまとまりのある英文を読みます。そのあとで，クエスチョンズと言って，その英文について三つの質問をします。その答えとして最もふさわしいものを，質問に続いて読まれるa，b，c，dの中から一つ選び，記号で答えなさい。答えは，大文字，小文字どちらでも構いません。なお，英文・質問・答えの選択肢は全体を通して2回読まれます。
では，始めます。

Jim, a thirty-eight-year-old freelance graphic designer, had what he called a lifelong addiction to sweets — he never met a jelly bean he didn't like. He was intrigued by a study I mentioned in class that found that leaving candy out in a visible place can increase people's general self-control (if they routinely resist the temptation). Jim worked from home, and often moved between his office and other rooms in his house. He decided to put a glass jar of jelly beans in the hallway that he would have to pass every time he left or returned to his office. He didn't ban all sweets, but did institute a "no candy from the candy jar" rule to challenge his self-control muscle.

The first day, the instinct to pop a few jelly beans in his mouth was automatic and difficult to stop. But over the week, saying no got easier. Seeing the candy reminded Jim of his goal to exercise his willpower to say no. Surprised by his success, he started stepping away from his desk more often just to get some extra "exercise" in. Though Jim had initially worried that the visible temptation would exhaust his willpower, he found the process energizing. When he returned to his office after resisting the candy jar, he felt motivated. Jim was astonished that something he thought was completely out of his control could change so quickly when he set a small challenge for himself and committed to it.

Questions

No. 1 What did Jim try not to eat?

a. Snacks.

b. All the sweets.

c. Jelly beans.

d. A candy jar.

No. 2 What helped Jim remember his goal to control his eating impulse?

a. Seeing the candy jar in the hallway did.

b. Staying in his office all day long did.

c. Putting the candy jar on his desk did.

d. Getting some exercise in a training room did.

No. 3 What is true about the passage?

a. Jim's willpower didn't make a difference in getting exercise.

b. The speaker was attracted to the research Jim mentioned in class about self-control.

c. Jim never found candy he liked until he made a decision to avoid eating sweets.

d. Something out of his control could change easily when Jim made a small effort for himself.

4　次に4の問題に移ります。問題は，No. 1とNo. 2の2問です。

これから，英語による対話文を読みます。次の(　　)のところに入る英語を聞き取り，書きなさい。対話文はそれぞれ2回読まれます。

では，始めます。

No. 1

M: Now, let's think about fixing up the downstairs bathroom.

W: OK, but we're already over budget. I'm not sure we can (afford to replace all the tiles and repaint the walls) now.

No. 2

W: Finally, we got our bonuses! What are you going to do with yours, Charlie?

M: I'm planning to (invest all of it in stocks for my retirement).

これで，リスニング・テストを終わります。次の問題に移ってください。

(☆☆☆◎◎◎)

【２】次の英文や対話文の中の(　　)に最も適するものを，以下のア～エの中からそれぞれ一つずつ選び，記号で答えなさい。

1　Since the launch of the health food campaign, the sales of organic foods (　　) at Kerokero Foods.

ア　increase　　イ　was increased　　ウ　has been increased

エ　have been increasing

2 This may sound ( ), but I think we need a hyphen between these two words.

ア numerical イ trivial ウ portable エ authentic

3 Advance Telecommunications announced that the cause of yesterday's network disruption is still ( ) investigation.

ア over イ with ウ among エ under

4 ( ) more than 2,000 people, Sunrise Manufacturing is one of the most important businesses in the town.

ア Employ イ Employed ウ Employing

エ Employment

5 A: The weather is absolutely beautiful today, isn't it?

B: Yes, I ( ) it was like this more often.

ア hope イ desire ウ want エ wish

6 Students in the science club ( ) on a field trip to the botanical gardens last Thursday.

ア caused イ went ウ chose エ completed

7 There are twenty students in the class, most of ( ) study very hard.

ア who イ which ウ whose エ whom

8 His sales talk sounds ( ). I can hardly believe what he said.

ア fishy イ collective ウ trustworthy エ reliable

9 Customers are expressing outrage at the charges banks ( ) on them for using automated teller machines.

ア compose イ dispose ウ impose エ oppose

10 How did you ( ) this information? It's supposed to be confidential.

ア get by イ come by ウ slip up エ keep up

11 The best way to ( ) after an exhausting day is to take a hot, long bath.

ア wind down イ bubble up ウ work out エ strip away

12 I couldn't follow all of Samantha's speech, but I understood enough to get the ( ) of what she was saying.

ア drone イ gall ウ drawl エ gist

13　Cathy didn't like what the interior designer had done. She preferred simple elegance, but her room now looked outright (　　).

ア　shrewd　　イ　extinct　　ウ　gaudy　　エ　fervent

14　The audience in the hall was (　　) by the stunning performance of the orchestra.

ア　mesmerized　　イ　eradicated　　ウ　disguised

エ　modulated

15　A: Aren't you dressed rather (　　) for such a cold day?

B: Don't worry. I am going to put on some more clothes before I go for a walk.

ア　testily　　イ　scantily　　ウ　murkily　　エ　haughtily

(☆☆☆☆◎◎◎◎)

【3】次の英文を読んで，以下の問いに答えなさい。

Chaos and conflict roiled the Mediterranean in the first century B.C. Against a backdrop of famine, disease and the assassinations of Julius Caesar and other leaders, the Roman Republic collapsed, and the Roman Empire rose in its place.

Social unrest no doubt contributed to that; politics can unhinge a society. But so can (1)something arguably more powerful. Scientists last month announced evidence that a volcanic eruption in a remote island, nearly 10,000 kilometers away from the Italian peninsula, contributed to the Roman Republic's demise.

That eruption — and others before it and since — played a role in changing the course of history.

In recent years, geoscientists, historians and archaeologists have joined up to study the societal impacts of large eruptions. They rely on an ①amalgam of records — ice cores, historical chronicles and climate modeling — to determine how civilizations like Ptolemaic Egypt and pre-Columbian Mesoamerica were affected.

At the Desert Research Institute in Reno, Nevada, it's not unusual to find researchers often study in puffy parkas and wool hats handling chunks of ice in a minus 20 degree Celsius "cold room." Ice cores, drilled from glaciers, hide bits of volcanic material that rained down from long-ago eruptions. Joseph McConnell, a climate scientist at the Desert Research Institute in Reno, Nevada, looks for that debris.

Using an instrument they designed and built, they melt the ice and pipe the water into an array of sensors. With hundreds of feet of tubing, the setup looks downright chaotic, but it's exquisitely sensitive.

The sensors pinpoint many substances, including about 30 different elements, and they do so by catching just tiny whiffs. "They have sensitivities of parts per quadrillion," Dr. McConnell said.

Volcanic ash, generally known as tephra, sometimes hides in ice. It can be tied to a specific volcano. "The tephra comes from the magma itself," said Michael Sigl, a chemist at the University of Bern in Switzerland who collaborates with Dr. McConnell. "It carries the composition of the rocks."

Sulfur is also indicative of a past eruption. Sulfur dioxide, a gas commonly belched by erupting volcanoes, reacts with water in the atmosphere to create sulfate aerosols. These tiny particles can ② linger in the stratosphere for years, riding wind currents, but they, like tephra, eventually fall back to Earth.

The ice also carries a time stamp. Dr. McConnell and his colleagues look for variations in elements like sodium, which is found in sea spray that's seasonally blown inland. By counting annual variations in these elements, it's possible to trace the passage of time, he said, "like a tree-ring record."

He and a team analyzed six ice cores drilled in the Arctic. In layers of ice corresponding to the early months of 43 B.C., they spotted (X).

Researchers have previously hypothesized that an environmental trigger may have helped set in motion the famines and social unrest that plagued the Mediterranean region at the time.

But until now, "There hasn't been the kind of data that these scholars brought forth to really get (2)their theory into the mainstream," said Jessica Clark, a historian of the Roman Republic at Florida State University who was not involved in the research.

Gill Plunkett, a paleoecologist at Queen's University Belfast, extracted 35 pieces of tephra from the ice and pored over the rock chemistry of likely volcanic suspects. Okmok, in Alaska's Aleutian Islands, turned out to be the best match.

This eruption was one of the largest of the last few millenniums, the team concluded, and the sulfate aerosols it created remained in the stratosphere for years. These particles reflect sunlight, which means they can temporarily alter Earth's climate. There's evidence that the Northern Hemisphere was colder than normal around 43 B.C. Trees across Europe grew slower that year. Using climate models to simulate the impact of an Okmok eruption, the team estimated that parts of the Mediterranean would have cooled by as much as 7.4 degrees Celsius. Rain patterns changed as well — some regions would have been drenched by 400 percent more precipitation than normal, the modeling revealed. These conditions likely would have decimated crops, the team said.

(　Y　) records note famines. In 43 B.C., Mark Antony, the Roman military leader, and his army had to subsist on wild fruit, roots, bark and "animals never tasted before," the philosopher Plutarch wrote. For a society already reeling from Caesar's assassination the year before, such conditions might have worsened unrest, the researchers concluded.

Dr. McConnell, who published the team's results in Proceedings of the National Academy of Sciences, said, "It's an incredible coincidence that it happened exactly in the waning years of the Roman Republic when things were falling apart."

(Katherine Kornei, "The End of Ancient Rome Is Linked to an Eruption" , *The New York Times International Weekly.* July 12, 2020 による。ただし，設問の都合で一部省略及び改変している。)

1　下線部(1)について，科学者が証拠として示したことを，本文に即して日本語で書きなさい。

2　下線部①，②を別の語で言い換えたとき，最も意味の近いものを，次のア～エの中からそれぞれ一つずつ選び，記号で答えなさい。

①　ア　mixture　イ　fraction　ウ　technique　エ　summary

②　ア　collide　イ　decline　ウ　develop　エ　stay

3　本文中の空欄(　X　)，(　Y　)に入る英語として最も適切なものを，次のア～エの中からそれぞれ一つずつ選び，記号で答えなさい。

X　ア　a surprising lack of tephra, sulfur dioxide and other elements like sodium

　イ　a significant difference between the amount of sulfur and that of tephra

　ウ　historical evidence that the Roman Republic was beginning to fall apart

　エ　large jumps in sulfur and bits of material that were probably tephra

Y　ア　Empirical　イ　Environmental　ウ　Historical

　エ　Physiological

4　下線部(2)が指す内容を，本文に即して日本語で書きなさい。

5　本文の内容に即して，次の問いに英語で答えなさい。

(1)　What does Dr. McConnell look for at the Desert Research Institute in Reno, Nevada?

(2)　According to Dr. McConnell, what can researchers do by counting annual variations in elements in the ice?

6　本文の内容に最も合うものを，次のア～エの中から一つ選び，記号で答えなさい。

ア　Evidence shows that a far-off volcanic eruption triggered another eruption.

イ　Historical chronicles show how many pieces of tephra are contained in ice cores.

ウ　It is most likely that Okmok erupted around 43 B.C., affecting the climate in Rome.

エ　The device Dr. McConnell used was so sensitive that it often broke during experiments.

(☆☆☆◎◎◎◎)

【中学校】

【1】次の英文を読んで，以下の問いに答えなさい。

One linguist had American co-workers who moved to Japan when their children were three and five years old. Her co-worker said that he expected his children to pick up Japanese easily, whereas he and his wife would have to work hard to learn it. This person's beliefs about the ease with which his children would acquire Japanese reflect something known as the Critical Period Hypothesis (CPH).

The CPH proposes that there is (1)a critical period for language acquisition. What this means is that for a linguistic system to be fully acquired, it must be acquired by a certain age. The term critical period comes out of biology and what we know about how certain aspects of biological development take place. For instance, there is a critical period for imprinting in ducklings. When ducklings are born, there is a certain window of time in which they will bond with the mother duck, and whatever animal they see during that critical period is the animal that they imprint on. It's important to note that this function is input dependent (it depends on access to a specific kind of stimuli in the real world), and that a lack of access to the critical stimuli does not ①entail no ability whatsoever. Instead, it means that ducklings might look to a member of another species to be their caregivers.

The CPH for language acquisition comes from Eric Lenneberg's 1967 book, *The Biological Foundations of Language*. On the basis of the neurological correlates for human language, evidence from children who do not succeed in learning an *L1, and because child language acquisition takes place during a period of time that is marked by a lot of neurological activity, (2)Lenneberg argued that L1 acquisition is subject to critical period effects. Specifically, Lenneberg argued that if children are not exposed to an L1 by the age of about five, they will not acquire language. Although most ②proponents of a CPH for adult L2 acquisition cite Lenneberg, he limited his proposal to child L1 acquisition. He mentions L2 acquisition almost in passing, stating that if someone is of average intelligence, that person can learn another language after the beginning of what he calls "their second decade." He adds that the incidence of "language-learning blocks" increases after puberty. He ends by saying that because natural languages tend to resemble each other in so many ways, the ability to acquire another language is present in humans.

Although Lenneberg says nothing directly about a critical period for L2 acquisition, there is some circumstantial evidence for a critical period for child language acquisition. One piece of evidence comes from the case of Genie. Genie was locked in a closet by her step-father at a young age and was deprived of any linguistic input. When she was discovered by child protective services, she was 13. Despite receiving intensive interventions to teach her English, she never developed the ability to speak fluently. Although she acquired some vocabulary, her language production lacked syntactic structure and also lacked systematic morphological marking. We should avoid drawing too many conclusions from the case of Genie, though. The fact is, Genie's childhood was marked by severe and lengthy emotional and physical abuse, part of which included linguistic deprivation. In short, her language deficits could be related to the cognitive and emotional problems stemming from the abuse she endured. This is one of the major problems with directly testing the CPH: Most of the cases we have of people who lack exposure to language do so because they have been deprived of the social environment necessary for all kinds of healthy human development, including the development of human language. In fact, it is impossible to directly test the CPH because to do so would essentially involve depriving infants and children of human contact. Thus, although the evidence for critical period effects in L1 is suggestive, (3)<u>it is impossible to test the CPH directly</u>.

(注)L1：第一言語(生まれて最初に習得した言語：first language)

(Bill VanPatten, Megan Smith and Alessandro G. Benati, *Key Questions in Second Language Acquisition − An Introduction* による。ただし，設問の都合で一部省略及び改変している。)

1　下線部①，②の英語の定義として最もよくあてはまるものを，次のア～エの中からそれぞれ一つずつ選び，記号で答えなさい。

①　ア　to involve something that cannot be avoided

　　イ　to find a way of dealing with a problem or difficult situation

　　ウ　to make something full of something

　　エ　to plan or organize something in advance

②　ア　a person who studies something carefully and tries to discover new facts about it

　　イ　an idea that you think is true although you may not be able to prove it

　　ウ　a person who supports an idea or course of action

　　エ　a scientific test that is carried out in order to study what happens and to gain new knowledge

2　下線部(1)の用語は何に由来しているか，本文に即して日本語で書きなさい。

3　下線部(2)に関して，Lennebergが具体的に主張したことは何か，本文に即して日本語で書きなさい。

4　下線部(3)のように筆者が述べるのはなぜか，本文に即して日本語で書きなさい。

5　本文の内容に即して，次の問いに英語で答えなさい。

(1)　According to Lenneberg, what is possible for people who have an ordinary intellectual capacity?

(2)　How much did Genie improve her speaking ability after being taught

English?

6　本文の内容に最も合うものを，次のア～エの中から一つ選び，記号で答えなさい。

ア　The co-worker of the linguist supposed that his children would acquire Japanese as easily as he and his wife did.

イ　It is possible that ducklings might recognize a member of another species as their caregivers because of imprinting.

ウ　Lenneberg concludes that the ability to acquire another language cannot be found in humans.

エ　Lenneberg argues that there is some circumstantial evidence for a critical period for L2 acquisition.

(☆☆☆◎◎◎◎)

【2】次の1，2について，指示に従って答えなさい。

1　次の日本語を英語に直しなさい。

人は自分に画期的な影響を及ぼすかもしれない本に，まったく偶然出くわすかもしれない。

2　文部科学省では，個別最適な学びと協働的な学びの一体的な充実など，教育の質を向上させるために，「GIGAスクール構想」を推進しているところであり，児童生徒の1人1台端末及び通信ネットワーク等の学校ICT環境の下での新しい学びが本格的に開始されている。あなたは外国語の授業で1人1台端末を生徒にどのように活用させるか。また，その活用には，生徒のコミュニケーションを図る資質・能力を育成する上で，どのような効果があると考えるか。学習指導要領の趣旨を踏まえ，100語程度の英語で書きなさい。ただし，語数には，句読点や符号は含まないものとする。なお，解答の総語数を記入すること。

(☆☆☆☆◎◎◎◎◎)

【高等学校】

【1】次の英文を読んで，以下の問いに答えなさい。

Memory is an area of research in psychology that has probably generated more studies than any other. Two aspects of memory research are relevant to understanding language acquisition and content learning in CBLT: encoding (the internalization of knowledge) and retrieval (recognizing or recalling what we have learned). The term working memory (also referred to as short-term memory) refers to the processing of information that is in focus at a given moment and may or may not be encoded in long-term memory. For example, we use our working memory as we try to learn a phone number or a vocabulary list or to understand an explanation in a science textbook or a rule in a grammar book. Unless we have repeated opportunities to process the information that was briefly in focus in working memory, we are not likely to store it in long-term memory for retrieval at a later time.

One important fact about memory is that the capacity of working memory is limited while the capacity of long-term memory — though perhaps not (　X　) — is very large indeed. The analogy often offered is that working memory is like (1)<u>a computer's RAM</u>, while long-term memory is like the computer's ROM. The computer's ROM capacity is very large, but only a limited amount of material can be processed in RAM. Like all analogies, this one has limitations, but it reflects the fact that we cannot 'think about' everything at once and that most of what we know is not in our active focus at any given time. The goal of learning is to be able to access elements of what is stored in long-term memory and to bring it into focus when you need it.

Research evidence of skill learning shows that, in order to learn something, we must first perceive or notice it (Schmidt, 1990; 2001). We pay attention to it within the limitations of our working memory. When this occurs, we may or may not be aware of it or able to remember that we noticed it. Researchers have developed ways of showing how our cognitive processing may be at work on something that we are not aware of having noticed. One example is in (2)<u>priming studies</u>, where language users, including second language learners, are more likely to use a particular word or language pattern if it has recently been used by their interlocutor in the conversation (Trofimovich & McDonough, 2011). Even if they cannot report having heard or noticed the word or pattern, it affects their behavior in measurable ways, in terms of both frequency and accuracy, showing that at some level, it has engaged their cognitive processing. Once again we see the importance of repeated exposure to material to be learned, sometimes in contexts of direct and focused instruction, sometimes in contexts where the material is present but not in focus.

One critical aspect of encoding new information is the connections that are made between that new information and other bits of information — old and new. When we encounter a new word, we may pay attention to the way it is spelled, what it means, how it sounds, what other words it reminds us of, the other words that occur with it. (3)<u>All of these things that we notice</u> can become attached to the new word in networks of associations. Repeated encounters with the word give us new opportunities for adding new associations to that word's network. The more associations a word or phrase has, the more avenues we have for retrieving it later. This is related to the notion of depth of processing (Craik, 2002).

The research on retrieval of previously learned knowledge is complex and fascinating, and some of the findings are quite surprising. For example, psychologists have found that one of the best ways to learn something is to test yourself on it. That is, instead of reading a list or a paragraph over and over again, it is more effective to put it aside and (　Y　), or to answer questions about it. This is referred to as 'effortful retrieval' or the 'test effect' (Bjork, 1994; Roediger & Karpicke, 2006). The test effect is often studied in combination with the spacing effect. When spaced practice is combined with the need to recall the material rather than have it presented again, long-term learning is enhanced. Thus, when we are learning a second language, we benefit from being placed in situations where we have to reach into our memory for something that we know but cannot yet access easily. The more often we do this, the greater the likelihood that eventually the knowledge will be accessible automatically.

(Patsy M. Lightbown, *Focus on Content-Based Language Teaching*による。ただし，設問の都合で一部省略及び改変している。)

1　本文中の空欄(　X　), (　Y　)に入る英語として最も適切なものを，次のア～オの中からそれぞれ一つずつ選び，記号で答えなさい。

X　ア　analogous　イ　insecure　ウ　infinite　エ　seamless
　　オ　ubiquitous

Y　ア　encode it in short-term memory
　　イ　find another one to concentrate on
　　ウ　pay less attention to the details of it
　　エ　try to remember it without looking at it
　　オ　try not to boost your working memory

2　下線部(1)ではどのようなことが可能か，本文に即して日本語で書きなさい。

3　下線部(2)の研究において，どのような結果が示されたか，本文に即して日本語で書きなさい。

4　下線部(3)が指す内容を，本文に即して日本語で書きなさい。

5　本文の内容に即して，次の問いに英語で答えなさい。

(1)　What happens if we do not have repeated, opportunities to process information that is briefly in focus?

(2)　When we pay attention to something to be learned within the limitations of our working memory, is it certain that we will be unable to remember that we perceived it?

6　本文の内容に最も合うものを，次のア～オの中から一つ選び，記号で答えなさい。

ア　A variety of items can be connected to new information, which may hinder us from recalling it later.

イ　Better long-term learning can be achieved when we are trying to retrieve information from memory.

ウ　We use our long-term memory when we process information that is in focus at a given moment.

エ　Direct and focused instruction enables us to test ourselves on research material more effectively.

オ　The capacity of working memory can be expanded if we encounter many different types of information.

(☆☆☆◎◎◎◎)

【2】次の1，2について，指示に従って答えなさい。

1　次の日本語を英語に直しなさい。

地元の食材を特徴とした新しい料理をメニューに追加したことで，顧客から好意的な反応があった。

2　「高等学校学習指導要領」(平成30年3月告示)の「第2章　第8節　外国語　第3款　英語に関する各科目にわたる指導計画の作成と内容の取扱い」において，「生徒が身に付けるべき資質・能力や生徒の実態，教材の内容などに応じて，視聴覚教材やコンピュータ，情報通信ネットワーク，教育機器などを有効活用」すると示されている。あなたは，ICT機器をどのように指導に取り入れるか。また，その活用にはどのような効果があると考えるか。学習指導要領の趣旨を踏まえ，100語程度の英語で書きなさい。ただし，語数には，句読点や符号は含まないものとする。なお，解答の総語数を記入すること。

(☆☆☆☆◎◎◎◎◎)

解答・解説

【中高共通】

【1】1　No. 1　b　No. 2　a　2　No. 1　b　No. 2　d　No. 3　c　3　No. 1　c　No. 2　a　No. 3　d　4　No. 1　afford to replace all the tiles and repaint the walls　No. 2　invest all of it in stocks for my retirement

〈解説〉問題用紙に質問文や選択肢が印刷されていないので，英文，質問文，選択肢のすべてを正確に聞き取る力が問われている。設問1は短い応答文，設問2は短い対話文で，ともに放送は1回のみ。設問3は250語程度のパッセージ，設問4は対話文の一部のディクテーションで，ともに放送は2回ある。　1　No.1　Let's call it a dayは「これで(仕事を)終わりにしよう」という意味の頻出の会話表現。　No.2　pros and consは「メリットとデメリット」の意。　2　No.1　男性の2回目の発話「裁縫は得意だったことがないんだ」に対して女性は2回目の発話で「学ぶべき時よ」と応じておりcが適切。　No.2　結婚式のギフトを何にすべきか聞いてきた女性に対し，男性の2回目の発話で「僕は何も思い浮かばないから自分で考えるべきだよ」と返しておりdが適切。No.3　男性の2回目の発話で母親と話していることがわかり，3回目の発話で「量が多そうだから一緒に来てほしい」と言っている。ここから母親は息子と一緒にクリーニング店に行って預けたものを取りに行くと考えられcが適切。　3　No.1　第1段落の内容から男性はjelly beansを食べないようにしていることが判断できる。　No.2　第1段落後ろの2文の内容に一致するのはaとなる。　No.3　第2段落最終文の内容に一致するのはdとなる。　4　英文は2回読まれ，長さもそれほどでもないため1語1語を聞き逃さないようにしたい。

【2】1　エ　2　イ　3　エ　4　ウ　5　エ　6　イ　7　エ　8　ア　9　ウ　10　イ　11　ア　12　エ　13　ウ

14　ア　　15　イ

〈解説〉1　冒頭にSince「～以来」があるので現在完了形であるウとエに絞られ，salesは複数形のためそれに対応した動詞の形のエが適切。　2　空所の後の「2つの語の間にハイフンが必要」というのは「ささいなこと」なのでイが適切。　3　under investigationで「調査中」の意。　4　分詞構文が用いられており，主語は雇う側のSunrise Manufacturingなので現在分詞形のウが適切。　5「もっとしょっちゅうこんな天気だったらなあ」という意味の文でI wish＋仮定法過去で現実には叶わない願望を表す。　6　go on a tripで「旅行に行く」の意。　7　人を表す関係代名詞はofの後はwhomを用いる。　8　fishyは「怪しい，うさんくさい」の意で2文目の内容と合致する。　9　impose on～で「～を課す」の意。　10　come byで「手に入れる」の意。　11　wind downで「くつろぐ」の意。　12　get the gist of～で「～の要領を得る，コツをつかむ」の意。　13　gaudyは「派手な，けばけばしい」の意。彼女の好みはシンプルな優雅さなのに，実際の部屋はそうではなくインテリアデザイナーの仕事が気に入らなかったという文意になる。　14　mesmerizedは「魅了された」の意。　15　dress scantilyで「薄着で」の意。

【3】1　イタリア半島からほぼ1万キロメートル離れた島の火山の噴火が，共和制ローマの崩壊の一因になったこと。　2　①　ア　　②　エ　3　X　エ　　Y　ウ　　4　環境的なきっかけが，当時地中海地方を苦しめた飢饉や社会不安の発生を助長したかもしれないこと。

5　(1)　He looks for bits of volcanic material that rained down from long-ago eruptions.　　(2)　They can trace the passage of time.　　6　ウ

〈解説〉1　社会を混乱させた「もっと強力なもの」は直後の文のa volcanic eruption以下を指すためこの部分を適切に日本語にまとめればよい。　2　①　amalgamは「(さまざまな要素の)混合」の意で，最も近いのはアのmixtureとなる。　②　lingerは「残存する」の意で最も近いのはエのstayとなる。　3　X　空所から2つ前の段落で，大気中で硫黄が水と反応して硫酸塩エアロゾルが作られ，これらの微小な粒子は空中にとどまるが火山灰は地面に落ちてくるという内容が述べられている。この地面に落ちてきた比較的大きな火山灰等が氷から発見されているのが空所の段落で述べられている内容と判断でき，エが適切となる。　Y　空所の次の文で紀元前43年に飢えを避けるためローマの軍隊が野生の果物や今まで味わったことのない動物等を食べて生きていたという「歴史の記録」が述べられている。　4　下線部の前段落の研究者の仮説がtheir theoryを指す。よってthat節以下を適切な日本語でまとめればよい。　5　(1)　第5段落の内容が問われている。質問文に対する答えになるようにlook forの目的語を明示して英文を組み立てる。　(2)　第10段落3文目が該当箇所となる。質問文に対する答えになるよう，動詞・目的語を明示して英文を組み立てる。　6　本文全体より，紀元前43年の火山の噴火がローマの気候や人々にも大きな影響を与えたことが読み取れるため，ウが適切。

【中学校】

【1】1　①　ア　　②　ウ　　2　生物学や生物学的発達の特定の状況がどのように生じてくるかについての知識。　　3　もし子供がおよそ5歳までに第1言語に接しなければ，言語を習得しないだろうということ。　　4　本質的に乳幼児や子供から人と触れ合う機会を奪うことを伴うだろうから。　　5　(1)　They can learn another language after the beginning of what he calls “their second decade.”　　(2)　She never developed the ability to speak fluently.　　6　イ

〈解説〉1　①　entailは「～を必然的に伴う」の意でアが最も近い。　②　proponentは「支持者，賛成者」の意でウが最も近い。　2　設問の解答は下線部の文の2つ後の文で述べられている。come out of～が「～から生まれる，出てくる」という意味なので，of以下の内容を適切な日本語でまとめればよい。　3　下線部の文の次の文のspecificallyは「具体的に」の意。よってこの文で具体的な主張が述べられていると読み取れ，適切な日本語でまとめればよい。　4　下線部の文の前文

のbecause節に理由が述べられており，この部分を適切な日本語でまとめればよい。　5　(1)　第3段落第5文が解答箇所となる。設問文のpeople who have an ordinary intellectual capacityは，本文中のsomeone is of average intelligenceを言い換えたものなので，that以下を質問への答えとしてふさわしい形で英文を組み立てればよい。　(2)　第4段落5文目が解答箇所となる。問われているのはGenieの会話能力の上達度合のため，Despite receiving intensive interventions to teach her Englishの部分は不要。　6　第2段落最終文の内容がイと一致する。

【2】1　You may come upon books entirely by chance which may have a revolutionary effect upon you.　2　I would like to give a tablet to each student mainly for active speaking and listening practice. That will make it easier for students to listen to English words and sentences recorded in the textbooks. It is also possible for teachers to have them repeat after the sounds and read aloud for practice in the classroom. In addition, at home, students themselves can record their own voice on a tablet and compare the native speaker's pronunciation to their own. As a result, students can improve their speaking and listening abilities for better communication not only in the classroom but also at home. (102 words)

〈解説〉1　come upon～「～に出くわす」，by chance「偶然に」，have an effect on～「～に影響を及ぼす」といった熟語と，問題文の日本語に合致した単語を用いて英文を組み立てればよい。entirelyはby chanceを修飾して「全く偶然に」となる。　2　解答例ではICT機器をリスニングとスピーキングの練習に用いることを提案している。また，教室において教師主導で行う英語学習だけでなく，生徒自身が自宅でも自分の音声を録音してネイティブスピーカーと比較したりするなど，より良いコミュニケーションができるための学習を，教室だけでなく自宅でも行えることを，効果として挙げている

【高等学校】

【1】1　X　ウ　　Y　エ　　2　限られた量の情報だけが処理されること。　　3　第2言語学習者を含めた言語使用者は，ある特定の単語や言語形式が最近の会話の中で話し相手から使われると，その語や形式を使う確率がより高くなること。　　4　新出語の綴り，意味，発音，その語が想起させる他の語，その語と共起する他の語。

5　(1)　We are not likely to store it in long-term memory for retrieval at a later time.　　(2)　No, it isn't.　　6　イ

〈解説〉1　X　空所を含む文は「長期記憶の容量は－おそらく(　　)ではないが－非常に大きい」の意。よってウのinfinite「無限な」が適切。Y　空所を含む文の前文でone of the best ways to learn something is to test yourself on it「何かを学ぶ最も良い方法の一つはそれについて自分自身にテストをすることである」とある。この内容と合致するのはエ「それを見ないで記憶するように努める」となる。　2　下線部の次の文のonly a limited amount of material can be processed in RAMを適切な日本語にまとめればよい。　3　下線部直後の関係詞where以下の内容を適切な日本語にまとめればよい。　4　下線部の直前の文から，「私たちが注目するすべてのこと」を適切な日本語にまとめればよい。

5　(1)　第1段落最終文のwe are not likely to～が該当箇所となる。

(2)「知覚したことを思い出せなくなるのは確実か」という問いに対し，第3段落第1～4文の内容から解答すればよい。　6　最終段落後ろから3文目の内容がイと一致する。

【2】1　The addition of a new dish to the menu, featuring local food, resulted in favorable feedback from customers.　　2　I would like to suggest that ICT devices should be utilized for English reading and composition classes. For example, when teachers request students to explain the content of reading material in a textbook, students can anonymously announce their answer and opinion without hesitation via the device. Not only each answer or opinion but also feedback from a teacher for it can be shared by everyone much more easily and immediately. Students can improve their ability of description by learning from different mistakes by others. In addition, they can also deepen and broaden their perspective by obtaining different opinions from others. (100 words)

〈解説〉1　主語を無生物のThe addition of a new dish to the menuとし，featuring local foodがa new dishを修飾する。動詞はresult in「～という結果になる」を用いればよい。「好意的な反応」はfavorable feedbackとする。　2　高等学校学習指導要領解説外国語編・英語編では，出題の項目について，「写真や映像などを見せることで，理解を促進し，現実感や臨場感を与え，学びの動機付けやきっかけを与えることができる」，「インターネット等を活用することで，学校外へと広がる，現実との結び付きの濃い発展学習を実現することができる」，「コンピュータや情報通信ネットワークを使うことによって，教材に関する資料や情報を入手したり，電子メールによって情報を英語で発信したりすることもできる」ことを挙げ，「このような活動を通して，生徒一人一人が主体的に世界と関わっていこうとする態度を育成することもできる」と解説している。こうしたことを踏まえて，どのような活用法が考えられるか具体的な意見を述べればよい。解答例では，ICT機器を英作文やリーディングの授業に活用することを挙げている。例えば，リーディング教材の内容を生徒に説明させるとき，生徒は匿名で気兼ねなく発表でき，教師のフィードバックも含めてすぐに全員に共有できることを利点として述べている。効果として，生徒の表現力向上や，自分の見解を深め広げることが期待できる。

2022年度　実施問題

【中高共通】

【１】(放送による問題)これはリスニング・テストです。放送の指示に従って答えなさい。

ただいまから，リスニング・テストを行います。問題は，1，2，3，4の四つです。聞いている間にメモを取っても構いません。

1　では，1の問題から始めます。問題は，No. 1とNo. 2の2問です。

これから読まれる英文に対する応答として最もふさわしいものを，続いて読まれるa，b，cの中から一つ選び，記号で答えなさい。答えは，大文字，小文字どちらでも構いません。なお，英文と応答は1度しか読まれません。

では，始めます。

No. 1　Why does page ten come after page eleven?

a. Because she came here after nine.

b. It came straight from the top.

c. They must have been mixed up somehow.

No. 2　Gee, your roommates make a lot of noise, don't they?

a. You can say that again!

b. I heard the news over the radio.

c. Sorry, they are quite expensive.

2　次に，2の問題に移ります。問題は，No. 1からNo. 3までの3問です。

これから，短い対話文を読みます。そのあとでクエスチョンと言っ

て質問します。その答えとして最もふさわしいものを，続いて読まれるa，b，c，dの中から一つ選び，記号で答えなさい。答えは，大文字，小文字どちらでも構いません。なお，対話文・質問・答えの選択肢は1度しか読まれません。

では，始めます。

No. 1

M : Today is sure to be a scorcher.

W : You're telling me! It's only 8:00 in the morning and it's already almost 30 degrees.

M : According to the weather forecast, it might rain this evening. That might be refreshing.

W : Let's hope so.

Question : What does the man imply about the weather?

a. He wishes it were cooler.

b. He thinks it is refreshing.

c. He likes hot weather.

d. He does not want it to rain.

No. 2

W : Bobby, weren't you supposed to bring the pile of flyers to the mailroom?

M : Right. But first, could you tell me where we keep the list of former customers? I can't find it in the database.

W : That's because it's not there. The customer information is stored in the mailroom only.

M : Oh, OK. The clerks there will know where to send those advertisements, then.

Question : According to the woman, how is the information protected?

a. By having it sent by e-mail.

b. By frequently changing a password.

c. By restricting access to the room.

d. By keeping it in one specific place.

No. 3

W : I see that the first bus has arrived. What time will the second bus be arriving?

M : I heard that it got caught in some heavy traffic coming off the Expressway, but I expect it to be pulling in at any minute now. Will that throw off the schedule?

W : I don't think so. I want everyone to enter the museum together, so we'll have the people from the first bus wait until it gets here.

M : They won't have to wait too long.

Question : What caused the second bus to be delayed?

a. The timetable of the tour was altered.

b. The traffic accident happened on the Expressway.

c. There were too many automobiles at the exit ramp.

d. The Expressway was closed for the time being.

3　次に3の問題に移ります。問題は，No. 1からNo. 3までの3問です。

これから，あるまとまりのある英文を読みます。そのあとで，クエスチョンズと言って，その英文について三つの質問をします。その答えとして最もふさわしいものを，質問に続いて読まれるa，b，c，dの中から一つ選び，記号で答えなさい。答えは，大文字，小文字どちらでも構いません。なお，英文・質問・答えの選択肢は全体を通して2回読まれます。

では，始めます。

Although snow's natural color may be white, it has been known to take on more hypnotizing hues.

According to Kenneth Libbrecht, a professor of physics at the California

Institute of Technology, snowpack, icebergs and glaciers can sometimes appear blue when light enters their bellies through cracks and crevices and gets trapped. As this light travels within the snow and ice, countless ice crystals scatter it on its journey. The farther it travels, the more times it scatters. Because water and ice "preferentially absorb more red light than blue light," when the light rays finally emerge from the snow layers, it's the shorter blue wavelengths rather than the longer red wavelengths that reflect toward our eyes. The longer the scattering repeats, the more noticeable the blue hue will be. The National Snow and Ice Data Center suggests snow depths of at least a few feet are needed to see any tint at all.

Pink or red-tinted snow — nicknamed "watermelon snow" — has also been documented. Its color comes courtesy of a type of cold-loving freshwater algae living within the snowpack, which is red. Similarly, other particles and organisms can tint snow, too. Because of this, Libbrecht admits that, hypothetically, snow could assume any color of the rainbow.

Of course, it's no mystery where one color of snow comes from; if you see yellow snow, it's a safe bet animal tracks are nearby.

Questions

No. 1 What do ice crystals scatter within the snow and ice?

a. Light.

b. Cracks and crevices.

c. Snow layers.

d. Snow depths.

No. 2 Which best summarizes the research by Kenneth Libbrecht?

a. More blue light tends to be absorbed by water and ice than red light, so they appear red to our eyes.

b. Less red light tends to be absorbed by water and ice than blue light, so they appear blue to our eyes.

c. More red light tends to be absorbed by water and ice than blue light, so they appear red to our eyes.

d. Less blue light tends to be absorbed by water and ice than red light, so they appear blue to our eyes.

No. 3　What is true about the passage?

a. Kenneth Libbrecht is one of the distinguished scientists majoring in hypnotism.

b. There should be snow depths of a few feet or more in order to see snow in any colors.

c. Sometimes snow appears pink or red due to particles of watermelon in the snowpack.

d. Yellow snow suggests that there should be a safe place not far away.

4　次に4の問題に移ります。問題は，No. 1とNo. 2の2問です。

これから，英語による対話文を読みます。(　　)のところに入る英語を聞き取り，書きなさい。対話文はそれぞれ2回読まれます。

では，始めます。

No. 1

M : He said he would write the thesis of 50 pages on macroeconomics. Did he make it?

W : Why not? (His behavior is consistent with what he says).

No. 2

W : I realized that comedies are never funnier than in a packed movie house.

M : Exactly. It shows we (are all influenced by peer pressure and social norms).

これで，リスニング・テストを終わります。次の問題に移ってください。

(☆☆☆◎◎◎◎)

【2】次の英文や対話文の中の(　　)に最も適するものを，以下のア～エの中からそれぞれ一つずつ選び，記号で答えなさい。

1　All employees (　　) security passwords have not been changed for over a month are reminded via e-mail to change them.

ア　why　　イ　whose　　ウ　who　　エ　whomever

2　Please take (　　) with you and tell me what you think of them tomorrow.

ア　these books of his　　イ　these his books

ウ　his books of these　　エ　his these books

3　It's (　　) each of you to help make the project a success.

ア　as to　　イ　on account of　　ウ　on top of　　エ　up to

4　Simpson Catering can supply a wide range of entertainment (　　) its food and beverage services.

ア　in addition to　　イ　as far as　　ウ　in the face of

エ　on the verge of

5　Different (　　) Mike and David were, they had something in common.

ア　unless　　イ　as　　ウ　if　　エ　how

6　The school cafeteria is not large enough to (　　) all the students at the same time.

ア　integrate　　イ　compromise　　ウ　accommodate

エ　customize

7　You don't have to hesitate to take this gift. It's a just (　　) for your effort.

ア　deserve　　イ　deserved　　ウ　reward　　エ　rewarded

8　A: I want to ask Joanne out to dinner, but I'm worried she might say no.

B: You shouldn't be so (　　). If you really like her, just go right up and ask her.

ア　prospective　　イ　innumerable　　ウ　instrumental

エ　timid

9　The nation's (　　) in table tennis is clear from the fact that its players usually come in first place in international tournaments.

ア　dominance　　イ　resemblance　　ウ　declaration

エ　contradiction

10　It took much longer than expected to (　　) all of the duties handed down by my predecessor.

ア　respond　　イ　console　　ウ　accomplish　　エ　intersect

11　The champion golfer had little time to (　　) her victory at the competition. Within days, she was already training for the next tournament.

ア　savor　　イ　trespass　　ウ　abduct　　エ　intimidate

12　Although Kevin was (　　) by his friend's suggestion that they start an editing company together, he decided to stay with his job at the newspaper.

ア　dispatched　　イ　deducted　　ウ　abridged　　エ　intrigued

13　Rebecca was extremely nervous at the beginning of her first recital. She (　　) all her courage and began to play the piano.

ア　sent out　　イ　plumped up　　ウ　rounded off

エ　summoned up

14　The baseball player's fans were (　　) when he suddenly announced his retirement. Everyone had expected him to play for at least two more seasons.

ア　obligated　　イ　entrusted　　ウ　stunned　　エ　elongated

15　A: This cactus on my desk isn't doing very well.

B: Don't water it so much. It's a desert plant, you know, so it's best suited to (　　) conditions.

ア　soggy　　イ　muggy　　ウ　sleek　　エ　arid

(☆☆☆◎◎◎◎)

【3】次の英文を読んで，以下の問いに答えなさい。

The story of written language — and therefore of punctuation — will never come to an end. The language changes as we use it. New technologies like book printing and digital distribution on the web provide guidance and frameworks for how we write. (1)<u>Those of us who are preoccupied with the written language</u> need to remind each other that the development of language cannot be reduced to a simple technological determinism. This is primarily something we must do ourselves.

We write better, faster and more effectively if we use punctuation marks deliberately, consistently and in a way that more or less corresponds to the ①<u>conventions</u> agreed on by our society. To write is to communicate and, like so many others, the word 'communication' also has its origins in Latin: *communicare*. The word is to do with fellowship, understanding and connections. If we are to communicate well when we write, we (X). So there is still a need for a few common ground rules for punctuation as well. The more we have in common when we communicate, the better we will understand one another.

Today, everyone who owns a smartphone possesses a means of publication capable of distributing a message that in theory can reach the entire world in seconds. However, we also know that our messages are not necessarily registered, understood and interpreted by recipients in the way we hope and expect. Technology has given every person the potential status of editor, so the struggle for attention has become that much harder. In our time it is easier than ever before to get a word in but more difficult to be heard — not to say listened to. If we wish to be understood, we cannot write according to the post-modernist credo (Y).

Neurolinguistic research confirms what we believe: correct punctuation helps us to understand the writings of others more quickly. In a study from 2018, the American researchers Heggie and Wade-Woolley conclude that punctuation sends the reader a message about how the text is to be read. When we read, we divide the text into units that we think belong together. If the punctuation is conventional, the text rapidly delivers the desired meaning and possible misunderstandings are avoided. The researchers Drury, Baum, Valeriote and Steinhauer summed it up in a similar way in a study from 2016. They measured brain activity during reading in order to find out how the inner voice produced by reading affects the understanding. The results? English-speaking readers rely on the commas when they are trying to understand a text. The same results had previously been found among German and Chinese readers (but not among the Dutch, something the researchers will investigate further in order to find out why). Nevertheless, (2)the main conclusion of the research is clear: when you use commas in the way the reader expects them to be used, your message will get through better and more quickly.

Back in antiquity, Aristophanes was the first to create a system in which the comma, full stop and semicolon would help to promote clearer communication. Later, punctuation had its ups and downs, especially the latter, but in the Renaissance Aldo Manuzio and like-minded contemporaries succeeded in putting in place a punctuation system that became standard in our western language community. I believe that, as a starting point, we should keep to a standard of this kind when we write formally and professionally. If the boundaries are generous, there is a decent amount of tolerance for personal preferences, fun and wriggle-room within the standard.

Common language codes were one of the driving forces behind the great advances in Europe 500 years ago, with a common punctuation system as one of the foundations. In *The Creative Society*, Lars Tvede wrote that common language codes in particular are an ②indispensable condition if we in the west continue to desire dynamism and creativity.

In his massive tome *The History and Power of Writing*, the French historian Henri-Jean Martin emphasises the idea that grammar is the mother of all creative disciplines and logic made it possible to shape the rules for the particular logic of writing.

(Bård Borch Michalsen, *Signs of Civilisation*による。ただし，設問の都合で一部省略及び改変している。)

1　下線部(1)がしなければならないのはどのようなことか，本文に即して日本語で書きなさい。

2　下線部①，②を別の語で言い換えたとき，最も意味の近いものを，次のア～エの中からそれぞれ一つずつ選び，記号で答えなさい。

①　ア　contributions　イ　formulas　ウ　proponents
　　エ　metaphors

②　ア　decent　イ　equivalent　ウ　clinical
　　エ　crucial

3　本文中の空欄(　X　)，(　Y　)に入る英語として最も適切なものを，次のア～エの中からそれぞれ一つずつ選び，記号で答えなさい。

X　ア　probably use fewer punctuation marks than ever before, and put less emphasis on the rules of grammar

　イ　neither have to know the rules of punctuation nor have positive and valid reasons for not following them

　ウ　can write a great many things in the course of one short day, and the variety also applies to punctuation

　エ　cannot all keep to individual private rules for how we are to write words, build up sentences or punctuate

Y　ア　*anything goes*　イ　*time flies*　ウ　*hit the books*
　エ　*in hot water*

4　下線部(2)が指す内容を，本文に即して日本語で書きなさい。

5　本文の内容に即して，次の英文の(　　)に入る適切な英語を書きなさい。

(1)　(　　) is am example of a device which enables us to distribute messages quickly on the web.

(2)　Dutch readers (　　), and the researchers will study more to know why.

6　本文の内容に最も合うものを，次のア～オの中から一つ選び，記号で答えなさい。

ア　How much punctuation people share is scarcely related with their mutual understanding when communicating.

イ　In the age of digital distribution to recipients all over the world, we have to endure incredible hardships to get a word in.

ウ　Neurolinguistic is a field of study that the author and other linguists abandon as a means to conduct their research.

エ　A punctuation system that became standard was introduced by Aldo Manuzio and like-minded contemporaries.

オ　In a great book written by a French historian, grammar is treated as something irrelevant to creative disciplines.

(☆☆☆◎◎◎◎)

【中学校】

【1】次の英文を読んで，以下の問いに答えなさい。

How are we expected to grade 30 research papers in the space of 48 hours so that they can be handed back while the feedback will still do the most good? The answer, of course, is rubrics. Rubrics are wonderful time savers and, for many of us, when first starting to use rubrics, timeliness is the main ①virtue that justifies their use. Rubrics allow us to meet the deadline posed by student attention spans and expectations and to do it without sacrificing the need for that feedback to be detailed and specific to each student's individual case.

As many of us know, most students make the same or similar mistakes on any given assignment. The combination of mistakes may be different and individual, but the actual mistakes are much the same. As a result, when we seriously try to offer specific, individual feedback to each student in note form, we often find ourselves writing variations on the same themes on most of the papers.

(1)A rubric eliminates this problem. In a rubric, we simply incorporate easily predictable notes into the "descriptions of dimensions" portion of the rubric. Then, when grading time comes, all we need do is circle or check off all comments that apply to each specific student and perhaps add a note here and there where the rubric does not cover what was done precisely enough, where added emphasis is needed, or where the connection between one or more aspects of the student's performance needs to be stressed. The use of the rubric does not, of course, preclude notes specific to the student that can be placed on the rubric, the paper itself, or elsewhere. The evaluative process of grading remains the same, as does the specificity of the feedback, but the time taken to transmit the feedback to the student is cut by at least 50% and often more.

The result is an easier grading process for us, and timely, detailed, often easier-to-read feedback for the student.

It's a vicious cycle. Students *say* they want detailed feedback so that they can know what they are doing right so they can keep doing it, as well as what they are doing wrong so that they can improve.

Yet, as we often discover, students barely seem to read, let alone absorb, the extended notes on their work that took up so much of our grading time. In time, (2)some of us may become discouraged and stop writing such detailed notes. If this continues, eventually we may find that our written comments are confined to terse statements such as "lacks ②cohesion, needs more references, organized, C ＋."

Students are understandably confused and discouraged by such laconic remarks, and here too, research bears them out. Brinko (1993) found that feedback was most effective when it contained as much information as possible rather than simply evaluating the level of the work. The same study revealed, however, that including a description of the highest level of achievement possible was also useful to students. Balancing (3)these two findings is where rubrics excel.

The demand for an explanation of the highest level of achievement possible and detailed feedback is fulfilled in the rubric itself. The highest level descriptions of the dimensions are, in fact, the highest level of achievement possible, whereas the remaining levels, circled or checked off, are typed versions of the notes we regularly write on student work explaining how and where they failed to meet that highest level. The student still receives all the necessary details about how and where the assignment did or did not achieve its goal, and even suggestions (in the form of the higher levels of descriptions) as to how it might have been done better.

Moreover, because we discuss the rubric and thereby the grading criteria in class, the student has a much better idea of what these details mean. Even when we make extensive notes and students actually do read them, there can still be quite a gap between comments and student understanding of expectations. For example, students may not have been acquainted with terms such as *context*, *analysis*, or *citations* before the rubric discussion began, but by the time they receive their graded work back, such words should have clear meaning for them.

(Dannelle D. Stevens and Antonia J. Levi, *Introduction to Rubrics* による。ただし，設問の都合で一部省略及び改変している。)

1　下線部①，②の英語の定義として最もよくあてはまるものを，次のア～エの中からそれぞれ一つずつ選び，記号で答えなさい。

①　ア　a fault in something or disadvantage of something

イ　an attractive or useful quality

ウ　the subject or main idea in a talk, piece of writing or work of art

エ　the state of feeling nervous or worried that something bad is going to happen

②　ア　all the words that a person knows or uses

イ　the things that are contained in something

ウ　a relationship, based on grammar or meaning, between two parts of a piece of writing

エ　a strong feeling of interest and enjoyment about something and eagerness to be involved in it

2　下線部(1)について，ルーブリックは具体的にどのような問題を取り除くか，本文に即して日本語で書きなさい。

3　下線部(2)のようになる原因として述べられていることを，本文に即して日本語で書きなさい。

4　下線部(3)について，一番目に述べられていることを，本文に即して日本語で書きなさい。

5　本文の内容に即して，次の問いに英語で答えなさい。

(1)　When giving feedback to students through rubrics, what proportion of time can teachers save?

(2)　What helps students to make up the gap between comments in the notes and their understanding of expectations?

6　本文の内容に最も合うものを，次のア～エの中から一つ選び，記号で答えなさい。

ア　Rubrics must tell students the deadline of their assignments because teachers think timeliness is necessary.

イ　In a rubric, teachers shouldn't add detailed notes because they are included in the descriptions of dimensions.

ウ　Students want detailed feedback to their assignments to know what they are doing right and what they are doing wrong.

エ　If teachers give their students brief comments such as "needs more references", they will get motivated.

(☆☆☆◎◎◎◎)

【2】次の1，2について，指示に従って答えなさい。

1　次の日本語を英語に直しなさい。

その視覚的性質のため，漫画は日本語に興味がある外国人にとって優れた学習用教材になる可能性がある。

2 「中学校学習指導要領」(平成29年3月告示)の「第2章　第9節　外国語　第2　各言語の目標及び内容等　3　指導計画の作成と内容の取扱い」には，「授業は英語で行うことを基本とする」と示されている。英語で授業を行うことの利点や効果と，英語で授業を行う際の留意点を，学習指導要領の趣旨を踏まえ，100語程度の英語で書きなさい。ただし，語数には，句読点や符号は含まないものとする。なお，解答の総語数を記入すること。

(☆☆☆◎◎◎◎)

【高等学校】

【1】次の英文を読んで，以下の問いに答えなさい。

The fact that languages carve up space in different ways is challenging for the view that a set of basic universal primitive spatial concepts underlie all spatial language (Levinson and Meira 2003; Bowernan 1996). For example, containment and support relations do not always cluster in the same way across languages when speakers of different languages are charged with sorting or describing spatial scenes. While English distinguishes between containment (*in*) and support (*on*) relations, Dutch is among a cluster of languages that more finely differentiates support relations, with a distinction between vertical attachment (*aan*: a picture on a wall, a handle on a door), and horizontal support (*op*: a cup on a table). In contrast, Spanish collapses containment and support relations with a single term, *en*, appropriate for containment and support (Bowerman 1996). Such differences lead to two questions that (　X　) mention. First, does the language one learns affect how one structures space? Second, do speakers of different languages actually "think" spatially in different ways? I take each of these issues in turn.

It is tempting to think that (　Y　). Indeed, with respect to *in* and *on*, differences in the way Korean and English languages carve up these relations have been the subject of a series of fascinating studies. While English distinguishes between containment and support events as the end points of motion actions, Korean distinguishes between tight-fit and loose-fit path events. In Korean the verb *kkita* is used for tight-fit path events (putting a video cassette in a video cassette box/putting a lid on a jar) while *nehta* is used for loose-fit containment paths and *nohta* for loose-fit support relations (Bowerman 1996). Choi et al. (1999), using a preferential looking method, showed that 1.5-2 year old Korean and English learning children already look at language-appropriate aspects of spatial relations when looking at visual scenes paired with words in their language. However, (1)McDonough et al. (2003) and Hespos and Spelke (2004) found that younger infants learning Korean or English look at both geometric distinctions between containment and support and tight-fit loose-fit distinctions, suggesting that learning a language might focus on some perceptual distinctions more than others, rather than language structuring space uniquely for that language. Indeed, as I reviewed above, even English adults are sensitive to degrees of location control when using *in* and *on*, and therefore it might be mistaken to argue that language completely filters out distinctions. However, one has to be cautious; as Casasola (2008) notes, it is likely that the extent to which language structures spatial categories in development varies as a function of spatial category.

It has also been claimed that the language one speaks affects performance on a range of non-linguistic tasks (i.e., a test of "linguistic relativity"). A much-discussed example is that of Pederson and colleagues (1998), who found differences across a range of tasks between speakers of languages differing in their use of reference frames. For example, (2)Tzeltal speakers, who use the absolute frame of reference even in small-scale/table-top space, have a tendency, when they rotate 180 degrees, to rearrange objects absolutely, while Dutch and English speakers rotate the object arrangement in alignment with body rotation. The interpretation of these results as evidence for a strong form of the Whorfian hypotheses has been controversial. What *is* clear is that speakers of languages can use their language as a tool to aid performance on non-linguistic tasks. However, while speakers of a language may use the distinctions they have in their language when performing non-linguistic tasks, those distinctions may not capture how those terms are actually used within a language by speakers.

(3)<u>It</u> is obvious that spatial language is a natural place to start to examine the spatial constructs that are important for language. This brief (and highly selective) review of empirical research on spatial language has illustrated how experimental approaches to spatial language have helped to unpack the multiple constraints underpinning the mapping between language and space. Cross-linguistic data collected using multiple methods will continue to play an important role in understanding not only the extent of possible universal perceptual parameters underpinning spatial language across languages, but also the full range of constraints speakers may employ to use the spatial language they have within their own language.

(Kenny R. Coventry, *Cognitive Linguistics Key Topics* Chapter 3: Space による。ただし，設問の都合で一部省略及び改変している。)

1　オランダ語の***aan***と***op***にはどのような違いがあるのか，本文に即して日本語で書きなさい。

2　本文中の空欄(　X　), (　Y　)に入る英語として最も適切なものを，次のア～オの中からそれぞれ一つずつ選び，記号で答えなさい。

X　ア　foil　　イ　enact　　ウ　merit　　エ　rehash　　オ　infer

Y　ア　the researchers use a methodology designed to elicit spatial demonstratives without speakers realizing that their language was being tested

イ　the distinctions a language makes are revealing about the type of non-linguistic concepts and processes that speakers of that language employ

ウ　it has been long noted that spatial terms are ambiguous, both in terms of the same words cropping up in spatial and non-spatial contexts

エ　an important warning is to note that the experimental approach we have overviewed should not be viewed as a substitute for other methods

オ　one can define spatial language as language that enables a hearer to narrow a search (usually visual) for the location of an object

3　下線部(1)は，発見したことをもとに，どのようなことを主張しているか，本文に即して日本語で書きなさい。

4　下線部(2)に示されるTzeltal speakersの行動の傾向に対し，同様のことがあったとき，オランダ語や英語の話者はどのように対応するか，本文に即して日本語で書きなさい。

5　下線部(3)が指す内容を，本文に即して日本語で書きなさい。

6　本文の内容に即して，次の問いに英語で答えなさい。

In the preferential looking method Choi et al. used in their work, what were shown to the children?

7　本文の内容に最も合うものを，次のア～オの中から一つ選び，記号で答えなさい。

ア　Speakers who don't have experience distinguishing *in* and *on* lack a capacity for sorting or describing spatial scenes.

イ　In English, *in* and *on* are used to distinguish two different relations, while *en* in Spanish is appropriate for the two relations.

ウ　One Korean word is referred to as an example of a verb that speakers adopt for both tight-fit and loose-fit path events.

エ　The author provides a result of a research that shows clear evidence for a strong form of the Whorfian hypotheses.

オ　Cross linguistic data is of importance in curtailing the extent of universal perceptual parameters across languages.

(☆☆☆◎◎◎◎)

【2】次の1，2について，指示に従って答えなさい。

1　次の日本語を英語に直しなさい。

国際感覚を持っている人は，国際問題を，偏見のない視点から考えることを嫌がらない。

2「高等学校学習指導要領」(平成30年3月告示)の「第2章　第8節　外国語　第2款　各科目　第4　論理・表現Ⅰ」の「1　目標　(1)　話すこと[やり取り]　イ」において，「日常的な話題や社会的な話題について，使用する語句や文，対話の展開などにおいて，多くの支援を活用すれば，ディベートやディスカッションなどの活動を通して，聞いたり読んだりしたことを活用しながら，基本的な語句や文を用いて，意見や主張などを論理の構成や展開を工夫して話して伝え合うことができるようにする。」と示されている。あなたは「論理・表現Ⅰ」において，生徒をどのように支援するか。またその支援にはどのような効果があると考えるか。学習指導要領の趣旨を踏まえ，100語程度の英語で書きなさい。ただし，語数には，句読点や符号は含まないものとする。なお，解答の総語数を記入すること。

(☆☆☆◎◎◎◎)

解答・解説

【中高共通】

【1】1　No. 1　c　No. 2　a　2　No. 1　a　No. 2　d　No. 3　c　3　No. 1　a　No. 2　d　No. 3　b　4　No. 1　His behavior is consistent with what he says　No. 2　are all influenced by peer pressure and social norms

〈解説〉山形県のリスニングテストでは文字情報が一切ない。よって，英文，質問文，選択肢すべてを正確に聴き取る力が要求される。

1　短い質問文に対して，読み上げられる選択肢から答えを選ぶ3択形式。放送は1度のみ。　No. 1「なぜ10ページが11ページの後に来ているのか」に対して「ごちゃまぜにされてしまったに違いない」。
No. 2「おやおや，また君のルームメートが騒いでいるね」に対して「本当にそうだ」。You can say that again.「全くだ」。　2　短い対話文と質問文を聞いて，答えを選ぶ最も一般的な形式。内容は日常的な会話で，放送は1度のみ。　3　200語程度の英文と質問文を聞いて，答えを選ぶ形式。話題は雪の塊・氷山・氷河などの色合い。放送は2度あるので，1度目は全体の流れを把握しながら，2度目は答えとなる箇所に注意しながら聞く。　4　男性の発話があり，それに応じた女性の発話の一部を書きとるディクテーション問題。聞き取る英文を推測できる。No. 1の男性の発話は「彼は50ページのマクロ経済学の論文を書くと言っていたね。書けたのかな」。No. 2は「コメディは満員の映画館で見るのが一番面白いと思ったよ」。

【2】1　イ　2　ア　3　エ　4　ア　5　イ　6　ウ　7　ウ
8　エ　9　ア　10　ウ　11　ア　12　エ　13　エ
14　ウ　15　エ

〈解説〉1「セキュリティパスワードを1カ月以上変更していない従業員は全員，メールで変更するよう注意喚起されている」。従業員のセキュリティパスワードを指すので，所有の意味を表す関係代名詞が適切。
2　所有格は指示代名詞thisと並べて使わない。代わりに〈of＋所有格〉を名詞の後につける。　3「プロジェクトを成功させるのを手伝うかどうかは個々に任せる」。up to～「～次第で」。　4「Simpson Cateringは飲食のサービスに加えて，様々なもてなしを提供することができる」。in addition to～「～に加えて」。　5「MikeとDavidは似ていなかったが」。譲歩節中の倒置。〈形容詞[副詞]＋as[though]＋S＋V〉。
6　accommodate～「～を収容する」。　7　a reward for effort「努力に対する報酬」。　8　timid「臆病な」。　9　dominance「優勢(な状態)」。
10　accomplish～「～を成し遂げる」。　11「優勝したゴルフ選手は大会の勝利をかみしめる時間はなかった」。savor～「～を楽しむ，味わう」。　12「Kevinは一緒に編集会社を設立しようという友人の提案に興味をそそられたが，新聞社の仕事を続けることに決めた」。intrigue～「～の興味を引き付ける」。　13　summon up one's courage「勇気を奮い立たせる」。　14　stun「驚かせる，当惑させる」。　15「知っての通り，それは砂漠の植物だから，乾燥した状態が最適だ」。arid「乾いた，湿気のない」。

【3】1　言語の発展は，単純な科学技術による決定論へと帰することはないということを，お互いに思い出させること。　2　①　イ　②　エ　3　X　エ　Y　ア　4　読み手が予測するような使い方でカンマを使えば，メッセージはよりよく，すばやく伝わること。　5　(1)　A smartphone　(2)　don't rely on the commas when they are trying to understand a text　6　エ

〈解説〉1　下線部(1)は「書き言葉に頭を占められている人」。need to以下を訳出する。　2　①　convention「しきたり，慣習」。formula「方策，基本原則」。　②　indispensable「必須の」。crucial「不可欠の，極めて重要な」。　3　X　空所にはエが入り，「書く時に上手くコミュニケーションをとるつもりなら，どのように書き，文を組み立て，句読点を打つかについてすべて個人の規則だけに従うことはできない」となる。そして「句読点について共通の基本原則が必要だ」という内容が空所後に続く。　Y「理解されることを望むのであれば，脱近代主義者の信条『何でもあり』に従って書くことはできない」。anything goes「何でもまかり通る」，time flies「時がたつのは早い」，hit the books「一生懸命勉強する」，in hot water「苦境にあって」。　4　下線部(2)は「調査の主な結論」。直後のコロン以下を訳出する。in the way＋S＋V「SがVする方法で」。　5　(1)　第3段落1文目参照。「スマートフォンはウェブ上ですぐにメッセージを広めることを可能にするデバイスの一例である」となる。　(2)　第4段落8文目，9文目より，英語，ドイツ語，中国語を話す読者は本文を読もうとするとき，カン

マに依存するが，オランダ人読者はそうではない，となる。　6　第5段落2文目参照。エ「標準となった句読点のシステムはAldo Manuzioや同じ考えを持つ当時の人々によって導入された」が正しい。なお，Aldo Manuzioは15世紀末にイタリア・ベネチアに印刷所を興したルネサンス期の出版人。商業印刷の父といわれる。

【中学校】

【1】1　①　イ　　②　ウ　　2　生徒個々に具体的なフィードバックを記述して示そうとするときに，同じ話題について多種多様な記述をしてしまうということ。　　3　評価の時間の多くを割く生徒の作品に対する長い記述を，生徒は吸収するどころか，ほとんど読みもしないこと。　　4　フィードバックは，単に作品の到達度を評価するよりも，できる限り多くの情報が含まれている方が効果的であること。5　(1)　At least 50% and often more.　　(2)　Discussing the rubric and thereby the grading criteria in class does.　　6　ウ

〈解説〉1　①　virtue「長所」なので，イ「魅力的または有益な性質」。②　cohesion「まとまり」なので，ウ「文書の2つのパート間の文法や意味に基づいた関係」。　2　下線部(1)は「ルーブリック(学習到達度を一覧表の形で示す評価規準)はこの問題を取り除く」。直前の第2段落の3文目を訳出する。in note form「メモ形式で」。　3　下線部(2)は「やる気を失う者もいる」。直前の1文がその理由に当たる。barely～「ほとんど～ない」。let alone～「～はもちろん，まして～なんて」。extended「延長された，長くされた」。　4　下線部(3)は「これら2つの発見」。第7段落2文目，3文目に述べられているBrinkoの2つの発見を指す。一番目は，feedback was most effective when it contained as much information as possible rather than simply evaluating the level of the workであり，二番目は，including a description of the highest level of achievement possible was also useful to studentsで，「達成可能な最もハイレベルの記述を盛り込むことも生徒にとって有益であること」。
5　(1)　質問は「ルーブリックを通して生徒にフィードバックを与え

るとき，教師はどれくらいの時間を節約できるか」。第3段落の最終文参照。「少なくとも50パーセントで，ときにそれ以上」。　(2)　質問は「メモのコメントと期待されていることを生徒が理解することの間のギャップを埋めるのに何が役立つか」。最終段落参照。「教師が書いた広範囲にわたるメモを生徒が実際に読んでも，コメントと期待されていることを生徒が理解することの間にギャップがある」が，「ルーブリックと，授業の評価規準について議論するので，生徒はこれらの詳細が何を意味するのかをよりよく理解する」とある。よって，「ルーブリックと，それに従って授業の評価規準を議論することが役立つ」。
6　第5段落の2文目に「改善できるように何を誤っているのかだけでなく，正しいことを続けられるよう，正しくできているのは何かわかるよう詳細なフィードバックが欲しいと生徒は言っている」とある。よって，ウ「生徒は，何が正しくて何が誤っているかわかるよう，課題に対して詳細なフィードバックを欲している」が正しい。

【2】1　Because of its visual nature, manga can be an excellent learning resource for foreigners who are interested in Japanese.　　2〔解答例〕I think teachers should conduct English classes principally in English to cultivate students' communication abilities. In such classes, students can be constantly exposed to English and they can make use of English as a means of communication. To carry it out, the important thing is to make sure of the students' comprehension. If an unfamiliar word appears in the text, teachers pause the class for rephrasing it. Or students can look for the word in the dictionary. In the process, the use of Japanese can be minimized. Establishing these situations intentionally motivates them to interact in English. (97 words)
〈解説〉1　because of～「～のため」。「～可能性がある」はcanで簡単に表すことができる。be likely to～なども可。　2　中学校学習指導要領では，外国語科の「指導計画の作成と内容の取扱い」の項で，「生徒が英語に触れる機会を充実するとともに，授業を実際のコミュニケーションの場面とするため，授業は英語で行うことを基本とする。その

際，生徒の理解の程度に応じた英語を用いるようにすること」と述べている。これを踏まえ，解答例では，英語で授業を行えば生徒が英語に触れる機会が常にあり，コミュニケーションの手段として英語を使うことができるようになることを利点として挙げ，わからない語彙が出てきたら，生徒にわかるように言い直したり辞書をひかせたりするなどして，生徒の理解を確認することが大切であることを留意点として挙げている。最後に，こうして授業中に日本語の使用を最低限に抑えることで，生徒たちの英語による対話が意欲的になるとまとめている。

【高等学校】

【1】1　垂直方向の付着なのか，水平方向の支持であるかの違い。
2　X　ウ　　Y　イ　　3　言語はその言語独自の空間を構成するということではなく，ある言語を学ぶことによって，ある知覚的区別に他の区別よりも焦点が当たるのかもしれないということ。　　4　体の回転に合わせて物の配置を回転させる。　　5　言語にとって重要な空間構成を調査するには，空間言語から始めるのが自然であること。
6　Visual scenes paired with words in their language were shown.　　7　イ

〈解説〉1　第1段落3文目後半参照。*ann*はvertical attachment，*op*はhorizontal supportを表す。　2　X　空所にはmeritが入り「このような違いは言及に値する2つの疑問につながる」となる。merit～「～に値する」。　Y　空所にはイが入り「言語が引き起こす区別は，非言語的概念の型やその言語の話し手が用いるプロセスについて明らかになってきていると考えがちである」となる。直後に，韓国語と英語を例に，「実際，それらの違いは一連の興味深い研究主題である」と続く。
3　下線部(1)の研究者たちが発見したことは「韓国語や英語を学ぶ幼児は，包含と支持，きつい接合とゆるい接合を幾何学的に区別している」ということ。主張していることは，同文のsuggesting that以下を訳出する。　4　ツェルタル語話者は180度回転する時，物を並べ替えようとする。対してオランダ語や英語話者はどう対応するか。while以下を訳出する。　5　It is obvious that～「～は明らかである」という文型なので，that以下を訳出する。　6　問いは「Choiらの研究における選好注視法で，子どもたちに何が示されたか」。第2段落5文目，when looking at visual scenes paired with words in their languageを使って答える。　7　第1段落の3文目，4文目より，イ「英語では*in*と*on*が2つの異なる関係を区別するために使われるが，スペイン語では*en*が2つの関係を表すのにあてられる」が正しい。

【2】1　A person who is internationally-minded is willing to think over international problems from an unbiased standpoint.　　2〔解答例〕First, I'll try to divide students into pairs or small groups to work so that they can help each other. Second, I'll choose the topic which they relate to. Each student works on the same topic several times in different pairs or groups. Then the teams swap their roles. That will increase the repertoire of possible things to say and the chance to think more about the issue. Apart from judging which has done better, I'll record such activities for later playback. While reviewing, I can give additional instruction that may be involved, such as the specific vocabulary or expressions. (100 words)

〈解説〉1　解答例は,「～を嫌がらない」を「喜んで～する」と肯定形ですっきりと表現している。hesitate to～「～することを厭う」なども否定形にして可。「偏見のない」はunprejudiced，impartialなどでも可。
2 「論理・表現Ⅰ」の目標を踏まえ，解答例では，ペアやグループなど形態の工夫や，賛否両方の立場を経験させる支援を挙げている。また，効果としては，自分が表現したいことのレパートリーを増やすことができ，トピックについてより深く考える機会となることを挙げている。解答例のほかにも，目標中の文言「聞いたり読んだりしたことを活用しながら」に絡めて，生徒が表現するモデルとなるような題材を準備することや，モデルを通して論理の構成や展開の仕方を十分に身に付けた上で活動を行うことなどについて言及することもできるだろう。

2021年度　実施問題

【中高共通】

【1】(放送による問題)これはリスニング・テストです。放送の指示に従って答えなさい。

ただいまから，リスニング・テストを行います。問題は，1，2，3，4の四つです。聞いている間にメモを取っても構いません。

1　では，1の問題から始めます。問題は，No. 1とNo. 2の2問です。

これから読まれる英文に対する応答として最もふさわしいものを，続いて読まれるa，b，cの中から一つ選び，記号で答えなさい。答えは，大文字，小文字どちらでも構いません。なお，英文と応答は1度しか読まれません。

では，始めます。

No. 1　Weren't you going to rearrange the books on the shelf?

a.　I'll be going with him.

b.　We are just about to.

c.　John has arranged to see me.

No. 2　How much do I owe you for dinner last night?

a.　That's all right. It's on me.

b.　It was very appetizing. Thank you.

c.　I didn't own anything at all.

2　次に，2の問題に移ります。問題は，No. 1からNo. 3までの3問です。

これから，短い対話文を読みます。そのあとでクエスチョンと言って質問します。その答えとして最もふさわしいものを，続いて読まれ

るa，b，c，dの中から一つ選び，記号で答えなさい。答えは，大文字，小文字どちらでも構いません。なお，対話文・質問・答えの選択肢は1度しか読まれません。

では，始めます。

No. 1

M : Have you already decided the courses for next year?

W : Yes, but I want to take some extra courses. Is there anything interesting?

M : Well, philosophy seems quite satisfying, and involves a lot of reading.

W : Then you can count me out.

Question : What does the woman mean when she says, "You can count me out"?

a. She prefers mathematics to philosophy.

b. She thinks the course should be interesting, too.

c. She knows a lot about the course.

d. She will not take the course.

No. 2

W : I'm sorry to interrupt, but do you know where the projector is? I need it for my class, which starts in twenty minutes.

M : Isn't it in the cabinet in the multipurpose room? That's where I saw it last.

W : I've already looked in there, and I didn't see it in the conference room, either.

M : Wait, then you should ask Lala. Yesterday she was here until seven preparing for her presentation. She can probably tell you where it is.

Question : What has the woman been looking for?

a. A cabinet.

b. A room.

c. A colleague.

d. A device.

No. 3　(効果音：電話)

W : Hello, this is George Hotel. How may I help you?

M : Hello. I just received an e-mail from you confirming my booking, but would it be possible to book two rooms, not one?

W : OK, could you tell me your confirmation number, please? I'll check your reservation and whether a room is available on that date.

M : Sure. It's 8-3-1-1-4-9-0.

W : Well, another single room is still available. If you'd like, I'll reserve it for you and send you an updated confirmation message.

Question : Why is the man calling?

a. To send a renewed message.

b. To make a change to the reservation.

c. To attach a registration form.

d. To enter an online check-in site.

3　次に3の問題に移ります。問題は，No. 1からNo. 3までの3問です。

これから，あるまとまりのある英文を読みます。そのあとで，クエスチョンズと言って，その英文について三つの質問をします。その答えとして最もふさわしいものを，質問に続いて読まれるa，b，c，dの中から一つ選び，記号で答えなさい。答えは，大文字，小文字どちらでも構いません。なお，英文・質問・答えの選択肢は全体を通して2回読まれます。

では，始めます。

At least in the short term, AI and robotics are unlikely to completely eliminate entire industries. Jobs that require specialization in a narrow range of routinized activities will be automated. But it will be much more difficult to replace humans with machines in less routine jobs that demand the simultaneous use of a wide range of skills and involve dealing with unforeseen scenarios. Take healthcare, for example. Many doctors focus almost exclusively on processing information: they absorb medical data, analyze it, and produce a diagnosis. Nurses, in contrast, need good motor and emotional skills in order to give a painful injection, replace a bandage, or restrain a violent patient. Therefore we will probably have an AI family doctor on our smartphone decades before we have a reliable nurse robot. The human care industry — which takes care of the sick, the young, and the elderly — is likely to remain a human bastion for a long time. Indeed, as people live longer and have fewer children, care of the elderly will probably be one of the fastest-growing sectors in the human labor market.

Alongside care, creativity too poses particularly difficult hurdles for automation. We don't need humans to sell us music anymore — we can download it directly online — but the composers, musicians, singers, and DJs are still flesh and blood. We rely on their creativity not just to produce completely new music but also to choose among a mind-boggling range of available possibilities.

Questions

No. 1　What is the main topic of this passage?

a.　The imperfect nature of AI and robotics.

b.　The potential risks of leading a routinized life.

c.　The urgent need for mechanical healthcare.

d.　The various possibilities in automated creative activities.

No. 2　What are nurses required to do?

a.　To resolve medical data.

b.　To make a diagnosis.

c.　To employ emotional skills.

d.　To disregard a violent patient.

No. 3　What is true about the passage?

a.　Routinized activities are crucial for many international companies.

b.　Doctors who give patients a painful injection can sympathize with them.

c.　An AI doctor on the smartphone will appear ten years after a nurse robot.

d.　Neither healthcare nor music composition has been successfully automated yet.

4　次に4の問題に移ります。問題は，No. 1とNo. 2の2問です。

これから，英語による対話文を読みます。(　　)のところに入る英語を聞き取り，書きなさい。対話文はそれぞれ2回読まれます。

では，始めます。

No. 1

W : I'm wondering which restaurant to take my parents to. Adam tells me Antonio's is the finest.

M : Does he? Then, (I couldn't agree with him more on that).

No. 2

M : Can you look at this e-mail? It doesn't make any sense to me.

W : It says it's (intended solely for the use of the individual to whom) it is addressed.

これで，リスニング・テストを終わります。次の問題に移ってください。

(☆☆☆◎◎◎◎◎)

【2】次の英文や対話文の中の(　　)に最も適するものを，下のア～エの中からそれぞれ一つずつ選び，記号で答えなさい。

1　The professor was unable to attend the party (　　) the late arrival of his plane.

ア　in spite of　　イ　due to　　ウ　instead of　　エ　by way of

2　As soon as the star player came on, the soccer game (　　).

ア　had been excited　　イ　became excited　　ウ　had been exciting

エ　became exciting

3　Psychology is an area (　　) my son has been familiar since he was a college student.

ア　whether　　イ　to which　　ウ　which　　エ　with which

4　Peter will soon work at ABC Hospital as a doctor, so he wants to know (　　) the distance is from here to there.

ア　what　　イ　that　　ウ　how　　エ　whether

5　(　　) anyone see him in the city, let me know as soon as possible.

ア　Since　　イ　As　　ウ　Would　　エ　Should

6　The light in the room was so (　　) that I couldn't read the book.

ア　dim　　イ　vague　　ウ　fragile　　エ　stubborn

7　He was standing with his eyes (　　) on the picture.

ア　fix　　イ　fixed　　ウ　have fixed　　エ　are fixing

8　A: Are you and John getting married?

B: We hope (　　).

ア　do　　イ　done　　ウ　them　　エ　to

9　There used to be a sign on the wall. It (　　) "Watch your step."

ア　saw　　イ　looked　　ウ　wrote　　エ　read

10　Yesterday Mary (　　) an old friend. They hadn't seen each other for more than twenty years.

ア　stuck in　　イ　kicked up　　ウ　bumped into

エ　jumped through

11　A: I got my finger caught in the door and now it is (　　), doctor.

B: Yes, it looks painful. I will see if it's broken.

ア　flimsy　　イ　swollen　　ウ　stale　　エ　invalid

12　His (　　) in the gallery will surely make him a famous artist one day.

ア deferment　イ freight　ウ ingenuity　エ haughtiness

13 The man apologized (　　) for being late. His client had waited for over two hours.

ア notoriously　イ ornamentally　ウ profusely

エ inherently

14 Our company could only reach a (　　) agreement after months of negotiations.

ア chronological　イ sublime　ウ tentative

エ contemporary

15 Bread prices have been raised in order to (　　) the higher cost of wheat.

ア resume　イ confiscate　ウ condone　エ offset

(☆☆☆☆◎◎◎◎◎)

【3】次の英文を読んで，あとの問いに答えなさい。

In February 1990, on its way out of the solar system after encounters with Jupiter and Saturn, the Voyager I probe beamed back the first image of our entire solar system as it might appear to visitors from another star. The picture is dominated by a single bright star, our Sun, seen from 6 billion kilometres away, 40 times the distance from which we are used to seeing it. The planets are scarcely visible. The Earth itself is smaller than one picture element in Voyager's camera, its faint light caught in what looks like a sunbeam. This is our whole world, seemingly just a speck of dust. But to any alien visitor with the right instruments, that tiny blue world would immediately attract attention. Unlike the giant stormy gas bags of the outer planets, cold, dry Mars, or the acid steam-bath of Venus, the Earth (　X　). Water exists in all three phases - liquid, ice, and steam. The atmospheric composition is not that of a dead world that has reached equilibrium but one that is active and must be constantly renewed. There is oxygen, ozone, and traces of hydrocarbons; things that would not exist together for long if they were not constantly renewed by living processes. This alone would attract the attention of our alien visitors, even if they could not catch the constant ①chatter of our communications, radio and television.

Geophysics goes way above our heads. I don't (Y) but that the physical influence of our planet extends far above its solid surface, way out into what we regard as empty space. But it is not empty. We live in a series of bubbles nested like Russian dolls one within another. The Earth's sphere of influence lies within the greater bubble dominated by our Sun. (1)That in turn lies within overlapping bubbles blown by the expanding debris of exploding stars or supernovae, long, long ago. They are all within our Milky Way galaxy, which is in turn a member of a supercluster of galaxies within the known universe, which itself may be a bubble in a quantum foam of worlds.

The Earth's atmosphere and magnetic field shield us, for the most part, from the radiation hazards from space. Without this protection, life on the Earth's surface would be threatened by solar ultraviolet and X-rays as well as cosmic rays, high-energy particles from violent events throughout the galaxy. There is also a permanent gale of particles, mostly hydrogen nuclei or protons, blowing outwards from the Sun. This solar wind speeds past the Earth at typical velocities of around 400 kilometres per second, and goes three times faster during a solar storm. It extends for billions of kilometres out into space, beyond all the planets and maybe beyond the orbits of comets, which reach out many thousands of times further from the Sun than does the Earth. The solar wind is very tenuous but it is sufficient to blow out the tails of comets as they come closer in to the heart of the solar system, so the tails always point away from the Sun. It also features in imaginative proposals for propelling spacecraft with vast gossamer-thin solar sails.

(2)The Earth is sheltered from the solar wind by its magnetic field, the magnetosphere. Because the solar wind is electrically charged it represents an electrical current, which cannot cross magnetic field lines. Instead, it compresses the Earth's magnetosphere on the sunward side, like the bow wave of a ship at sea, and stretches it out into a long tail down-wind which reaches almost as far as the orbit of the Moon. Charged particles caught within the magnetosphere build up in belts between the field lines where they are forced to spiral, generating radiation. These radiation belts were first ②detected in 1958 when James van Allen flew the first Geiger counter in space on board the American Explorer 1 satellite. They are areas to be avoided by spacecraft hoping for a long life and would be lethal to unprotected astronauts.

Where the Earth's magnetic field lines dive down towards the poles, solar wind particles can enter the atmosphere, sending atoms ricocheting downwards to produce spectacular auroral displays. At the top of the atmosphere, the hydrogen ions of the solar wind itself produce a pink haze. Lower down, oxygen ions produce a ruby-red glow, while nitrogen ions in the stratosphere cause violet blue and red auroras. Occasionally, magnetic field lines in the solar wind are forced close to those of the Earth, causing them to reconnect, often with spectacular releases of energy which extend the auroral displays.

(Martin Redfern, *THE EARTH: A Very Short Introduction* による。ただし，設問の都合で一部省略及び改変している。)

1　下線部①，②を別の語で言い換えたとき，最も意味の近いものを，次のア～エの中からそれぞれ一つずつ選び，記号で答えなさい。

①　ア　profile　イ　babble　ウ　hostile　エ　globule

②　ア　colonized　イ　rebelled　ウ　incited　エ　spotted

2　本文中の空欄(　X　)，(　Y　)に入る英語として最も適切なものを，次のア～エの中からそれぞれ一つずつ選び，記号で答えなさい。

X　ア　is floating in the blackness of space
　　イ　tells how it has been weathered
　　ウ　is a dusty glow of our planetary system
　　エ　has everything just right

Y　ア　mean by that that it is incomprehensible
　　イ　deny that the surface of the Earth is solid
　　ウ　think that it can give any clues about the issue

エ　have a giant edifice that we can stand on

3　下線部(1)が示すものを，本文中から5語以上で抜き出して書きなさい。

4　下線部(2)について，なぜそのようになるのか，本文に即して日本語で書きなさい。

5　本文の内容に即して，次の問いに英語で答えなさい。

(1)　By what are we protected from solar ultraviolet, X-rays, and cosmic rays?

(2)　Why do the tails of comets point away from the Sun?

6　本文の内容に最も合うものを，次のア～オの中から一つ選び，記号で答えなさい。

ア　The first image of the solar system from the Voyager I was sent from 40 times the distance between the Sun and the Earth.

イ　Alien visitors faced an ambitious challenge to invent a tool which would enable them to get rid of dust in space, but it was unsuccessful.

ウ　The Earth's magnetic field is sometimes toxic because it generates a permanent gale of particles blowing outwards from the Sun.

エ　The radiation belts are vital when launching spacecraft into space, and for the survival of astronauts on their journey to the Moon.

オ　Auroral displays are extended when some ions of the solar wind make greater energy because it is very windy on the surface of the Earth.

(☆☆☆☆◎◎◎◎◎)

【中学校】

【1】次の英文を読んで，あとの問いに答えなさい。

There is still no generally accepted way of classifying tasks. By and large pedagogical ①accounts of tasks have continued to distinguish tasks in terms of the operations learners are required to carry out when they perform them. Willis (1996), for example, distinguished six types — listing, ordering and sequencing. comparing, problem solving, sharing personal experiences and creative. Other ways of classifying tasks have emerged from research that has investigated the communicative and cognitive processes involved in performing different tasks. This has led to (1)a set of features such as whether a task requires one-way or two-way communication and whether the outcome is closed or open. For example, 'Spot the Difference' (a task where students have to work together to identify the differences in two similar pictures) is a two-way, closed task. A jigsaw task where information is split among a number of learners is a two-way, open task.

There are a number of other pedagogically useful ways of classifying tasks. An important distinction is between *real-world* and *pedagogic tasks*. The former are tasks that have situational authenticity; that is, they are based on tasks that can be found in real life (i.e. target tasks). An example might be a task where two students take on the roles of hotel receptionist and ②prospective guest where the latter has to make a booking for a room based on the information provided by the former. A pedagogic task lacks situational authenticity but must still display interactional authenticity (i.e. results in the kind of natural language use found in the world outside the classroom). An example is (2)the Spot the Difference task. It is very unlikely that two people would engage in talk aimed at identifying the differences in two pictures but this task can result in patterns of turn taking and repair of misunderstandings that are typical of everyday talk and thus achieve interactional authenticity. Real-world tasks are required in specific purpose language courses but in general-purpose courses it is likely that many of the tasks will be pedagogic in nature.

A task can be *input-based* requiring learners to simply process the oral or written information provided and demonstrate their understanding of it (for example by drawing a picture or making a model) or it can be *output-based*, requiring the learner to speak or write to achieve the task outcome. This distinction is important because, as Prabhu (1987) noted, beginner learners cannot be expected to use the *L2 productively so task-based learning must initially be input-driven.

Tasks can also be unfocused or focused (Ellis, 2003). An *unfocused task* is intended to elicit general samples of language. (3)A *focused task* must satisfy the general criteria for a task but is designed in such a way as to orientate learners to the use of a particular linguistic feature. This possibility was explored by Loschky and Bley-Vroman (1993). They suggested that a task could be designed in such a way that it made the processing of a particular grammatical structure 'natural' (i.e. 'the task lends itself, in some natural way, to the frequent use of the structure' (1993)), 'useful' (i.e. the use of the structure is very helpful for performing the task)or 'essential' (i.e. successful performance of the task is only possible if the structure is used). Advocates of task-based language teaching differ in their views about the inclusion of focused tasks. I will argue they have a role to play. However, both Skehan (1998) and Long (2015) favour a curriculum consisting only of unfocused tasks.

Long (1985) proposed that the tasks to be included in a course should be needs-based. That is, the starting point is the identification of the target tasks that a specific group of learners need to be able to perform to 'function ③adequately in a particular target domain' (1985). Long (2015) has continued to emphasize the importance of needs analysis as a basis for task selection. There is an obvious advantage in such an approach as it helps to ensure the relevance of the content of a task-based course.

(注)　*L2：第2言語(母語を学んだ後に学ぶ言語：second language)

(Rod Ellis, *Reflections on Task-Based Language Teaching* による。ただし，設問の都合で一部省略及び改変している。)

1　下線部①～③の英語の定義として最もよくあてはまるものを，次のア～エの中からそれぞれ一つずつ選び，記号で答えなさい。

①　ア　a large important organization that has a particular purpose

イ　a person who knows a lot about a particular subject because they have studied it in detail

ウ　an explanation or a description of an idea, a theory or a process

エ　a word or symbol that represents an amount or a quantity

② ア　happening or done quickly and without warning

イ　expected to do something or to become something

ウ　famous and much admired, especially because of what you have achieved

エ　extremely unpleasant, especially in a way that offends people

③ ア　in a way that is satisfactory or acceptable in quality or quantity

イ　very quickly and in a very short time

ウ　used to emphasize that something is very true or obvious

エ　approximately but not exactly

2　下線部(1)は，どのような研究がもとになっているか，本文の内容に即して日本語で書きなさい。

3　下線部(2)がsituational authenticity を持たないのはなぜか，本文の内容に即して日本語で書きなさい。

4　下線部(3)は，学習者が何に関心を持つように設定されるのか，本文の内容に即して日本語で書きなさい。

5　本文の内容に即して，次の問いに英語で答えなさい。

(1)　What do the learners who engage in an input-based task process?

(2)　According to Long, why can needs analysis as a basis for task selection be beneficial?

6　本文の内容に最も合うものを，次のア～エの中から一つ選び，記号で答えなさい。

ア　Spot the Difference is a task typed as ordering and sequencing according to Willis's distinction of tasks.

イ　Real-world tasks, which have situational authenticity, are required in specific purpose language courses.

ウ　Beginner learners cannot use the L2 productively because task-based learning is initially input-driven.

エ　Some linguists say that no tasks should be natural, useful and essential when they are used in a curriculum.

(☆☆☆☆◎◎◎◎◎)

【2】次の1，2について，指示に従って答えなさい。

1　次の日本語を英語に直しなさい。

生活の利便性と環境保全のバランスをいかにとるかということが，我々が直面している大きな課題である。

2　「中学校学習指導要領」(平成29年3月告示)の「第2章　第9節　外国語　第2　各言語の目標及び内容等　3　指導計画の作成と内容の取扱い」では，「指導計画の作成に当たっては，小学校や高等学校における指導との接続に留意」するなど，異校種との円滑な学びの接続を求めています。小学校における指導との接続の観点から，あなたは中学校第1学年でどのような授業を構成しますか。小学校との接続の留意点に触れながら，学習指導要領の趣旨を踏まえ，100語程度の英語で書きなさい。ただし，語数には，句読点や符号は含まないものとします。なお，解答の総語数を記入すること。

(☆☆☆☆◎◎◎◎◎)

【高等学校】

【1】次の英文を読んで，あとの問いに答えなさい。

Data-driven learning (DDL) was first proposed by Johns (1991) who defined it as the direct use of corpus data in the language teaching process. As an inductive approach, it is based on the premise that learners engage in their own linguistic analysis in which they focus on specific linguistic features. As Chambers (2010) notes, such corpus-aided learning can take different forms and range from concordances prepared by the teacher to learners' autonomous corpus consultation. Decisions as to which form should be used are likely to be influenced by the level and needs of our students.

There are several major benefits of DDL that are emphasized by its proponents. First of all, DDL promotes learners' active role in their linguistic development by encouraging them to discover regularities in language as it is used across natural contexts. As highlighted by Johns's (1997) oft-quoted metaphor, in DDL learners perform the role of detectives in the classroom and each of them can become a Sherlock Holmes. Since DDL gives learners "direct access to the data" (Johns 1991), classroom work becomes an inductive, student-centered approach with each learner carrying out their own linguistic analysis. Further advantages of DDL are discussed by Gilmore (2015), who states that the direct use of corpora allows learners to immerse themselves in natural data and test their hypotheses about specific linguistic features. Thus, not only does DDL raise learners' awareness of the way language is used in real-life communicative situations but it also develops their autonomy by encouraging them to take responsibility for their own learning.

(1)<u>Such an understanding of the teaching process has important consequences for the role of teachers</u>; they are no longer the only source of knowledge in the classroom but rather they facilitate the learning process and assist learners with their discovery. Crucially, teachers can also profit enormously from corpus consultation and analysis. Cobb and Boulton (2015) state that corpora can be treated as a tool which boosts teachers' confidence, especially in situations when they are unsure of their own linguistic competence. As shown by Römer (2009), many teachers who teach a language that is not their mother tongue do not trust their *L2 linguistic competence and consequently seek guidance on specific language features. Also, O'Keeffe et al. (2007) point out that corpora can be used as a resource for teachers "who wish to either improve their own language awareness" or need answers to some unexpected questions that might come up during classes. Corpora can also be used as repositories of sample sentences that demonstrate the use of a given word or chunk.

Up to this point our discussion has (X) around the positive aspects of

DDL. However, there are also certain challenges that the implementation of DDL might entail (Gilquin and Granger 2010; Boulton 2009). First, DDL might be difficult to implement because of practicalities such as a lack of computers or corpus software. Even though technological advances have transformed the way foreign languages are taught these days, practicing teachers can easily imagine a situation in which access to fifteen computers during a language class might become problematic. In such cases, an alternative form of DDL is preparing paper-based concordances and giving them to students as worksheets. This form of DDL is probably more time-consuming than computer-based concordancing but it is worth considering if you or your students face the problem of limited access to technology.

(　Y　) Irrespective of the form of presentation (on computer vs. on paper), some students might find it difficult to process large amounts of data, in particular when they represent lower levels of proficiency. As Yoon and Hirvela (2004) warn, from the perspective of students, analyzing concordances might seem time-consuming, tedious and off-putting, and DDL may not necessarily be perceived as a worthwhile classroom activity.

However, as Boulton's (2010) research demonstrates, if DDL is well planned and relies on carefully selected materials (e.g. paper-based corpus activities), it can be successfully implemented with learners at lower levels of proficiency. It appears that the attitude of a given teacher is of crucial importance; that is, he or she needs to know what their students are capable of and how the use of corpus data will impact on the learning experience as a whole. It goes without saying that to avoid failure in the implementation of DDL, learners ought to be informed well in advance that they will participate in a hands-on approach and they need to be prepared that this approach requires their active involvement.

(注)　*L2：第2言語(母語を学んだ後に学ぶ言語：second language)

(Pawel Szudarski, *Corpus Linguistics for Vocabulary*による。ただし，設問の都合で一部省略及び改変している。)

1　DDLはどのような前提に基づいているものか，本文に即して日本語で書きなさい。

2　DDLの利点として，一つ目に述べられていることを，本文に即して日本語で書きなさい。

3　下線部(1)について，DDLにおける教師の役割は何か，本文に即して日本語で書きなさい。

4　本文中の空欄(　X　)，(　Y　)に入る語または文として最も適切なものを，次のア～オの中からそれぞれ一つずつ選び，記号で答えなさい。

X　ア　revolved　　イ　admonished　　ウ　duplicated

　　エ　mocked　　オ　tampered

Y　ア　Despite this rather gloomy situation, we can also observe some positive changes in the DDL classrooms.

　　イ　A related problem that might interfere with the successful use of corpus is teachers' lack of expertise in corpora.

　　ウ　The most basic type of corpus analysis is checking the frequency of occurrence of a given word or a phrase.

　　エ　From an empirical point of view, it is worth comparing the language of textbooks with that of authentic interactions.

　　オ　Another thorny issue that should be mentioned is the potential of overwhelming students with corpus data.

5　DDLの失敗を避けるため，指導者は学習者をどのような状態にしてDDLに取り組ませるべきか，本文に即して日本語で書きなさい。

6　本文の内容に即して，次の問いに英語で答えなさい。

What can teachers who are trying to implement DDL do when they face a lack of computers in their language classes?

7　本文の内容に最も合うものを，次のア～オの中から一つ選び，記号で答えなさい。

ア　Learners' autonomous corpus consultation is not considered to be corpus-aided learning because teachers cannot evaluate it precisely enough.

イ　How much responsibility learners feel for their own language learning relies on how much communication they have in their real-life situations.

ウ　Immersing teachers in natural data consequently impedes the development of their own linguistic competence, causing them to lose confidence.

エ　In case teachers are asked questions they are unprepared for in their classes, they can depend on corpora to find the answers.

オ　Teachers who aim to practice DDL should know learners' proficiency of the second language except for those with inadequate motivation.

(☆☆☆☆☆◎◎◎◎◎)

【2】次の1，2について，指示に従って答えなさい。

1　次の日本語を英語に直しなさい。

世の中は，あなたが一生を費やしても吸収しきれないほどの多くの情報で溢れている。

2　次の表は，平成30年度「英語教育実施状況調査」概要における「CAN-DO リスト」形式による学習到達目標の設定等の状況【高等学校】を示したものです。この表からどのような問題点が読み取れますか。また，その問題点を踏まえ，どのような指導が求められているとあなたは考えますか。「高等学校学習指導要領」(平成30年3月告示)の趣旨を踏まえ，100語程度の英語で書きなさい。ただし，語数には，句読点や符号は含まないものとします。なお，総語数を記入すること。

	「CAN-DO リスト」形式による学習到達目標を設定している学校の割合	「CAN-DO リスト」形式による学習到達目標の達成状況を把握している学校の割合
平成 28 年度	88.1%	41.6%
平成 29 年度	94.5%	51.9%
平成 30 年度	95.0%	55.2%

(☆☆☆☆◎◎◎◎◎)

解答・解説

【中高共通】

【1】1 No. 1 b No. 2 a 2 No. 1 d No. 2 d No. 3 b 3 No. 1 a No. 2 c No. 3 d 4 No. 1 I couldn't agree with him more on that No. 2 intended solely for the use of the individual to whom

〈解説〉リスニングテストの質問文や選択肢は問題用紙に印刷されていないので，すべて聴き取った範囲で解答しなければならない。1～3は選択問題，4は記述式問題で，放送回数は1と2が1回のみ，3と4は2回である。 1 英文に対して適切な応答を選択する問題である。

No.1 過去の予定を聞かれ，その予定を実行したかには返答せず，「今やることろだ」と返答している。be about to do「まさに～するところだ」。 No.2 返答として具体的な金額を言うものと期待しがちだが，それを覆して「私のおごりです」と答えている。 It's on～.「～のおごりだ」。 2 会話文の内容についての質問である。

No.1 count～outは「～を数に入れない，除外する」という意味。男性から「哲学は満足すると思うし，たくさん本を読むことになる」と言われ，自分は(本をたくさん読みたくないので)哲学を取らないという意味で使われている。 No.2 女性の最初の発言の「プロジェクターがどこにあるか知っていますか」から，探しているものはprojectorを別の言葉で言い換えたdevice「機器」だと判断する。　No.3　男性の最初の発言で，「部屋を1つではなく，2つ予約することは可能ですか」と電話をした理由を告げているので，「予約の変更をするため」と考える。　3　250語程度のパッセージの内容に関する3つの質問に答える問題である。細部を問われる問題もあり難易度は高い。
No.1　ある程度分量のある英文は，最初にその主題や目的が述べられる。本パッセージでは，冒頭にAI and robotics are unlikely to completely eliminate entire industries.とあり，これからこの話題を展開していくと判断する。よって，これと同じ内容を別の表現で言い換えた「AIとロボットの不完全性」が適切。　No.2　第1段落の6文目に，「看護師は，痛みを伴う注射をしたり，包帯の交換をしたり，暴力的な患者を拘束したりするために，運動能力や情緒的なスキルが必要である」と述べている。　No.3　第1段落の3文目に，ルーティンワークではないものは，機械が人間に取って代わることははるかに難しいだろうと述べている。その例として，4文目～第1段落の最後まではhealthcareの仕事が取り上げられ，第2段落では音楽関係などのクリエイティブな仕事が取り上げられていることから判断する。　4　対話文の一部を記述するディクテーション問題。ナチュラルスピードでネイティブの英語を聴きなれておく練習が必要である。また，単純なスペルミスをしないように。　No.1　with himは「ウィズィム」のように，more on thatは「モアロンナッ」のように聞こえる。文尾の破裂音(この場合は[t]音)は発音されない。　No.2　solelyの1つ目の[l]音は日本語の「ウ」に近い音で「ソウウリー」のように聞こえ，intended solelyは「インテンディッ ソウウリー」のように聞こえる。

【2】1　イ　2　エ　3　エ　4　ア　5　エ　6　ア　7　イ　8　エ　9　エ　10　ウ　11　イ　12　ウ　13　ウ　14　ウ　15　エ

〈解説〉1　教授がパーティーに出席できなかった理由を述べていること

から，原因・理由を表す熟語を選ぶ。　2　スター選手が出場したのが過去で，その同じ時に試合が面白くなったと考え，過去形にする。主節の主語はthe soccer gameなので，試合は人を「興奮させる」と考え，現在分詞にする。　3　主節は，Psychology is an areaとmy son has been familiar withが関係代名詞whichを使って1つになった文。withがwhichの前に来ている。be familiar with～で「～に精通している」という意味。　4　What is the distance from～to …「～から…の距離はどのくらいですか」という意味。How far is it from～to …?と同じ意味。

5　疑問文でもないのにshouldが文頭にある場合，If S＋should＋V～, S＋V～.のif節のifをとり，shouldをSの前に置き，倒置した文だと考える。　6　「部屋の明かりはとても～なので本を読むことができなかった」から「薄暗い」と判断する。　7　付帯状況のwithは，〈with＋O～〉の形で使う。目的語(名詞)のあとにbe動詞が入ると，文になる関係の語を選ぶ。his eyes (were) fixed on the pictureのように，wereが入ることで1つの文(この場合，受動態の文)になっている。

8　We hope to (get married)だと考える。　9　readには「～は…と書いてある」という意味がある。　10「昨日メアリーは旧友に～。彼らはお互いに20年以上会っていなかった」から「偶然出会う」と考える。

11　指がドアに挟まったから今どのような状態なのかと考え，「腫れた」と判断する。　12　「画廊にある彼の～はきっといつか彼を有名なアーティストにするだろう」から「創造性」だと判断する。

13　apologize profuselyで「深くわびる」という意味になる。

14「数カ月の交渉の後，私たちの会社は，～な合意に達しただけだった」から「暫定の」だと判断する。　15「パンの値段は小麦の値段の高騰を～するために値上げされた」から「相殺する」だと判断する。

【3】1　①　イ　　②　エ　　2　X　エ　　Y　ア　　3　the greater bubble dominated by our Sun　　4　太陽風は帯電していて，電流に相当し，それは磁力線を超えることができないから。　　5　(1)　By the Earth’s atmosphere and magnetic field.　　(2)　Because they are blown out by the solar wind.　6　ア

〈解説〉1　①　chatter「おしゃべりする」と同義の単語を選ぶ。
②　detect「見つける，検出する」と同義の単語を選ぶ。　2　X　空所を含む文の意味は，「木星型惑星(外惑星)の巨大な嵐のようなガス球や，冷たく乾燥した火星，酸性の蒸し風呂の金星とは異なり，地球は～」。これに続いて，「水は液体，氷，水蒸気の三相すべてに存在し～酸素，オゾン，微量の炭化水素があり～」と，地球がどういう惑星なのか説明している。よって，空所は，他の惑星と違って「すべてが整っている」ため，エイリアンの訪問者の注意を引くだろう，と考えるのが適切。　Y　空所を含む文の直前のgoes way above our headsの意味には，「はるか頭上を越える」と「理解をはるかに超える」があるが，実際に「地球の物理的な影響力は固体表面のはるか上にまで，私たちが何もない空間とみなしているところにまで，及んでいる」と考える。
3　下線部(1)の直前に「地球の影響範囲は，太陽に支配された大きな泡の中にある。」とあり，in turn「次に」のあとに，「その大きな泡は，はるか昔に爆発した星や超新星の破片によって吹き飛ばされた泡の重なり合いの中にある」と続くと考える。　4　下線部(2)の理由は，直後のBecause以降に述べられている。electrically charged「帯電した」，electrical current「電流」，magnetic field line「磁力線」。　5　(1)　第3段落2文目に「この保護がなければ，太陽紫外線やX線だけでなく，宇宙線すなわち銀河系内の激しい出来事から発生する高エネルギー粒子の影響で，地球の生命は脅かされることになる」とある。「この保護」が何を指すかは，1文目にある「地球の大気と磁場は，宇宙からの放射線の脅威から私たちを守っている」から判断できる。
(2)　第3段落6文目の前半に「太陽風は非常に弱いが，彗星の尾が太陽系の中心部に近づくにつれて，彗星の尾を吹き飛ばすのには十分で」とあり，彗星の尾が常に太陽から離れた方へ向いている理由が述べられている。　6　第1段落の2文目に「この画像(＝the first image of our entire solar system)は，私たちが見慣れている距離の40倍の60億キロ離れた場所から見た太陽という1つの明るい星が中心となっている」とあり，アと一致する。

【中学校】

【1】1　①　ウ　　②　イ　　③　ア　　2　様々なタスクを行うことに関わる，コミュニケーション上の認知的処理についての研究。
3　二人の人が，二枚の絵の違いを明らかにすることを目的として会話を行うことはありそうにないから。　　4　特定の言語特性の使用。
5　(1)　They process the oral or written information provided.
(2)　Because it helps to ensure the relevance of the content of a task-based course.　　6　イ

〈解説〉1　①　1　account of～で「～の説明」。本文中の文意は「タスクの教育学的な説明では，学習者がタスクを実行する際に求められる操作の観点からタスクを区別してきた」である。　②　prospectiveで「有望な，見込みのある，予想される」。本文中の文意は「例として，2人の学生がホテルの受付係と見込みのある客の役割を担い，後者が前者から提供された情報に基づいて部屋の予約をしなければならないという課題が考えられる」である。　③　adequatelyで「十分に，適切に」。本文中の文意は「つまり，特定の学習者グループが特定の目標領域で十分に機能するために必要な目標課題を特定することが出発点である」である。　2　下線部を含む文の冒頭のThisは，その直前の文で述べている「タスクを分類する他の方法は，様々なタスクを行うことに関わるコミュニケーション上の認知的処理を調査した研究から生まれたもの」を指す。その研究をもとに「タスクが一方通行か双方向のコミュニケーションを必要とするかどうか，結果がクローズドかオープンかどうかなどの特徴へと導いた」と考える。　3　the Spot the Difference taskの説明は，第1段落6文目に「似たような2つの絵の違いを一緒に確認する課題は，双方向のクローズドな課題である」とある。また，situational authenticityの説明は，第2段落3文目のthat is以下に「実際の生活の中で見られる課題(目標とする課題)に基づいている」とある。また，下線部(2)の直後の文で，このようなタスクのための会話が行われることはありそうにないと述べられている。　4　focused taskがどのように設計されているかは，下線部(3)を含む文のas to以降に「学習者が特定の言語的特徴を使用するように方向付けられるように」と述べられている。　5　(1)　第3段落の1文目にinput-based taskでは，学習者が口頭と文書で提供される情報をインプットして，処理すると述べられている。　(2)　第5段落の3文目にニーズ分析の重要性を強調し続けていると述べられていて，続く最終文で「そのような手法」(＝ニーズ分析)の利点として，as以降に「タスクベースのコースの内容の関連性を確保するのに役立つ」と述べられている。　6　第2段落の3文目にThe former are tasks that have situational authenticityとあり，同段落の最終文にReal-world tasks are required in specific purpose language coursesとあることから，イと一致する。

【２】1　We are faced with a big problem of how we should keep the balance between the convenience of life and the environmental preservation.

2　〔解答例〕First of all, I will check if my students have fully acquired what they learned in elementary schools. If they have not, I will start our class reviewing basic English knowledge and skills to help students smoothly move on to junior high school curriculum. Second, in order to foster students' interest in foreign countries and English language, I will introduce informative topics which shows different cultures and lifestyles in the world. It is also important to encourage students not to feel embarrassed about speaking English. Therefore, I would like to offer students a lot of opportunities to talk with each other at an early stage in my class. (108 words)

〈解説〉1「我々は大きな課題(問題)に直面している」という文を作り，「生活の利便性と環境保全のバランスをいかにとるか」を，「課題」の後ろに置くことで，後ろから説明する。「いかに我々はAとBのバランスをとるべきか」はHow should we keep the balance between A and B?となる。この疑問文をofの目的語にするので，間接疑問で肯定文の語順にする。　2　解答例では，小学校で学んだことが身についているかを確認し，無理なく中学校の内容に移行できるよう基礎の復習からスタートすることを挙げている。さらに，生徒の興味を育めるような海外の話題を教材として導入することを挙げ，また，生徒が英語を話すことをためらわないように，授業の早い時期から生徒同士の対話の機会を設けることを述べている。

【高等学校】

【1】1　学習者は彼ら自身の言語的分析に取り組み，その中で特定の言語特徴に注目するという前提。　2　学習者が，自然な文脈の中で使われている言語の規則性を発見し，彼らの言語の発達に主体的になるようにする。　3　学習者が学びやすくなるようにして，彼らの発見を支援すること。　4　X　ア　Y　オ　5　実用的な学習法に取り組むということを事前に知っており，またその学習に主体的に取り組んでいかなければならないという心構えを持った状態。

6　They can prepare paper-based concordances and give them to students as worksheets.　7　エ

〈解説〉1　第1段落の冒頭に「データ駆動型学習(DDL)は，～」とあり，DDLの説明をし，2文目で，「帰納的アプローチとして，それ(DDL)は～という前提に基づいている。」と述べ，on the premise that～以降に，どういう前提か述べられている。engage in～「～に従事する」，focus on～「～に焦点を当てる」。　2　第2段落の最初に，There are several major benefits of DDLと，DDLの利点があるとし，2文目に「まず第1に～」と1つ目の利点が述べられている。　3　下線部の直後のセミコロン(；)以下で，教師は今までのような教室での唯一の知識源ではなく，とあり，後半のbut rather～以降にDDLにおける教師の役割が述べられている。　4　X「議論はDDLの肯定的な側面を～」とあることから判断する。revolve around～で「～を中心に展開する」。　Y　第4段落ではコーパスのマイナスの側面である，「コンピュータやコーパス・ソフトウェアの不足などの現実的な問題から，DDLの実装が困難な場合」を取り上げ，第5段落では，空所の直後で「プレゼンテーションの形式(コンピュータ上と紙上)にかかわらず，学生の中には大量のデータを処理するのが難しいと感じる人もいるかもしれない」と，別の問題を取り上げて話を展開していることから判断する。　5　第6段落の最終文の前半に「DDLの実施で失敗しないためには，～」とあり，DDLへの取り組ませ方が述べられている。～be informed that…「～は…を知らされる」，in advance「前もって」。　6　言語の授業でコンピュータの不足に直面した場合には，第4段落の5文目に，In such cases「このような場合」(＝言語の授業中に15台のコンピュータにアクセスすることが問題となる状況)以降に，どう対処するかが述べられている。　7　第3段落の5文目に，O'Keeffe et al.がコーパスの使われ方を2つ述べていて，その2つ目に「あるいは授業中に出てくるかもしれない予期せぬ質問への答えを必要としている場合のリソースとして使用できる」と述べている。これがエと一致する。

【2】1　The world is filled with more information than you can absorb even if you devote your life to doing so.　2　The number of schools that set achievement goals in CAN-DO lists is increasing, while only about half of them keep track of students' achievement status. The CAN-DO list will motivate your students to learn English because they can recognize exactly which goal they are expected to accomplish. Once students consider the goals are achievable, they will be likely to study harder to make it . Also, by reviewing their self-evaluation in the list, they will become aware which skills and abilities they should improve. Therefore, teachers should set proper goals each time, review the self-evaluation lists with students regularly, give them advice to achieve goals and encourage them to keep up their efforts. (112 words)

〈解説〉1「世の中はより多くの情報で溢れている(満ちている)という文を作り，その中の「より多くの情報」を「たとえあなたがそうすることに一生を費やしても吸収することができるよりも」が後ろから説明する。「～で溢れている」はbe filled with～，「たとえ～でも」はeven if

S+V～，「～を…に費やす(捧げる)」はdevote～to…で表す。　2　解答例では，CAN-DOリストを作成してもその達成度を把握していない学校が約半数に上り，その目標設定を活かしきれていないことを述べている。CAN-DOリストは，目標到達のためにどのようなスキルや能力を伸ばせばよいかわかるため，生徒にとって学習の動機付けになるものである。よって教師は，達成可能な目標を設定して生徒に達成への意欲をもたせ，定期的に振り返りを行ってゴール達成への助言をし，生徒が学びを継続できるよう励ますようにすることが述べられている。

2020年度　実施問題

【中高共通】

【1】(放送による問題)これはリスニング・テストです。放送の指示に従って答えなさい。

ただいまから，リスニング・テストを行います。問題は，1，2，3，4の四つです。聞いている間にメモを取っても構いません。

1　では，1の問題から始めます。問題は，No. 1とNo. 2の2問です。

これから読まれる英文に対する応答として最もふさわしいものを，続いて読まれるa，b，cの中から一つ選び，記号で答えなさい。答えは，大文字，小文字どちらでも構いません。なお，英文と応答は1度しか読まれません。

では，始めます。

No. 1　Why don't we get a new microwave?

a.　The manual is here.

b.　Because these dishes are microwave safe.

c.　Do you think we can afford it?

No. 2　Where can I borrow a computer for my presentation?

a.　You can use mine.

b.　During the next project.

c.　It's been great, thanks.

2　次に，2の問題に移ります。問題は，No. 1からNo. 3までの3問です。

これから，短い対話文を読みます。そのあとでクエスチョンと言って質問します。その答えとして最もふさわしいものを，続いて読まれ

るa，b，c，dの中から一つ選び，記号で答えなさい。答えは，大文字，小文字どちらでも構いません。なお，対話文・質問・答えの選択肢は1度しか読まれません。

では，始めます。

No. 1

M: I booked a room for your lecture next week.

W: Thanks. By the way, I'm looking for a restaurant to hold a party after the lecture. Do you know any good places?

M: How about the Italian restaurant right next door? Let me give you the phone number by e-mail.

Question: What does the man offer to do?

a. Reserve a room.

b. Send a phone number.

c. Borrow a book about Italian restaurants.

d. Provide an e-mail address.

No. 2

M: I've got some information about a convention in New York next month. I can't go, but maybe you will be interested.

W: What's it about? I'd like to go if the event is on politics.

M: Oh, I should have mentioned that first. Yes, it's a politics and diplomatic relations event.

W: Is it? Well, I think I might go.

Question: What is the main topic of the conversation?

a. A seasonal event.

b. A convention.

c. A university course.

d. A tour guide.

No. 3

M: Hi, I'm interested in one of the paintings in the gallery. Can you tell me how much it is?

W: Sure. Which one?

M: That one in the middle. The artist's name is Hudson Laird.

W: Oh, yes. He has become rather famous recently. It's 135,000 dollars.

M: Uh ... I think I'll pass. Unfortunately, it's out of my price range.

Question:　What does the man mean when he says, "I think I'll pass" ?

a.　He browses in the gallery.

b.　He expects to be admitted.

c.　He will not buy the item.

d.　He is ready for a test.

3　次に3の問題に移ります。問題は，No. 1からNo. 3までの3問です。

　これから，あるまとまりのある英文を読みます。そのあとで，クエスチョンズと言って，その英文について三つの質問をします。その答えとして最もふさわしいものを，質問に続いて読まれるa，b，c，dの中から一つ選び，記号で答えなさい。答えは，大文字，小文字どちらでも構いません。なお，英文・質問・答えの選択肢は全体を通して2回読まれます。

　では，始めます。

For many sports, the ultimate goal would be to go one step further and make it onto the Olympic schedule. But not in the case of kendo. Many in the sport's global community are set against that, saying it would spell the end of kendo as they know it.

If kendo were a straightforward contest like table tennis or archery, making it conform to International Olympic Committee standards would not be difficult. The sport, however, has a highly subjective scoring system that values form and execution as much as the result.

Unlike Olympic fencing, which keeps score with electronic sensors that light up when the target is hit, a game-winning perfect strike in kendo, known as *ippon*, cannot be measured electronically; instead, it is a judgment call made by at least two out of the three referees.

The ingredients of that perfection are so nebulous that referees are notorious for bad calls. Nevertheless, for many kendo fighters, a referee's call is preferable to the flash of a light; for them, the technology would degrade the beauty of victory. The really important part of scoring is the process of initiating the attack, identifying a target, striking that target with correct posture and full spirit and then showing continued physical and mental alertness.

Questions

No. 1　What is the main topic of this passage?

a.　The ultimate goal of showing physical and mental alertness.
b.　The history of electronic scoring systems in the Olympic Games.
c.　How to become a skillful player in traditional sports.
d.　The beauty of victory that can't be measured by technology.

No. 2　What is required when scoring at the Olympic events?

a.　Subjectivity in anyone's view.
b.　Clear and concrete rules.
c.　Impressiveness in form and execution.
d.　Swiftness in course of play.

No. 3　Why do many kendo fighters prefer a referee's call?

a.　Because the electronic scoring system would be too subjective.
b.　Because the referee's call is always accurate.
c.　Because the electronic scoring system would not measure the process of *ippon*.

d.　Because the referee's call is made by a few people.

4　次に4の問題に移ります。問題は，No. 1とNo. 2の2問です。
これから，英語による対話文を読みます。(　　)のところに入る英語を聞き取り，書きなさい。対話文はそれぞれ2回読まれます。
では，始めます。

No. 1
W: I'm working on a paper for history class, but I have forgotten when the deadline is.
M: I heard that it (is to be submitted by next Wednesday at the latest).

No. 2
M: How was your game last weekend?
W: Well, (had it not been for our great aggressive play), we would have lost it.

これで，リスニング・テストを終わります。次の問題に移ってください。

(☆☆☆◎◎◎◎◎)

【2】次の英文や対話文の中の(　　)に最も適するものを，下のア～エの中からそれぞれ一つずつ選び，記号で答えなさい。

1　We should be (　　) of each other's ideas, no matter how much we disagree.
ア　respecting　　イ　respective　　ウ　respectful
エ　respectable

2　My parents have many (　　) they like to do in their spare-time: they watch movies, play tennis, and so on.
ア　habits　　イ　exercises　　ウ　actions　　エ　activities

3　Mr. Sato is in a very difficult position (　　) decision he makes.

ア　where　　イ　whoever　　ウ　whatever　　エ　what

4　I recommended that he (　　) on time to the interview test.

ア　come　　イ　coming　　ウ　will come　　エ　would come

5　Today smartphones are so much (　　) that we assume everyone has one.

ア　granted　　イ　for granted　　ウ　taken for granted

エ　taken it for granted

6　A : Is Ken still using your bike?

B : Yes, I wonder when he (　　) it.

ア　has returned　　イ　returns　　ウ　returned　　エ　will return

7　There was (　　) audience at the concert yesterday.

ア　many　　イ　much　　ウ　a lot of　　エ　a large

8　I believe you are innocent, but your friends don't trust you. We have yet (　　) a witness who can prove what you are saying is true.

ア　find　　イ　found　　ウ　to find　　エ　finding

9　(　　) was her joy that she ran about the room.

ア　So　　イ　That　　ウ　What　　エ　Such

10　A: You are too late!

B: Sorry. Let me (　　) for it by treating you to dinner.

ア　make up　　イ　turn in　　ウ　get over　　エ　put out

11　The boy hated worms, so he wouldn't enter the house until all of them were (　　).

ア　suspended　　イ　exterminated　　ウ　diminished

エ　investigated

12　Nancy has a serious back problem. She now has (　　) pain and she is looking for a skillful doctor.

ア　chronic　　イ　obscure　　ウ　humble　　エ　deprived

13　The manual of my office includes a graph, which shows an (　　) of the shipping costs.

ア　approximation　　イ　association　　ウ　interpretation

エ　observation

14　The volcano near the small village has been (　　) for more than 100 years, but some professors predict that it could become active again.

ア　stale　　イ　drowsy　　ウ　dormant　　エ　trite

15　You are (　　) invited to attend the celebration of marriage of my daughter and John on June 25th.

ア　cordially　　イ　diagonally　　ウ　intermittently

エ　infectiously

(☆☆☆☆◎◎◎◎◎)

【3】次の英文を読んで，あとの問いに答えなさい。

It's a well-known fact that a translation is no substitute for the original.

It's also perfectly obvious that this is wrong. Translations ***are*** substitutes for original texts. You use them in the place of a work written in a language you cannot read with ease.

The claim that a translation is no substitute for an original is not the only piece of folk wisdom that isn't true. We happily utter sayings such as (1)<u>"crime doesn't pay" or "it never rains but it pours" or "the truth will out"</u> that fly in the face of the evidence — Russian mafiosi basking on the French Riviera, British drizzle, and family secrets that never get out. Adages of this sort don't have to be true to be useful. Typically, they serve to warn, console, or encourage other people in particular circumstances, not to establish a theory of justice, a weather forecasting system, or forensic science. That's why saying a translation is no substitute for the original misleads only those who take it to be a well-known fact. It's truly astounding how many people fall into the trap.

When you say "crime doesn't pay" to a teenager caught filching a DVD from a market stall, it does not matter whether you believe this to be true or not. You are trying to ①<u>steer</u> the young person toward acceptance of the eighth commandment and using a conventional phrase in the service of that moral aim.

Similarly, a schoolteacher who has just caught his students reading *The Outsider* in English when they were supposed to be preparing their lessons by reading Camus's novel in French may well admonish them by saying in an authoritative tone of voice, "A translation is no substitute for the original!" The students know it's not true because they have just been caught using the translation as a substitute for the original. But they also understand that the teacher used a piece of folk wisdom to say something else that really is true — that only by reading more French will they improve their language skills. (X)

Students eventually graduate and get jobs, and soon enough some of them start writing book reviews. In those circumstances, when they have to write about a work of foreign literature translated into English and are lost for a phrase to use, they may parrot the warning they first heard at school. In common with all things people say and write, however, the force of the saying that "a translation is no substitute for an original" is completely altered (2)<u>when the context of utterance is changed</u>.

In its new context, it means that the writer of the book review possesses sufficient knowledge of some original to be able to make a judgment that its translation is not a substitute for it. Whether or not the reviewer really has read the original work, the assertion that the translation does not constitute a substitute for it puts the reviewer in charge.

Using the adage in this way obviously affects the meaning of the word *substitute*. If, for example, I said, "Instant coffee is no substitute for espresso made from freshly ground beans," (3)<u>I would be wrong</u>, in the sense that the purpose of instant coffee is to serve as a substitute for more laborious ways of making the drink; but also right, as long as the word *substitute* is understood to mean "the same as," "as good as," or "equivalent to." Instant coffee is clearly not the same as espresso; many people regard it as not as good as espresso; and because preferences in the field of coffee are matters of individual taste, it is not ②unreasonable to treat powdered coffee as not equivalent to espresso. We do often say all these more explicit things about coffee. But it is not so straightforward when it comes to translation.

People who declare translations to be no substitute for the original imply that they possess the means to recognize and appreciate the real thing, (　Y　), original composition as opposed to a translation. Without this ability they could not possibly make the claim that they do. Just as an inability to distinguish two types of coffee would deprive you of any possibility of comparing them, so the ability to discriminate between "a translation" and "an original" is a basic requirement for anyone who wants to claim that one of them is not the same as, equivalent to, or as good as the other.

(David Bellos, *Is That a Fish in Your Ear?*による。ただし，設問の都合で一部省略及び改変している。)

1　下線部①，②を別の語で言い換えたとき，最も意味の近いものを，次のア～エの中からそれぞれ一つずつ選び，記号で答えなさい。

①　ア　counsel　　イ　humiliate　　ウ　decline
　　エ　assess

②　ア　disentangle　　イ　irrational　　ウ　unresponsive
　　エ　nonprofit

2　本文中の空欄(　X　)，(　Y　)に入る英文または語句として最も適切なものを，次のア～エの中からそれぞれ一つずつ選び，記号で答えなさい。

X　ア　The phrase is used to make the students be irresolute about dedicating themselves to learning French.

　イ　The teacher means to spur them into greater assiduity, not to speak the truth about translation.

　ウ　The use of adages is a practical way for teachers to attempt a new method of teaching translation of novels.

　エ　French has such distinctive characteristics due to its unique phonological system.

Y　ア　over and above　　イ　in the first place　　ウ　now and again
　　エ　that is to say

3　下線部(1)のような表現は，何をするのに役立つのか，本文に即して日本語で書きなさい。

4　下線部(2)において，“a translation is no substitute for an original” はどのようなことを意味するのか，本文に即して日本語で答えなさい。

5　下線部(3)について，どのような意味において正しくないのか，本文に即して日本語で答えなさい。

6　本文の内容に即して，次の問いに英語で答えなさい。

What do we need to have in order to compare instant coffee with espresso?

(☆☆☆☆◎◎◎◎◎)

【中学校】

【1】次の英文を読んで，あとの問いに答えなさい。

Input alone is not sufficient for acquisition, because when one hears language one can often interpret the meaning without the use of syntax. For example, if one hears only the words *dog*, *bit*, *girl*, regardless of the order in which those words occur, it is likely that the meaning *The dog bit the girl* is the one that will be assumed rather than the more unusual *The girl bit the dog*. Similarly, if one hears a sentence such as *This is bad story*, one can easily fill in the missing article. Little knowledge, other than knowing the meanings of the words and knowing something about real-world events, is needed.

This is not the case with language production or output, because one is forced to put the words into some order. Production then “may force the learner to move from semantic processing to syntactic processing” (Swain, 1985). In fact, the impetus for Swain’s original study was the lack of second language development by immersion children even after years of academic study in that second language. Swain studied children learning French in an immersion context, suggesting that (1)<u>what was lacking</u> in their development as native-like speakers of French was the opportunity to use language productively as opposed to using language merely for comprehension. She compared results on a number of different grammatical, discourse, and sociolinguistic measures of sixth grade children in a French immersion setting and sixth grade native French speaking children. The lack of proficiency on the part of the immersion children, coupled with their apparent lack of productive use of French, led Swain to suggest the crucial role for output in the development of a second language.

It is ①<u>trivial</u> to state that there is no better way to test the extent of one's knowledge (linguistic or otherwise) than to have to use that knowledge in some productive way — whether it be explaining a concept to someone (i.e., teaching) or writing a computer program, or, in the case of language learning, getting even a simple idea across. However, output has generally been seen not as a way of creating knowledge, but as a way of practicing already existing knowledge. In other words, output has traditionally been viewed as a way of practicing what has previously been learned. This was certainly the thrust behind early methods of language teaching in which the presentation-practice (i.e., drill and repetition) mode was in vogue. A second traditional role assigned to output was that it was the way in which additional (and perhaps richer) input could be ②<u>elicit</u>ed. The idea that output could be part of learning was not seriously contemplated prior to Swain's important paper in 1985, in which she introduced the notion of (2)<u>comprehensible output or "pushed" output</u>. What is meant by this concept is that learners are "pushed" or "stretched" in their production as a necessary part of making themselves understood. In so doing, they might modify a previous utterance or they might try out forms that they had not used before.

Comprehensible output refers to the need for a learner to be "pushed toward the delivery of a message that is not only conveyed, but that is conveyed precisely, coherently, and appropriately" (Swain, 1985). In a more recent explication of the concept, Swain claimed that "output may stimulate learners to move from the semantic, open-ended, nondeterministic, strategic processing prevalent in comprehension to the complete grammatical processing needed for accurate production. Output, thus, would seem to have a potentially significant role in the development of syntax and morphology" (Swain, 1995).

The question becomes: In what ways can output play a central role in the learning process? We consider four possible ways that output may provide learners with a forum for important language-learning functions: receiving crucial feedback for the ③verification of these hypotheses; testing hypotheses about the structures and meanings of the target language; developing automaticity in interlanguage production; and forcing a shift from more meaning-based processing of the second language to a more syntactic mode.

(Susan M. Gass and Larry Selinker, *Second Language Acquisition*による。ただし，設問の都合で一部省略及び改変している。)

1　下線部①～③の英語の定義として最もよくあてはまるものを，次のア～エの中からそれぞれ一つずつ選び，記号で答えなさい。

①　ア　being the only one of its kind
　　イ　not likely to move, change or fail
　　ウ　not worth considering
　　エ　being an essential part

②　ア　to become twisted in an untidy way
　　イ　to remove or get rid of
　　ウ　to keep a person or an animal alive and healthy
　　エ　to get information or a reaction from someone

③　ア　an official rule made by a government or some other authority
　　イ　discovering whether something is correct or true
　　ウ　a judgment or opinion about the value
　　エ　a large important organization that has a particular purpose

2　下線部(1)は何であったか，本文に即して日本語で書きなさい。

3　下線部(2)はどのようなことか，本文に即して日本語で答えなさい。

4　理解可能なアウトプットはどのような必要性について言及してい

るか，本文に即して日本語で答えなさい。

5　本文の内容に即して，次の問いに英語で答えなさい。

(1)　What was the stimulus for Swain's original study?

(2)　How many possible ways that output may provide learners with a forum for important language-learning functions does the author consider?

6　本文の内容に最も合うものを，次のア～エの中から一つ選び，記号で答えなさい。

ア　Input alone is effective for acquisition, because when we hear language we can interpret the meaning in the moment.

イ　The idea that output could be part of learning was seriously contemplated in 1980.

ウ　Getting a simple idea across is not a productive way in which learners' knowledge is used.

エ　Output has been viewed as a way of practicing what we have already learned.

(☆☆☆☆◎◎◎◎◎)

【2】次の1，2について，指示に従って答えなさい。

1　次の日本語を英語に直しなさい。

成功への決意が何よりも重要だということを，肝に銘じておきなさい。

2 「中学校学習指導要領」(平成29年3月告示)の「第2章　第9節　外国語　第2　各言語の目標及び内容等　1　目標　(3)　話すこと[やり取り]　ア」において，「関心のある事柄について，簡単な語句や文を用いて即興で伝え合うことができるようにする。」と示しています。生徒があらかじめ原稿を準備してから話すのではなく，その場で考えて意見や気持ちを伝え合うためには，どのように授業構成を工夫しますか。学習指導要領の趣旨を踏まえ，100語程度の英語で

書きなさい。ただし，語数には，句読点や符号は含まないものとします。なお，総語数を記入すること。

(☆☆☆☆◎◎◎◎◎)

【高等学校】

【1】次の英文を読んで，あとの問いに答えなさい。

In the middle of the twentieth century, one of the most popular pursuits for applied linguists was the study of two languages in contrast. Eventually the stockpile of comparative and contrastive data on a multitude of pairs of languages yielded what commonly came to be known as (1)<u>the Contrastive Analysis Hypothesis (CAH)</u>. Deeply rooted in the behavioristic and structuralist approaches of the day, the CAH claimed that the principal barrier to second language acquisition is the interference of the first language system with the second language system, and that a scientific, structural analysis of the two languages in question would yield a taxonomy of linguistic contrasts between them which in turn would enable linguists and language teachers to predict the difficulties a learner would encounter.

It was at that time considered feasible that the tools of structural linguistics, such as Fries's (1952) slot-filler grammar, would enable a linguist to accurately describe the two languages in question, and to match those two descriptions against each other to determine valid contrasts, or differences, between them. Behaviorism contributed to the notion that human behavior is the sum of its smallest parts and components, and therefore that language learning could be described as the acquisition of all of those discrete units. (2)<u>Moreover, human learning theories highlighted *interfering* elements of learning</u>, concluding that where no interference could be predicted, no difficulty would be experienced since one could *transfer* positively all other items in a language. The logical conclusion from these various psychological and linguistic assumptions was that second language learning basically involved the overcoming of the differences between the two linguistic systems — the native and target languages.

Intuitively the CAH has appeal in that we commonly observe in second language learners a plethora of errors attributable to the negative transfer of the native language to the target language. It is quite common, for example, to detect certain foreign accents and to be able to infer, from the speech of the learner alone, where the learner comes from. Native English speakers can easily identify the accents of English language learners from Germany, France, Spain, and Japan, for example. Such accents can even be represented in the written word. Consider Mark Twain's *The Innocents Abroad* (1869), in which the French-speaking guide introduces himself: (3)"If ze zhentlemans will to me make ze grande honneur to me rattain in hees serveece. I shall show to him everysing zat is magnifique to look upon in ze beautiful Paree. I speaky ze Angleesh parfaitmaw."

Some rather strong claims were made of the CAH by language teaching experts and linguists. One of the strongest was made by Robert Lado (1957) in the preface to *Linguistics Across Cultures*: "The plan of the book rests on the assumption that we can predict and describe the patterns that will cause difficulty in learning, and those that will not cause difficulty, by comparing systematically the language and the culture to be learned with the native language and culture of the student." Then, in the first chapter of the book, Lado continues: "in the comparison between native and foreign language lies the key to ease or difficulty in foreign language learning.... Those elements that are similar to [the learner's] native language will be simple for him and those elements that are different will be difficult." An equally strong claim was made by Banathy, Trager, and Waddle (1966): "The change that has to take place in the language behavior of a foreign language student can be equated with the differences between the structure of the student's native language and culture and that of the target language and culture."

Such claims were supported by what some researchers claimed to be an empirical method of prediction. A well-known model was offered by

Stockwell, Bowen, and Martin (1965), who posited what they called a hierarchy of difficulty by which a teacher or linguist could make a prediction of the relative difficulty of a given aspect of the target language. For phonological systems in contrast, Stockwell and his associates suggested eight possible degrees of difficulty. These degrees were based upon the notions of transfer (positive, negative, and zero) and of optional and obligatory choices of certain phonemes in the two languages in contrast. Through a very careful, systematic analysis of the properties of the two languages in reference to the hierarchy of difficulty, applied linguists were able to derive (4)a reasonably accurate inventory of phonological difficulties that a second language learner would encounter.

(H. Douglas Brown, *Principles of Language Learning and Teaching* による。ただし，設問の都合で一部省略及び改変している。)

1 下線部(1)CAHは二つのことを主張している。二つのことのうち，二番目に示された内容を，本文に即して日本語で書きなさい。

2 下線部(2)によって導かれた結論を，本文に即して日本語で書きなさい。

3 下線部(3)について，第二言語学習者がこのような文を作るのはなぜか。その理由を本文に即して日本語で書きなさい。

4 本文の内容に即して，次の問いに英語で答えなさい。

(1) According to the conclusion from the psychological and linguistic assumptions, what do second language learners have to do?

(2) According to Robert Lado, what kind of elements will be difficult for foreign language learners?

5 下線部(4)は何によって得られるか，本文に即して日本語で答えなさい。

6 本文の内容に最も合うものを，次のア～エの中から一つ選び，記号で答えなさい。

ア It was considered that Fries's slot-filler grammar would not help linguists determine valid contrasts of the two languages in question.

イ　A little vagueness of the accents of second language learners leads native speakers of the target language to be indecisive about where the learners are from.

ウ　Robert Lado states we can predict what will or will not cause difficulty in learning by comparing systematically the language and culture to be learned with the learners' native language and culture.

エ　Some teachers and linguists came to the conclusion that an empirical method of prediction such as a hierarchy of difficulty could be posited later.

(☆☆☆☆☆◎◎◎◎◎)

【2】次の1，2について，指示に従って答えなさい。

1　次の日本語を英語に直しなさい。

私たち人間は，失敗したり負けたりして初めて自分の間違いやいたらなさに気づく。

2　「高等学校学習指導要領」(平成30年3月告示)の「第2章　第8節　外国語　第2款　各科目　第1　英語コミュニケーションⅠ」の「2　内容　(3)の①のエの(ア)」には，「情報や考え，気持ちなどを即興で話して伝え合う活動」と示されています。即興で話す力を身に付けさせるために，あなたは「英語コミュニケーションⅠ」の授業でどのような指導を継続的に行いますか。学習指導要領の趣旨を踏まえ，100語程度の英語で書きなさい。ただし，語数には，句読点や符号は含まないものとします。なお，総語数を記入すること。

(☆☆☆☆◎◎◎◎◎)

解答・解説

【中高共通】

【1】1 No. 1 c　No. 2 a　2 No. 1 b　No. 2 b　No. 3 c　3 No. 1 d　No. 2 b　No. 3 c　4 No. 1 I heard that it (is to be submitted by next Wednesday at the latest).　No. 2 Well, (had it not been for our great aggressive play), we would have lost it.

〈解説〉リスニング問題の問題形式は多岐にわたっている。問題用紙には質問文・選択肢とも印刷されていないので，音声からの情報で解答しなければならない。1 No.1 Why don't we ～ ?「～しませんか?」に対して Do you think we can afford it?「それを買える余裕があると思うの?」と答えている。 No.2 Where can I borrow a computer ～ ?「どこで発表用のコンピューターを借りることができますか?」と尋ねているので，You can use mine.「私の(コンピューター)を使っていいですよ」と答えている。 2 No.1 男性は「メールでイタリアンレストランの電話番号を知らせます」と言っている。 No.2「来月ニューヨークで行われる会議の情報がある」という発言から始まり，そのテーマについて質問している。 No.3 ここでのpassは「いらない，結構だ」という意味。したがって勧められた絵画を買わないと考えられる。 3 No.1 第3段落のUnlike Olympic fencing ～ the three refereesで，フェンシングとは違って剣道の「一本」は電子機器を使って測れない，さらに最終段落1文目のfor them, the ～ beauty of victoryでテクノロジーが勝利の美の品位を下げると述べられている。 No.2 第2段落2文目に「剣道は主観的な点数のつけ方である」とあり，これはオリンピック委員会の基準に合わない。つまり，オリンピックでの採点基準として必要なものは客観的な数値やルールと考える。 No.3 第3段落より，剣道の「一本」を取るまでの過程を審査する電子機器を使った採点方式はないと考えることができる。 4 No.1 be動詞＋不定詞で予定を表している。 No.2 仮定法過去完了の従属節を答える。ifが省略された場合に倒置が起こることに注意する。

【2】1　ウ　2　エ　3　ウ　4　ア　5　ウ　6　エ　7　エ　8　ウ　9　エ　10　ア　11　イ　12　ア　13　ア　14　ウ　15　ア

〈解説〉1　be respectful of ～「～に敬意を示す」。respectの派生語はそれぞれ意味を整理して暗記しよう。　2　コロンの後の具体例(映画を観る，テニスをするなど)を参考に考える。activity「活動」。　3　直後に名詞をとれる語はwhateverとwhat。ここでのwhateverは副詞節を作っている。whatever decision he makesで「彼がどんな決断をしようとも」。　4　要求，命令，主張，提案などを表す動詞(ここではrecommend)のthat節では，動詞が「should＋動詞の原形」もしくは「動詞の原形」になる。　5　take A for granted「Aを当然のことであると考える」。本問では受動態になっている。　6　when以下がwonderの目的語で，「いつ～？」という意味の名詞節になっているので，未来を表す助動詞willを節内で使用することが可能。whenが「～する時」という意味の副詞節の場合は，たとえ内容が未来を表していてもwillが使えず，動詞を原形にする。　7　audienceを修飾する語としてふさわしいのはlarge。large audienceで「大勢の聴衆」という意味。　8　have yet to ～「まだ～していない」。　9　Such is S that …「Sはとても大きい～なので…」。元の文はHer joy was such that she ran about the room.で，本問は倒置構文である。　10　make up for ～「～の埋め合わせをする」。
11　exterminate「根絶する，一掃する」。　12　chronic「慢性の」。chronic pain「慢性の痛み」という意味で文意に合う。
13　approximation「概算，近似」。　14　dormant「休止中の」。dormant volcanoは「休火山」という意味。　15　invitedを修飾する副詞を選ぶ問題。cordially「心から，温かく」。diagonally「斜めに」，intermittently「途切れ途切れに」，infectiously「伝染して」。

【3】1 ① ア ② イ 2 X イ Y エ 3 特定の状況で他人に警告したり慰めたり勇気づけたりするのに役立つ。 4 書評の書き手が，その翻訳では原作の代用にはならないという判断を下すことができるほど，ある原作における十分な知識を持っているということ。 5 インスタントコーヒーの目的は，作るのに手間がかかるエスプレッソの代用品として役立つことであるという意味。
6 We need to have an ability to distinguish two types of coffee.
〈解説〉1 ① steerは「導く，操縦する」という意味。DVDを盗んだその若者を第八戒(モーゼの十戒の中の第八戒のこと，盗みを禁じている)に導くという意味になる。counselはadviseやguideの意味に近い。② unreasonableは「不合理な，道理をわきまえない」という意味。最も近いのはirrational。 2 X 教師から読むように言われた作品を，学生が翻訳版で読んでいたので，教師が格言(A translation is no substitute for the original)を使って，原文で読むように生徒を諭している場面であり，学生もただ教師がその格言を引用したに過ぎず，原語であるフランス語で読まなければ語学力が上がらないことを自覚している。これを踏まえて，その格言を用いて伝えたかったことは，イ「その教師は翻訳の真理について述べているのではなく，学生をより一生懸命勉強させようと励ました」となる。 Y 直前のthe real thingと直後のoriginal compositionの関係を考えると，that is to say「すなわち」が適切。 3 下線部の表現はそれぞれcrime doesn't pay「悪事はわりに合わない」，it never rains but it pours「降れば必ず土砂降り」，the truth will out「事実はすぐに表れる」という意味。これらが役立つ場面が書かれている箇所は同段落4文目である。解答欄の大きさを考えると，they serve to ～ in particular circumstancesまでをまとめる。 4 次の段落の1文目の先頭にあるits new contextは下線部のthe contextを指し，さらにitはa translation is no substitute for an originalを表しているので，これより後ろを解答としてまとめる。 5 直後にin the sense that ～「～という意味において」があるので，これ以降が該当箇所となる。serve as ～「～として役に立つ」，laborious「手間のかかる，面倒な」。

6　質問文の意味は「インスタントコーヒーとエスプレッソを比較するために必要なものは何か?」である。第7段落より，「その2つのコーヒーの違いを区別(認識)する能力を身につける必要がある」。別解としてWe need to develop an ability to recognize the differences between these two types of coffee.などが考えられる。

【中学校】

【1】1　①　ウ　②　エ　③　イ　2　言語を理解のためだけに使うということとは対照的に，言語を大いに使用する機会。　3　自分の言っていることを理解してもらうのに必要なことの一つとして，発話の際に学習者が「後押しされ」たり「伸長され」たりすること。　4　学習者が「内容を単に伝えるだけではなく，正確で，理路整然と，適切に伝える話し方へと後押しされる」必要性。　5　(1)　It was the lack of second language development by immersion children.

(2)　Four possible ways.　6　エ

〈解説〉1　①　trivialは「取るに足らない，つまらない」という意味。

②　elicitは「(応答・反応など)を引き出す」という意味。

③　verificationは「立証，確証」という意味。　2　下線部を含む文の主語はwhat was lacking，動詞はwas，補語はthe opportunityで第二文型であり，主語＝補語の関係が成り立つ。すなわち解答はthe opportunity以下となる。　3　直後にWhat is meant by this conceptとあり，this conceptが指す内容は下線部なので，解答はその後のlearners are "pushed"～ making themselves understoodまでとなる。　4　第4段落1文目のto be以下を和訳する。thatはmessageを先行詞とする主格の関係代名詞である。　5　(1)　第2段落3文目を見る。impetusが問題文のstimulusに言い換えられていることに注目する。解答はthe stimulusを代名詞itに変えて書き始めること。　(2)　問題文がHow manyから始まっているので数を問われていることに注意する。最終段落2文目を参照する。　6　ア　第1段落1文目に合わない。　イ　第3段落6文目に合わない。　ウ　第3段落1文目に合わない。　エ　第3段落2文目に合致

する。

【2】1　Keep in mind that nothing is more important than your own resolution to succeed.　　2　[解答例]　Impromptu speech is a speech you deliver without preparation. To better prepare for students to make an impromptu speech, first of all, we should show them the basic structure of an English speech, using some sample templates for their practice. And then instruct them to expand their ideas based on the keywords relevant to the topic, which is designed to attract their interests, and present their speeches in the classroom in one or two minutes. In addition, we should advice students to explain their ideas in simpler words. Also, it is important to create the relaxed atmosphere so that students do not be afraid of making mistakes. (107 Words)

〈解説〉1 「肝に銘じておく」は「心に留めておく」と考えてkeep O in mindを用いる。「成功への決意が何よりも重要だ」は最上級を用いてyour own resolution to succeed is the most important of allと表すこともできる。　2　新中学校学習指導要領(平成29年3月告示)では，従来ひとつの領域であった「話すこと」が，「話すこと[やり取り]」と「話すこと[発表]」の2つの領域に分けられ，より具体的かつ詳細な内容が提示されるようになった。今後は，新学習指導要領に基づきどのような授業を行えばよいか，自分なりに英語で意見を述べられるように準備しておきたい。解答例では，即興スピーチ(impromptu speech)をまずは定義し，即興で自分の考えを伝えるために，授業でどのような指導が必要かを述べている。まずスピーチのサンプルを示して英語のスピーチの基本構造を教え，生徒の興味・関心を引くトピックについて即興でスピーチをさせる。その際，できるだけ簡単な単語を使うよう指導し，また生徒が誤りをおそれないようにリラックスした雰囲気作りも大事である，とまとめている。

【高等学校】

【1】1　当該の二つの言語を科学的，構造的に分析すると，言語学的差異を分類する方法が生み出され，今度はそれによって，言語学者や語学教師は，学習者が直面する困難を予測できるようになるかもしれないということ。　2　言語的干渉が全く予測されない場合には，学習者は第二言語習得に全く困難を感じないだろうということ。

3　対象言語に対する母国語の負の転移が起こるから。

4　(1)　They have to overcome the differences between the system of the native language and that of the target language.　(2)　Those elements that are different from their native language will.　5　難易度の階層に関して，二つの言語の性質を念入りにかつ体系的に分析すること。

6　ウ

〈解説〉1　CAH(対照分析仮説)が主張している内容は，次の文のthe CAH claimed以下に書かれており，andはclaimの目的語に当たるthat節を2つつないでいることから，問題文より，解答はandの後ろの2つめのthat節以下をまとめる。in questionは「当該の，話題にしている」という意味で前のtwo languagesを修飾している。taxonomyは「分類」という意味。　2　直後のconcluding以下をまとめる。whereは「～する場合(所)で」という意味で副詞節を作っている。　3　前文より，下線部(3)はフランス語話者が*The Innocents Abroad*(1869)の中で自己紹介した英文。このような母語と英語が混じる文を作る原因は同段落1文目に述べられている。構文を分析すると，observeの目的語は，in second language learnersが間に入っているのでわかりにくくなっているが，a plethora of errorsである。さらにattributable「起因すると考えられて」以下の形容詞句がerrorsを修飾しており，この部分が解答となる。なお，言語習得関連の英文においてtransferは「転移」と訳すことが多い。

4　(1)　the conclusion from the psychological and linguistic assumptionsを手掛かりに当該箇所を探す。第2段落最終文より，第二言語学習には目標言語と母語の違いを克服することが必要だとわかる。

(2)　Robert Ladoを手掛かりに当該箇所を探す。第4段落4文目のthose

elements that are different will be difficultを引用し，解答の際にはdifferentの後に省略されている語を補うこと。　5　下線部を含む文の最初のThroughはここでは手段を表しているので，このThroughから始まる前置詞句が表す内容が解答となる。in reference to A「Aに関して」。　6　ア　第2段落1文目に合わない。　イ　第3段落2文目・3文目に合わない。indecisive「決定的ではない」。　ウ　第4段落2文目に合致する。　エ　最終段落1文目・2文目に合わない。

【2】1　It is not until we human beings experience failures or defeats that we notice our mistakes or shortcomings.　2　〔解答例〕I believe that students can make an impromptu speech based on the topics of the passages they read in class. In the process of making the instructional design, we should choose topics from the reading passage familiar to students, and explain them in Japanese to help students understand the content. After that, students are expected to make pairs and discuss their ideas about the passages with their partners without preparation using the words and expressions in the reading. In the next step, they are asked to make an impromptu speech in front of their classmates. These small steps will help them to develop their speaking skills. (106 Words)

〈解説〉1　it is not until ～ that …「～して初めて…する」を用いて書く。　2　新高等学校学習指導要領(平成30年3月告示)は，現行版から大幅に改訂された。従来の「コミュニケーション英語Ⅰ」は「英語コミュニケーションⅠ」として整理され，その目標についても「(1)聞くこと，(2)読むこと，(3)話すこと［やり取り］，(4)話すこと［発表］，(5)書くこと」の5つの領域に分けられ，より具体的かつ詳細な内容が提示されるようになった。今後は，新学習指導要領に基づきどのような授業を行えばよいか，自分なりに英語で意見を述べられるように準備しておきたい。解答例では，生徒に親しみのあるトピックについての英文を読ませ，内容理解を行った後，ペアワークでそれに関する自分たちの考えを即興で話させる。その際ハードルを下げるために，読んだ英文中の単語や表現を用いるよう指示する。さらに他の生徒の前で発表をさせるといった細かい段階を踏ませることが肝要である，とまとめている。

2019年度　実施問題

【中高共通】

【1】(放送による問題)　これはリスニング・テストです。放送の指示に従って答えなさい。

ただいまから，リスニング・テストを行います。問題は1，2，3，4の四つです。聞いている間にメモを取っても構いません。

1　では，1の問題から始めます。問題はNo. 1とNo. 2の2問です。

これから読まれる英文に対する応答として最もふさわしいものを，続いて読まれるa，b，cの中から一つ選び，記号で答えなさい。答えは，大文字，小文字どちらでも構いません。なお，英文と応答は1度しか読まれません。

では，始めます。

No. 1　Would you like to go to the concert of Tom's Band next Sunday?

(a)　Which movie is it in?

(b)　I didn't know that you could play the guitar.

(c)　I would rather prepare for next Monday's exam.

No. 2　Could you update our market share figures for the second quarter?

(a)　Sure. The new supermarket is near my house.

(b)　Certainly. How soon do you need them?

(c)　OK. It's on the third floor.

2　次に，2の問題に移ります。問題は，No. 1からNo. 3までの3問です。

これから，短い対話文を読みます。そのあとでクエスチョンと言って質問します。その答えとして最もふさわしいものを，続いて読まれ

るa，b，c，dの中から一つ選び，記号で答えなさい。答えは，大文字，小文字どちらでも構いません。なお，対話文・質問・答えの選択肢は1度しか読まれません。

では，始めます。

No. 1

M: What are you doing this long weekend?

W: I'm traveling alone to Okinawa. How about you?

M: I'm planning on relaxing at home. And I have a lot of things to do.

W: That sounds good, too.

Question: What is the man most likely to do this weekend?

(a) Go hiking.

(b) Take a bus.

(c) Go fishing.

(d) Make a shelf

No. 2

W: Shall we schedule the Spanish seminar for next Wednesday?

M: Sorry. Some of us will be on vacation from the beginning of next week until the following Tuesday.

W: OK. Let's plan to have it this Wednesday.

M: Sounds good.

Question: When will the Spanish seminar take place?

(a) Next Wednesday.

(b) Next Tuesday.

(c) This Wednesday.

(d) This Tuesday.

No. 3

M: Thank you for calling. This is George Hotel.

W: My name is Mika Sato. I have a reservation from tomorrow.

M: Yes, Ms. Sato. We have your reservation. It's for six days, from November 4 to November 9 . Is that correct?

W: That's correct. But can I stay two more days?

M: Let's see. Yes, you can keep your room for two more days through November 11.

Question: How long will the woman stay at the hotel?

(a) For five days.

(b) For six days.

(c) For seven days.

(d) For eight days.

3 次に3の問題に移ります。問題は，No. 1からNo. 3までの3問です。

これから，あるまとまりのある英文を読みます。そのあとで，クエスチョンズと言って，その英文について三つの質問をします。その答えとして最もふさわしいものを，質問に続いて読まれるa，b，c，dの中から一つ選び，記号で答えなさい。答えは，大文字，小文字どちらでも構いません。なお，英文・質問・答えの選択肢は全体を通して2回読まれます。

では，始めます。

In our globalized, technology-driven world, we have convinced ourselves that the route to excellence and progress lies in specialization. Consider entrepreneur Peter Thiel's recent argument that workers should make a lifelong commitment to a single career objective. Or the fact that fewer than 7% of U.S. undergraduates choose a major from among the humanities, opting instead for market-focused majors such as petroleum engineering or pharmaceutical marketing.

Superficially, this trend toward specialization makes sense. It does, after all, take sustained dedication to attain world-class expertise. But the implication that everyone should become an expert in one thing is dangerous because there is untold value in knowing a little about a lot.

University of Pennsylvania professor Philip Tetlock knows this well. His research has shown that in a variety of situations, certain nonexperts can actually make better predictions than experts, because they are better able to draw upon an eclectic array of perspectives. Such situations, of course, do not include, say, picking a surgical procedure, for which subject-matter expertise is an enormous asset. But they do include solving contemporary problems - inequality, climate change, policing - that require thinking broadly and smartly across many disciplines.

Questions

No. 1 What is the title of this passage?
- (a) The benefits of globalization.
- (b) The danger of having too many experts.
- (c) The students of the humanities and the science.
- (d) The key to solving climate change.

No. 2 According to entrepreneur Peter Thiel, what should workers make?
- (a) A lifelong commitment to a single career objective.
- (b) A technology-driven society.
- (c) A new application for petroleum engineering.
- (d) A route to excellence and progress.

No. 3 What has Philip Tetlock's research shown?
- (a) We don't have all solutions in this world.
- (b) Some experts can make better solutions than nonexperts.
- (c) Scientists can draw upon many kinds of perspectives.
- (d) Some nonexperts can make better predictions than experts.

4　次に4の問題に移ります。問題はNo. 1とNo. 2の2問です。

これから，英語による対話文を読みます。(　　)のところに入る英語を聞き取り，書きなさい。対話文はそれぞれ2回読まれます。

では，始めます。

No. 1

M: Have you seen my glasses?

W: Oh, again?

No. 2

W: I don't like getting older any more.

M: Why not? You can

これでリスニング・テストを終わります。次の問題に移ってください。

(☆☆◎◎◎)

【2】次の英文や対話文の中の(　　)に最も適するものを，下のア～エの中からそれぞれ一つずつ選び，記号で答えなさい。

1　On Sundays Nancy's family enjoys having (　　) discussions over a cup of coffee.

ア　lived　　イ　living　　ウ　alive　　エ　lively

2　It was much (　　) question, so nobody in my class was able to answer it.

ア　too difficult a　　イ　too difficult　　ウ　too a difficult

エ　a too difficult

3　Human beings differ from wild beasts (　　) they can think and speak.

ア　if not　　イ　in that　　ウ　to that　　エ　except that

4　A: When should I come here?

B: Please come at noon, (　　) the manager will be back in our office.

ア　by time　　イ　just by　　ウ　by which time　　エ　during

5 (　　) the night before, the street was wet and full of mud.

ア　Having rained　　イ　It having rained　　ウ　Having been rained

エ　It being rained

6 My parents are very displeased with the outcome because we (　　) the game against Sam's team last night.

ア　should win　　イ　will have won　　ウ　are to win

エ　could have won

7 A: Shall we go to see a movie this afternoon?

B: Sorry, my grandmother is seriously ill now. We have to take (　　) sitting with her in the hospital.

ア　terms　　イ　changes　　ウ　turns　　エ　orders

8 The Chinese pottery is a (　　) work of art, so it is displayed behind a thick pane of glass in his room.

ア　priceless　　イ　penniless　　ウ　worthless　　エ　valueless

9 The big tree in our village was (　　) by lightning two months ago.

ア　stuck　　イ　struck　　ウ　beaten　　エ　blown

10 It seems that John has little (　　) for jokes of any kind.

ア　ambition　　イ　annoyance　　ウ　expression　　エ　tolerance

11 The new treaty is scheduled to take effect in five years, but the countries concerned must first (　　) it.

ア　devastate　　イ　ratify　　ウ　atone　　エ　hamper

12 Bill is always arguing with her, and won't listen, (　　) take her advice.

ア　let alone　　イ　let by　　ウ　let down　　エ　let off

13 Certain forms of mental illness can be (　　) by food allergies.

ア　submerged　　イ　permeated　　ウ　replicated　　エ　triggered

14 Most researchers agree that children have an (　　) ability to acquire language.

ア　aerial　　イ　arbitrary　　ウ　innate　　エ　intimate

15 Nowadays the advanced technologies are regarded as safer and more efficient than their (　　).

ア　ancestors　　イ　predecessors　　ウ　prevision
エ　descendants

(☆☆◎◎◎)

【3】次の英文を読んで，あとの問いに答えなさい。

Many ①spurious rules start out as helpful hints intended to rescue indecisive writers from paralysis when faced with a choice provided by the richness of English. These guides for the perplexed also make the lives of copy editors easier, so they may get incorporated into style sheets. Before you know it, a rule of thumb morphs into a rule of grammar, and a perfectly innocuous (albeit second-choice) construction is demonized as incorrect. Nowhere is (1)this transition better documented than with the phony but ubiquitous rule on when to use *which* and when to use *that.*

According to the traditional rule, the choice depends on which of two kinds of relative clause the word is introducing. A nonrestrictive relative clause is set off by commas, dashes, or parentheses, and expresses a comment from the peanut gallery, as in *The pair of shoes, which cost five thousand dollars, was hideous.* A restrictive relative clause is essential to the meaning of the sentence, often because it pinpoints the referent of the noun from among a set of alternatives. (2)If we were narrating a documentary about Imelda Marcos's vast shoe collection and wanted to single out one of the pairs by how much she paid for it and then say something about that pair alone, we would write (3)*The pair of shoes that cost five thousand dollars was hideous.* The choice between *that* and *which*, according to the rule, is simple: nonrestrictive relative clauses take *which*; restrictive relative clauses take *that.*

One part of the rule is correct: it's odd to use *that* with a nonrestrictive relative clause, as in *The pair of shoes, that cost a thousand dollars, was hideous.* So odd, in fact, that few people write that way, rule or no rule.

The other part of the rule is utterly incorrect. There is nothing wrong with using *which* to introduce a restrictive relative clause, as in *The pair of shoes which cost five thousand dollars was hideous*. Indeed, with some restrictive relatives, *which* is the only option, such as *That which doesn't kill you makes you stronger* and *The book in which I scribbled my notes is worthless*. Even when *which* isn't mandatory, great writers have been using it for centuries, as in the King James Bible's "Render therefore unto Caesar the things which are Caesar's" and Franklin Roosevelt's "a day which will live in infamy." The linguist Geoffrey Pullum searched through a sample of classic novels by authors such as Dickens, Conrad, Melville, and Brontë and found that on average readers will bump into a restrictive relative clause with *which* by the time they are 3 percent of the way into it. Turning to (4)edited prose in twenty-first-century English, he found that *which* was used in about a fifth of the restrictive relative clauses in American newspapers and in more than half of those in British newspapers. Even the grammar nannies can't help themselves. In *The Elements of Style* E. B. White recommended "*which*-hunting," but in his classic essay "Death of a Pig" he wrote, "The premature ②expiration of a pig is, I soon discovered, a departure which the community marks solemnly on its calendar."

The spurious rule against restrictive *which* sprang from a daydream by Henry Fowler in *Modern English Usage* in 1926: "If writers would agree to regard *that* as the defining relative pronoun, & *which* as the non-defining, there would be much gain both in lucidity & in ease. Some there are who follow this principle now; but it would be idle to pretend that it is the practice either of most or of the best writers." The lexicographer Bergen Evans punctured the reverie with an observation that should be embossed on little cards and handed out to language pedants: "What is not the practice of most, or of the best, is not part of our common language."

So (5)what's a writer to do? The real decision is not whether to use *that* or *which* but whether to use a restrictive or a nonrestrictive relative clause. If a phrase which expresses a comment about a noun can be omitted without substantially changing the meaning, and if it would be pronounced after a slight pause and with its own intonation contour, then be sure to set it off with commas (or dashes or parentheses): *The Cambridge restaurant, which had failed to clean its grease trap, was infested with roaches.* Having done so, you don't have to worry about whether to use *that* or *which*, because if you're tempted to use *that* it means either that you are more than two hundred years old or that your ear for the English language is so mistuned that the choice of *that* and *which* is ③<u>the least of your worries</u>.

(Steven Pinker, *The Sense of Style* による。ただし，設問の都合で一部省略及び改変している。)

1　下線部①～③を別の語句で言い換えたとき，最も意味の近いものを，次のア～エの中からそれぞれ一つずつ選び，記号で答えなさい。

①　ア　abundant　イ　accurate　ウ　binary　エ　bogus

②　ア　digest　イ　debt　ウ　death　エ　dairy

③　ア　the thing which you have to be bothered about
　　イ　the thing which you shouldn't be bothered about
　　ウ　the thing which you'll count on the most
　　エ　the thing which you'll count on at last

2　下線部(1)が指す内容を日本語で書きなさい。

3　下線部(2)の場合に，下線部(3)のように書くのはなぜか。その理由を本文に即して日本語で書きなさい。

4　下線部(4)について，言語学者のGeoffrey Pullumが発見したのはどのようなことか，本文に即して日本語で書きなさい。

5　下線部(5)について，筆者が書き手にすすめているのは何をすることか，本文に即して日本語で書きなさい。

(☆☆☆◎◎◎)

【中学校】

【1】次の英文を読んで，あとの問いに答えなさい。

There are different kinds of language teachers: those who teach what is usually called 'mother tongue', the ①<u>dominant</u> language of a society (such as

French in France, Japanese in Japan); those who teach a dominant language in a society to newcomers to the society for whom it is a 'second language'; those who teach a language spoken in another country and learnt only in schools, colleges and universities - a 'foreign' language. All these teachers are handling one of the most important elements of humankind, for it is language that is one of the distinctive features of being human, one of the most important facilitating factors in the formation of human social groups, and at the same time one of the factors that separates groups from one another. (1) Language teachers have important responsibilities in ensuring that learners of any age - from kindergarten into schools and on into adult, lifelong education - acquire the practical skills of the languages they need. This includes reading and writing the language(s) they otherwise acquire naturally in their environment - their 'mother tongue(s)' or 'first language(s)' - because, although they will inevitably learn to speak, reading and writing do not come naturally and often do not come at all without great effort and application. Language teaching also includes teaching the practical skills in a language that are needed for a short term business or pleasure trip to another country. Teaching 'mother tongues' and 'languages for business' are two extremes of a continuum of skills and knowledge, and there is every kind of language teaching in between.

At the same time, language teachers are concerned with values, for values are ②inherent in any kind of teaching whether teachers and learners are aware of them or not. The teachers of 'mother tongue' have to reflect on what the language means for those who speak another language at home. They have to think about how their teaching is not only focused on practical skills but also creates a sense of living in a specific time and place, in a specific country, in a specific nation-state; language and identity are inseparable. Those who teach second and foreign languages have to think about how (2) the language is offering a new perspective, a challenge to the primary language of identity, and a different vision of the culture(s) in which they live and have hitherto taken for granted.

Language teaching has both practical purposes and challenging values. Language teachers can expect a career of 30-40 years and half way through this they may begin to feel that the vision they had as young teachers needs renewal. At the beginning of their careers, teachers are full of enthusiasm and visions - which may be indeterminate and not yet well formed - and to give shape to their enthusiasm they undertake (3)initial teacher training. This however tends to focus on the everyday issues of methods, classroom discipline and the problems that all new teachers face. It is important to temper this with engagement with the significance of language teaching for individuals, for societies, for teachers themselves. They need to maintain the knowledge that they are doing something worthwhile, even in the midst of their daily, often stressful work.

By mid-career, teachers have established a routine for dealing with ③discipline and similar issues even though it is in the nature of such things that they are never totally resolved. Mid-career teachers have different priorities and they are usually offered short in-service courses or sometimes they can attend Masters courses. Short courses may keep them up to date with new methods and recent policy changes but hardly give them the opportunity to renew their enthusiasm and vision. Longer courses should allow them to see their work in a wider educational context, but unfortunately longer courses are not offered to everyone.

(Michael Byram, *From Foreign Language Education to Education for Intercultural Citizenship* による。ただし，設問の都合で一部省略及び改変している。)

1　下線部①～③の英語の定義として最もよくあてはまるものを，次のア～エの中からそれぞれ一つずつ選び，記号で答えなさい。

①　ア　more powerful, important or noticeable than others

　　イ　continuing to exist for a long time or for all future time

　　ウ　usually good and special

エ　not very great in amount, number, or ability

② ア　average or usual, not different or special in any way

イ　almost the same, but not exactly the same

ウ　very large, serious, or important, when compared to other things

エ　existing in something as a permanent or characteristic attribute

③ ア　the practice of doing regularly without thinking about it

イ　the practice of acting as if you don't really feel sad

ウ　the practice of training people to obey rules and behave well

エ　the practice of talking with someone when you want to study

2　下線部(1)について，外国語の教師が保証するのは，全ての年齢の学習者が何をすることか，本文に即して日本語で書きなさい。

3　下線部(2)について，言語が提示するのはどのようなことか，本文に即して日本語で書きなさい。

4　若く経験の浅い教師が下線部(3)を受ける目的は何か，本文に即して日本語で書きなさい。

5　本文の内容に即して，次の問いに英語で答えなさい。

(1)　What do the teachers of mother tongue have to reflect on?

(2)　What may language teachers feel in the midst of their long career?

6　本文の内容に合うものを，次にア～エから一つ選び記号で答えなさい。

ア　Only the teachers of a second language handle one of the most important elements of humankind.

イ　Not all teachers can attend longer courses to see their work in a wider educational context.

ウ　Speaking, reading, and writing skills don't come naturally to language learners.

エ　Short courses hardly keep teachers up to date with new methods and recent policy changes.

(☆☆☆◎◎◎)

【2】次の1，2について，指示に従って答えなさい。

1　次の日本語を英語に直しなさい。

私は新しい英語の一節をひと目見て，自分が日本語に訳すことなく理解していることに気づいた。

2　「中学校学習指導要領」(平成20年3月告示)の「第2章　第9節　外国語　第2　各言語の目標及び内容等」では，「英語　2　内容　イ　話すこと　(ウ)」において，「聞いたり読んだりしたことなどについて，問答したり意見を述べ合ったりなどすること」としています。生徒が既習の表現を使うことができるようにするために，授業において英語で意見を述べ合う活動を取り入れるとしたら，あなたはどのような授業を行いますか。学習指導要領の趣旨を踏まえ，100語程度の英語で書きなさい。ただし，語数には，句読点や符号は含まないものとします。なお，解答の総語数を，(　　)の中に記入すること。

(☆☆☆◎◎◎)

【高等学校】

【1】次の英文を読んで，あとの問いに答えなさい。

Clearly, however we choose to define it, the very concept of demotivation draws attention to the unstable nature of motivation as something that (①) over time. This process of motivational flux or change in students' experiences of learning English seems to be of particular interest to researchers in Japan. I believe that (1)<u>one of the reasons for this</u> may lie in the structure of the Japanese educational system, which I sketched in fairly simplistic and hyperbolic terms earlier - that is, the high pressured 'exam hell' that characterizes students' learning experiences through high school and then the sudden transition to the 'four-year leisure-land existence' (Clark, 2010) of university life. Associated with this structure and its clear-cut division between school life and university life is an equally sharp contrast between the kinds of English language study to which students are exposed in the two settings. Learning English at school is equated with learning English for university entrance exams, with its focus on grammar, reading and vocabulary, or as Ryan and Makarova (2004) put it, those 'elements of English which are testable in a written examination requiring short answers, most of which can be graded by a computer'. As they note, this is despite highly publicized government-led attempts to give more emphasis to English listening and speaking skills. Put simply, oral communication skills are much less easily testable, and hence, tend to receive much less attention. On the other hand, learning English at university is more about learning English for communication, for which years of grappling with English language structures and vocabulary at junior and senior high school have not really prepared students. As Warrington and Jeffrey (2005) observe, (2)this can lead to students becoming 'confused or overwhelmed by the change' and becoming passive and demotivated in English classes at university.

In effect, there are major changes and dissonances in students' experiences of learning English as they progress through successive stages of education. In this connection, we might note here that from April 2011, the stages of English language education under focus also include elementary school, following the introduction of compulsory 'foreign language activities' - namely, English - from Grade 5 in public elementary schools. (　X　) Nakata's (2006) research monograph was perhaps the first major study to focus on the links between Japanese students' educational experiences and the development of their language learning motivation. More recently, researchers have compared the motivation of students at different stages of education, such as secondary and university (e.g. Ryan, 2009), or have conducted longitudinal investigations of students' motivation and learning experiences during a course of study (e.g. Nitta & Asano, 2010).

If we examine this body of research on Japanese students' motivational trajectories, (3)an interesting theme that seems to emerge is the potential impact of *initial motivational states or initial learning experiences* in shaping subsequent motivational trajectories. Simplifying somewhat, it seems that students who have low motivation when they begin their university English courses tend to remain rather poorly motivated and succumb to negative learning experiences. On the other hand, students who begin with high motivation are better able to sustain or recover their motivation despite challenges in their learning experiences. As Nitta and Asano (2010) suggest, 'initial motivational states can be a litmus test for predicting the success of classroom learning'. Moreover, looking further back to students' earlier experiences of learning English in school, it seems that the quality of these initial learning experiences may similarly function as a litmus test for students' long-term motivational trajectories and self-regulatory processes, as evidenced in Carpenter *et al.*'s (2009) study. Put simply, if students' first encounters with learning English at school are negative, the long-term motivational and self-regulatory prognosis is not good. At a local national level, this raises critical questions about the quality of now even younger pupils' first encounters with learning English in elementary school from April 2011.

(Ema Ushioda, *Foreign Language Motivation Research in Japan : An Insider' Perspective from Outside Japan* による。ただし，設問の都合で一部省略及び改変している。)

1　本文中の空欄(　①　)に入る語句として最も適切なものを，次のア～エの中から一つ選び,記号で答えなさい。

ア　binds and melts　　イ　ebbs and flows

ウ　flashes and vanishes　　エ　goes well and wrong

2　本文の内容に即して，次の問いに英語で答えなさい。

Why are oral communication skills often paid less attention to in Japan?

3　下線部(1)について，筆者が理由の一つであると考えていることは何か，本文に即して日本語で書きなさい。

4　下線部(2)が指す内容を日本語で書きなさい。

5　本文中の空欄(　X　)に入る英文として最も適するものを，次のア

～エの中から一つ選び，記号で答えなさい。

ア　From a professional perspective, my insider status stems from the fact that most of my language teaching experience in the decade before I began my doctoral research was with Japanese students of English.

イ　The survey uncovered a clear developing trend in teenagers' perceptions of English as the 'must-have' language, diminishing their interest in learning other foreign languages, including the traditional regional language, German.

ウ　This is particularly the case in the university sector because of problems of apathy, passivity or lack of learning purpose and engagement that commonly seem to characterize student learning in this setting.

エ　Under the circumstances, it is perhaps not surprising that researchers' attention has been drawn to exploring Japanese students' motivational trajectories through these transitions in their English learning experiences.

6　下線部(3)とはどのようなことか，本文に即して日本語で書きなさい。

(☆☆☆◎◎◎)

【2】次の1，2について，指示に従って答えなさい。

1　次の日本語を英語に直しなさい。

できるだけ多くの事に挑戦しなさい。経験はただでは手に入らないものだ。

2「高等学校学習指導要領」(平成21年3月告示)の「第2章　第8節　外国語　第2款　各科目　第6　英語表現Ⅱ」では，「1　目標」において，「事実や意見などを多様な観点から考察し，論理の展開や表現の方法を工夫しながら伝える能力を伸ばす」こととしています。「英語表現Ⅱ」の授業で単元のまとめの活動として生徒がプレゼンテーションを

するとしたら，あなたはどのように指導しますか。学習指導要領の趣旨を踏まえ，100語程度の英語で書きなさい。ただし，語数には，句読点や符号は含まないものとします。なお，解答の総語数を，(　　)の中に記入すること。

(☆☆☆◎◎◎)

解答・解説

【中高共通】

【1】1　No.1　c　　No.2　b　　2　No.1　d　　No.2　c　　No.3　d　　3　No.1　b　　No.2　a　　No.3　d　　4　No.1　Oh, again? (It seems like you lose something every day).　　No.2　Why not? You can (have more time to do what you like to do).

〈解説〉リスニング問題については，選択形式と記述式とで構成されている。短い質問に対する応答文を選択する問題，短い対話文や200語程度の英文とその内容についての質問を聞き答えを選択する問題，そして放送された英文を書き取る問題である。問題用紙には印刷されておらず，情報は音声のみであるので，集中して聞き取る必要がある。　1　No.1　(a)　Would you like ～？「～したいか？」に対してwould rather「むしろ～したい」と答えている。　(b)　Could you update ～で更新してくれないかと依頼をしているので，How soon…と期日を尋ねている。　2　No.1　(a)　家でリラックスをしたいということと，やらなければならないことがたくさんあるという発言からdが適切である。　No.2　(b)　来週の水曜日に予定しようという会話で始まったが，休暇をとる人がいるためLet's plan to have it this Wednesdayと発言している。　No.3　It's for six daysの予約を確認した後に you can keep your room for two more daysとあるので合計で8日間となる。　3　No.1　第2段落第3文 But the implication ～ a little about a lot.で，広く浅い知識にも計り知れない価値があるので，誰もが一つのことの専門家になるべきという考え方は危険だと言及している。　No.2　第1段落第2文でaと同じことを述べている。　No.3　第3段落第2文で言及している。draw upon「～を利用する」。　4　No.1　It seems like ～「～のような気がする」。　No.2　2回目のto doの部分を聞き逃さないように。

【2】1　エ　　2　ア　　3　イ　　4　ウ　　5　イ　　6　エ　　7　ウ　　8　ア　　9　イ　　10　エ　　11　イ　　12　ア　　13　エ　　14　ウ　　15　イ

〈解説〉1　lively discussion「活発な議論」。　2　much too difficult a questionはa difficult questionを全体で名詞扱いしたいところだが，tooは副詞であるため名詞を修飾することができない。副詞のルール通り形容詞であるdifficultの直前にtooを置きmuchはさらにtoo difficultの程度を表す副詞。　3　in that～「～という点で」。　4　by which timeのwhichは，接続詞と形容詞の働きを兼ねる関係形容詞。　5　主節の主語がthe streetで過去形であり，従節にはbeforeが見られることから時制は過去完了である。従節の主語が主節の主語と異なることが明らかなので，従節に天気を表すときの主語itを残した完了形の分詞構文となる。　6　仮定法過去完了。「昨夜，サムのチームとの試合に勝つことができたかもしれないので」。　7　take turns ～ing「交代で～する」。　8　priceless「(金で買えないほどの)非常に貴重な」。　9　strike「(雷などが)襲う」で，活用はstrike-struck-struck。　10　tolerance「寛容，耐性」。　11　ratify「承認する，批准する」。　12　let alone take her advice「彼女の助言を聞き入れるはずがない」。let aloneはふつう否定文の後で用いられる慣用句。意味は「～などとんでもない」。
13　trigger「誘発する」。　14　innate「生来の，先天的な」。
15　predecessor「前にあったもの」。

【3】1　①　エ　　②　ウ　　③　イ　　2　経験から得た方法が文法の規則に変わり，悪意のない文が間違いだとされること。　　3　制限

用法の関係節は「that」を使い，いくつかの選択肢から名詞が指すものに焦点を当てるから。　4　アメリカの新聞では約5分の1，イギリスの新聞では半分以上の制限用法の関係節において，「which」が使われているということ。　5　ある名詞について述べた句が本質的に意味が変わることなく省略でき，わずかな間のあとで発音されるならば，コンマをつけること。

〈解説〉1　①　spurious，bogusともに「偽の」という意味。

②　expiration「(期限・任期などの)満了」。直前のDeath of a Pigという語が判断のヒントになり，ここでは「死」を意味するとわかる。

③　the least「最小」，bother「悩ます」なので，「悩まされることはない」と考える。　2　直前の第1段落第3文を和訳する。　3　第2段落第6文から第3段落に非制限用法のwhich制限用法のthatに関する記述があるので，この部分をまとめる。　4　第4段落第6文のhe found that以下から文末までに，Geoffrey Pullumが発見したことが記述されている。

5　第6段落第3文のIf a phraseからwith commasまでの部分を訳出する。

【中学校】

【1】1　①　ア　②　エ　③　ウ　2　学習者が必要としている言語の実用的な技能を習得すること。　3　新しいものの見方や，自身の母国語が試されるような難題，学習者が生活し当然と考えてきた文化とは異なる考え。　4　教師になった当初に持っている情熱や理想を具現化するため。　5　(1)　They have to reflect on what the language means for those who speak another language at home.

(2)　They may feel that the vision they had as young teachers needs renewal.

6　イ

〈解説〉1　①　dominant「もっとも有力な」。　②　inherent「先天的な，天賦の」　③　discipline「訓練，修行」。　2　下線部(1)の直後のthat以下から文末のthey need.までを訳す。　3　下線部(2)の直後のa new perspectiveからand have hitherto taken for granted.までを訳す。take granted for～「～を当然のことと思う」，hitherto「これまで」。　4　下

線部(3)を含む第3段落第3文のAt the beginning ofからgive shape to their enthusiasmまでを訳す。　5　(1)　第2段落第2文のThe teachers of以下の記述を抜き出す。　(2)　第3段落第2文のthey may begin to feel以下の記述を抜き出す。　6　第4段落第4文に長期の研修は教師にとって有効であるが，誰でも受講できるわけではないと述べているので，イと一致する。

【2】1　I found myself understanding a new English passage at one glance, without translating it into Japanese.　2　(例)　For example, let the students write a map of the town they live. The students make some small groups, talk about their maps in order. At that time teachers show some fixed phrases which the students have already learned. Students can keep the conversation going to combine these phrases and change the groups. After group work they play a game to ask where the classmate want to go and guide to his destination. It's good practice for students to explain these things in English, and by using some fixed phrases in a small group, students who are not good at English have opportunities to use English proactively. (107 words)

〈解説〉1　「Oが～していることに気づく」はfind O～ingで表せる。「ひと目見て」はat a glanceでも可。　2　解答例では，自分が住む町の地図を生徒に描かせ，地図についての質疑や説明，道案内ゲーム等を行うグループ活動を提案している。このとき教師が既習の定型表現を提示することで，英語の得意でない生徒であっても積極的に英語を使う機会を得られるとしている。なお，本問は平成20年3月告示の現行中学校学習指導要領に即した出題であるが，新中学校学習指導要領(平成29年3月告示)では内容が大幅に改訂されていることに注意したい。例えば，現行では「イ　話すこと」というひとつの領域が，改訂では「エ　話すこと[やり取り]」と「オ　話すこと[発表]」の2つの領域に分けられている。より具体的かつ詳細な内容が提示されているので，今後は，新学習指導要領に基づきどのような授業を行えばよいか自分なりに意見をまとめておきたい。

【高等学校】

【1】1 イ　2 Because they are less easily testable.　3 高校での「受験地獄」から大学での「4年間のレジャーランド生活」へ突然移行すること。　4 大学での英語学習はコミュニケーションに重きを置いているが，生徒は中学校や高校では単語や文の意味を取るような学習しかしていないため，大学で英語を学習するための準備ができていないということ。　5 エ　6 生徒の学校における最初の英語学習が否定的なものであれば，長期にわたる英語学習への動機づけや学習に向かう姿勢もまた良好ではないということ。

〈解説〉1 文意は「意欲とは時間とともに～するように，本質的に不安定なものである」。したがってebbs and flows「潮が満ちては引く」が適切。　2 第1段落第7文のtend to receive much less attention を見つける。henceは「それゆえに」という意味の副詞なので，その直前の部分のoral communication skills are much less easily testableが解答となる。　3 下線部(1)の文を含む第1段落第3文で，要因はthe structure of the Japanese educational systemにあると述べ，さらにこのsystemがどんなものかをwhich以下で説明している。　4 第1段落第8文のlearning Englishから文末のstudentsまでに注目する。中学校・高等学校での英語学習と大学でのそれとは大きく異なっていることを述べている。grapple withには「取り組む」という意味がある。　5 第1段落第8文と第9文では，中学校・高等学校との英語学習と大学でのそれとのギャップが大きすぎて，英語学習へのモチベーションが低下することを述べている。続く第2段落第1文と第2文では，より早い段階である小学校から英語学習が開始されることになったと述べている。したがって，空欄にはエ「この状況下で，英語学習経験におけるこれらの変遷を通して日本の生徒の動機づけの過程に研究者がずっと関心を持ち続けていることは何ら不思議でない」が適切である。　6 第3段落第2文のstudents who haveから文末のlearning experiencesまでに，下線部(3)

が示すことが分かりやすく説明されている。

【2】1　Try as much as possible. Experience is one thing you can't get for nothing.　2　(例)　Teachers encourage the students to choose a topic from familiar problem or current affairs and to consider facts and opinions from various viewpoints. Teachers should get a grasp of intelligibility of a presenter and listener each other. A presenter should not be afraid of making grammatically mistakes. It's important that a presenter can express the opinion and improve the ability of communication through presentation. By using worksheet in the classroom, the students can evaluate each other and establish the presentation skill even more. Presentation is an excellent way to increase their vocabulary and improve basic skills in English. (98 words)

〈解説〉1　Experience is one thing you can't get for nothing.とは，オスカー・ワイルドの格言として有名である。　2　解答例では，生徒によく知っている問題や時事問題からトピックを選ばせ，さまざまな観点からその問題に関して考察させる。教師はプレゼンターと聞き手の理解度を把握しておく。目的はプレゼンテーションを通じて意見を述べたりコミュニケーションスキルを高めたりすることなので，文法的な誤りは気にしない。ワークシートを活用してお互いのプレゼンテーションを評価させ，さらにスキルを高めることを述べている。なお，本問は現行の高等学校学習指導要領(平成21年3月告示)からの出題であるが，新学習指導要領(平成30年3月告示)では，内容が大幅に改訂されているので注意されたい。例えば，現行版での「英語表現Ⅱ」は，「論理・表現Ⅱ」として整理され，その目標についても「(1)話すこと[やり取り]，(2)話すこと[発表]，(3)書くこと」の3領域に分類されて具体的な内容が詳述されている。早めに改訂版を入手し学習をすすめておきたい。

2018年度　実施問題

【中高共通】

【1】(放送による問題)　これはリスニング・テスト です。放送の指示に従って答えなさい。

ただいまから，リスニング・テストを行います。問題は1，2，3，4の四つです。聞いている間にメモを取っても構いません。

1　では，1の問題から始めます。問題はNo.1とNo.2の2問です。

これから読まれる英文に対する応答として最もふさわしいものを，続いて読まれるa，b，cの中から一つ選び，記号で答えなさい。答えは，大文字，小文字どちらでも構いません。なお，英文と応答は1度しか読まれません。

では，始めます。

No.1　Do you happen to know when the next sale at the bookstore is?

(a)　Yes, I will go to the sale and buy best-selling books.

(b)　No, I don't know how much the discount will be next month.

(c)　Oh, it starts on October 30th.

No.2　How much did it cost to launch our new model of this computer?

(a)　More than 50 models have been involved.

(b)　More than 500 million dollars.

(c)　It took more than 5 years.

2　次に，2の問題に移ります。問題は，No.1からNo.3までの3問です。

これから，短い対話文を読みます。そのあとでクエスチョンと言って質問します。その答えとして最もふさわしいものを，続いて読まれるa，b，c，dの中から一つ選び，記号で答えなさい。答えは，大文字，小文字どちらでも構いません。なお，対話文・質問・答えの選択肢は1度しか読まれません。
では，始めます。

No.1　W: I've had my eye on this brown shirt for a long time. What do you think?

M: To be honest, I think it will make you look a little older.

W: Do you like these green pants?

M: I don't really like this color. But they will look nice on you.

Question: What is she most likely to do next?

(a) Buy the green shirt.

(b) Try on the green pants.

(c) Buy the brown shoes.

(d) Try on the brown pants.

No.2　W: Hello. How can I help you?

M: I'd like two tickets for the music show at 7 o'clock tomorrow night.

W: I'm sorry. There are no more tickets for the show until next month.

M: Next month! But I'm leaving here next week. Well, thanks anyway.

Question: Why can't he buy the tickets?

(a) Because the show will be held tomorrow.

(b) Because the show has just started.

(c) Because there is only one ticket left at the theater.

(d) Because he will leave soon.

No.3　M: Front desk. Can I help you?

W: This is Nancy Anderson in Room 528. The fridge in my room is making an irritating humming sound.

M: I'm sorry, ma'am. I'll send someone to check for you right away.

W: My friend and I are going out for dinner. Would you get it fixed by around seven?

M: Of course, Ms. Anderson. Enjoy your dinner.

Question: What does the woman request that the front desk do?

(a) Fix the fridge this evening.

(b) Take her to dinner.

(c) Prepare another room for her.

(d) Bring dinner up to her room by seven.

3　次に3の問題に移ります。問題は，No.1からNo.3までの3問です。

これから，あるまとまりのある英文を読みます。そのあとで，クエスチョンと言って，その英文について三つの質問をします。その答えとして最もふさわしいものを，質問に続いて読まれるa，b，c，dの中から一つ選び，記号で答えなさい。答えは，大文字，小文字どちらでも構いません。なお，英文・質問・答えの選択肢は全体を通して2回読まれます。

では，始めます。

Boredom can be a powerful incentive. In 1997, Philippe Kahn was stuck in a hospital room with nothing to do. The software entrepreneur had been shooed away by his wife while she birthed their daughter, Sophie. So Kahn, who had been tinkering with technologies that share images instantly, jerry-built a device that could send a photo of his newborn to friends and family — in real time. Like any invention, the setup was crude: a digital camera connected to his flip-top cell phone, synched by a few lines of code he'd written on his laptop in the hospital. But the effect has transformed the world: Kahn's device captured his daughter's first moments and transmitted them instantly to more than 2,000 people.

Kahn soon refined his ad hoc prototype, and in 2000, a Japanese company used his technology to release the first commercially-available integrated camera phone. The phones were introduced to the U.S. market a few years later and soon became ubiquitous. Kahn's invention forever altered how we communicate, perceive and experience the world and laid the groundwork for smartphones and photo-sharing applications. Phones are now used to send hundreds of millions of images around the world every day — including a fair number of baby pictures.

Question

No.1　What is the title of this passage?

(a)　A powerful incentive for a job.

(b)　The history of cellphones.

(c)　The first cellphone picture.

(d)　How to send pictures to the world

No.2　Why did Kahn make the new device?

(a)　Because he wanted to send his daughter's first moments to his friends and family.

(b)　Because he needed to make a new software for the hospital.

(c)　Because he had nothing to do with his friends.

(d)　Because he connected his camera to his flip-top cell phone in the wrong way.

No.3　How was Kahn's invention refined?

(a)　It was introduced to a U.S. company and the company used his technology.

(b)　A Japanese company helped him to make a prototype.

(c)　He made his prototype and introduced it to the U.S. market.

(d)　A Japanese company used his technology and released the first camera phones.

4　次に4の問題に移ります。問題はNo.1とNo.2の2問です。

これから，英語による対話文を読みます。(　　)のところに入る英語を聞き取り，書きなさい。対話文はそれぞれ2回読まれます。

では，始めます。

No.1　W: Mr. White, we've finished making our reports.

M: Great. I'd (　　　　　　　　) of this class.

Na. 2　M: Look at these buildings. They were built about 400 years ago.

W: How unusual! The (　　　　　　　　).

これで，リスニング・テストを終わります。次の問題に移ってください。

(☆☆◎◎◎)

【2】次の対話文や英文の中の(　　)に最も適するものを，下のア～エの中からそれぞれ一つずつ選び，記号で答えなさい。

1　A: There are too many things! I can't remember everything. Do you have something (　　)?

B: Sure, you can use the notebook over there.

ア　to write　　イ　to write on　　ウ　to write with

エ　to write for

2　If I (　　) home one hour earlier, I wouldn't be involved in such a heavy traffic jam now.

ア　left　　イ　have left　　ウ　had left　　エ　had been left

3　A: What's wrong? Do you need some help?

B: Yes. We want to get a train ticket, but can't (　　) out how to use this machine.

ア take　　イ figure　　ウ let　　エ hold

4 In the 18th century, spectacular technological improvements happened in Britain, (　　) we call the Industrial Revolution.

ア where　　イ that　　ウ how　　エ which

5 Comparing Japan to Britain can be a bit like comparing "chalk and cheese", (　　) the English expression. It's so hard because they can be different even when things seem alike.

ア use　　イ to use　　ウ using　　エ used

6 Stevenson, (　　) in Edinburgh and educated at Edinburgh University, is the creator of *Treasure Island*.

ア bears　　イ was born　　ウ born　　エ been bearing

7 She was (　　) surprised to hear the news that she won the first prize in the contest that she didn't know what to say.

ア very　　イ enough　　ウ so　　エ quite

8 You should remember that it is generally thought that proper clothes (　　) for a lot in the business world.

ア count　　イ number　　ウ weight　　エ respect

9 (　　) is an explicit comparison of one thing with another. One example is "He is as brave as a lion."

ア Prose　　イ Verse　　ウ Metaphor　　エ Simile

10 A: This project is too tough for me! I don't think I can make it.

B: Yes, you can! Don't (　　) yourself short.

ア fall　　イ sell　　ウ run　　エ cut

11 A: I'm thirsty. Oh, here is a vending machine, but I don't have any coins (　　) me. Do you?

B: No, I left my wallet at home.

ア at　　イ in　　ウ of　　エ on

12 Of all the customs in the U.S., none is such a (　　) annoyance as tipping. On an average day you usually have to decide whether to tip and how much at least once.

ア regular　イ fatigued　ウ considerate　エ quite

13 By projecting current (　　) trends, we can predict that the birthrate will continue to fall in industrialized countries.

ア demographic　イ menial　ウ tantamount
エ dormant

14 When the committee met, they always started by having the (　　) of the previous meeting read out.

ア seconds　イ minutes　ウ hours　エ days

15 John is the best person to be the captain of our team. He has the (　　) of scoring goals when they are most needed.

ア detriment　イ novice　ウ qualm　エ knack

(☆☆◎◎◎)

【3】次の英文を読んで，あとの問いに答えなさい。

OK is the most amazing invention in the history of American English. It would not be much of an exaggeration to say that the modern world runs on OK (or plain lowercase *k*, if you are texting). We write those letters on documents to mark our approval. We speak them to express ①assent, or just to say we're listening. We accept a computer's actions by clicking on OK. And we also use OK to introduce matters of importance, or recall an audience's wandering attention.

Those are the simple obvious uses for OK, the ones we know well. In those situations, what a good friend OK is! A handy tool. An uncomplaining workhorse. Indeed, in America in the twenty-first century, it's hard to get through a conversation without a plentiful sprinkling of OK. It's the easiest way to signal agreement, whether with a written OK on a document or an OK spoken aloud:

OK, I'll go with you.

OK, you win.

At the start of a sentence, OK can also be a wakeup call, an alert, an attention getter, an announcement that something new is coming:

OK, I'll only say this once.

OK, I get it.

OK, let's start making our pinhole camera!

To begin to grasp the full import of the phenomenon that is OK, we need to step back and consider it from fresh perspectives. When we do, we find that OK is like blue jeans, Shakespeare, and light.

(1)OK is as American as jeans. In fact, it's very much like them. Nearly everyone uses both OK and jeans for everyday purposes, but not on formal occasions. And they are both American inventions of the nineteenth century that have spread to the far corners of the globe.

Less obviously, OK is also America's answer to Shakespeare. Or more precisely, OK *is* America's Shakespeare, a two-letter expression as potent (though perhaps not as poetic) as anything in the Bard's works. Like Shakespeare, OK is protean, ②pervasive, influential, and successful in its own day and in ours. But the similarity goes deeper.

Like Shakespeare, OK had (　a　) origins. This has set some critics on edge, prompting them to deny the attested origins in favor of more dignified ones. For Shakespeare, the anti-Stratfordians reason that the "poacher from Stratford," a commoner, could not have written the noble language of Shakespeare's plays and poems. No, those works of genius must have come from a nobleman like the Earl of Oxford, a scholar like Francis Bacon, a college-educated playwright like Christopher Marlowe (whose death in 1593 must have been faked), or royalty — maybe Queen Elizabeth.

Similarly, for OK, elitists find it beyond embarrassing to think that OK began as a joke misspelling for "all correct." Surely, they reason, an expression as serious and important as OK must have come from a more serious abbreviation, like "Old Kinderhook" for presidential candidate Martin Van Buren in the 1840 election. Or maybe it came from baker Otto Kimmel's supposed custom of imprinting his initials in vanilla cookies. Or wait —

maybe it was borrowed from another language, like Choctaw, Scottish, Greek, or Mandingo. All very tempting, but overwhelming evidence shows otherwise.

(2)Another thing OK and Shakespeare have in common is elusiveness. How do you properly spell OK? And is it a noun, verb, adjective, adverb, or interjection? Indeed, is it a word at all, an abbreviation, or something else? There are no simple answers to these questions. Similarly, the text of Shakespeare's plays can't be pinned down. The quarto and folio versions of the plays published during or shortly after Shakespeare's lifetime have significant differences, and it is hard to imagine the full text of either quarto or folio being spoken quickly enough to fit the "two hours traffic" stated in the prologue to *Romeo and Juliet.*

And light! Yes, OK is like light, in our post-Einsteinian understanding of that pervasive phenomenon. Before Einstein, physicists were puzzled: light sometimes appears to be a particle, sometimes a wave. Is light a wave or particle? Einstein's answer was "Yes, it's either, or both." That's the answer we have to give to the OK phenomenon. Is it a word or an abbreviation? Is it a noun, verb, adjective, adverb, interjection, or all of the above? The answer has to be "Yes, it's either, or both, or all." It's an old-fashioned joke with a postmodern ③punch line.

(Allan Metcalf, *OK: the improbable story of America's greatest word* による。ただし，設問の都合で一部省略及び改変している。)

1　下線部①～③を別の語句で言い換えたとき，最も意味の近いものを，次のア～エの中からそれぞれ一つずつ選び，記号で答えなさい。

①　ア　appointment　イ　agreement　ウ　assignment
　エ　attachment

②　ア　perpetual　イ　persistent　ウ　perverse
　エ　prevalent

③　ア　sentence that draws people's attention
　イ　statement that represents someone's opinion

ウ　phrase that makes the joke funny at the end

エ　clue that makes the question easy to answer

2　筆者が下線部(1)のように考える二つの理由を(ア)，(イ)とし，本文に即してそれぞれ日本語で書きなさい。ただし，解答の順序は問わない。

3　本文中の空欄(　a　)に入る語として最も適切なものを，次のア～エの中から一つ選び，記号で答えなさい。

ア　dreadful　　イ　esoteric　　ウ　noble　　エ　humble

4　筆者が下線部(2)のように考える理由を，本文の内容に即して日本語で簡潔に書きなさい。

5　本文の内容に即して，次の問いに英語で答えなさい。

(1)　According to the author, does the modern world run on OK?

(2)　How many examples does the author show when he considers the OK phenomenon from fresh perspectives?

6　本文の内容に合うものを，次のア～エの中から一つ選び，記号で答えなさい

ア　People can get ready to deal with something new to come if OK is put at the start of a sentence.

イ　Shakespeare is believed to have been a college-educated playwright in the nineteenth century.

ウ　An American baker borrowed OK from another language for imprinting it in his vanilla cookies.

エ　Einstein's idea that everything is defined as a certain object can be applied to the OK phenomenon.

(☆☆☆◎◎◎)

【中学校】

【1】次の英文を読んで，あとの問いに答えなさい。

We (the authors) taught together for five years at a secondary school near Toronto, Ontario, *Canada. Pine Ridge Secondary School is a high school with 2,000 students. The first-year French classes at Pine Ridge are available to students at the applied and academic class levels. Applied classes emphasize a more hands-on approach to the language, whereas the academic classes put more emphasis on concepts. Class sizes were approximately 25, and all students had studied French for four years before entering secondary school.

First, we would like to discuss small-group cooperative learning activities that enable students to develop their oral and ①aural skills in the second language. Our first technique is a great class builder. Class builders are important because they give students a chance to meet and feel comfortable working with a number of classmates before ongoing small groups are formed. Sometimes we assume, and incorrectly so, that all students in a class already know each other. Class-building activities help to break the ice, and thus, create a more relaxed atmosphere in the class.

This class-building activity we call *Mon Ami Imaginaire* (My Imaginary Friend). To begin the activity, (1)we usually model what we expect the students to do. By modeling, we increase the likelihood of students performing the task the way we believe it will work best: We stand in front of the class and put our arms around some fresh air which is *mon ami imaginaire*. We then introduce this friend in French to the class by saying: "*Je vous présente Sophia. Elle a les yeux bruns et les cheveux noirs. Elle habite en Italie et elle est actrice. Elle est très grande et elle aime regarder les films au cinéma. Sa nourriture favorite est le poulet rôti et elle adore le vin blanc.*" (Translation: "I present to you my imaginary friend. Her name is Sophia. She has brown eyes and black hair. She lives in Italy and is an actress. She is very tall and likes watching films in the cinema. Her favorite food is roast chicken and she just ②adores white wine.")

We then invite students to give back a full description of *mon ami imaginaire*. Once this is done, students create their own *ami imaginaire*. Students must include a name for their *ami* and four or five details. We ask students to practice the description in their heads until they are completely comfortable with it. Now the fun part begins: Students stand up and locate another student to talk to, and then present their *ami imaginaire* to that student, who in turn presents her or his *ami*. Also, all students must be able to describe their partner's imaginary friend because they will describe that *ami* to a new partner. This activity ③reinforces many of the important points of the lesson and builds descriptive vocabulary as well.

Once this part of the activity is completed, students move again, but this time they have a totally new *ami imaginaire* — the one their classmate just introduced to them. Students typically can rotate four or five times exchanging friends. After the fourth or fifth rotation, we stop the activity and ask a student for the name of the original *ami imaginaire* she or he created. Let's say the name was Vincent. We then find the last person in the class to be introduced to Vincent and ask that student to describe him. (2)It is really exciting to hear how close or far away the description of Vincent is from the original creation by double-checking with the student who first imagined Vincent.

We like *Mon Ami Imaginaire* because it includes face-to-face interaction as students are communicating directly with each other through this activity. It is important to note that, along with its advantages as a language learning activity, *Mon Ami Imaginaire* includes an important aspect of cooperative learning: (3)individual accountability. This is built into the activity because students know in advance that they will have to present their new friend to their classmates in the target language.

(注)　Canada requires that all students become bilingual in French and English.

(P. Jones and A.Taylor, *Using cooperative learning to teach French at the secondary school level* による。
ただし，設問の都合で一部省略および改変している。)

1　本文の内容に即して，次の問いに英語で答えなさい。

(1) Why do the authors adopt class-building activities in the classes of the first year?

(2) What do the students do before they create their own imaginary friends?

2 下線部①～③の英語の定義として最もよくあてはまるものを，次のア～エの中からそれぞれ一つずつ選び，記号で答えなさい。

① ア relating to visual art
イ relating to or involving the mouth
ウ relating to the sense of hearing
エ relating to seeing or sight

② ア to take liquid into your mouth and swallow it
イ to like something very much
ウ to decorate something
エ to include or contain something

③ ア to give support to an opinion or idea and make it stronger
イ to make part of a building or structure stronger
ウ to make a group of people stronger by adding people
エ to give a bond of friendship and make it stronger

3 筆者が下線部(1)を行う目的は何か，本文に即して日本語で書きなさい。

4 下線部(2)について，筆者が面白いと考えることは何か，本文に即して日本語で書きなさい。

5 "*Mon Ami Imaginaire*" という活動が，下線部(3)を含んでいる理由を，本文に即して日本語で書きなさい。

6 本文の内容に合うものを，次のア～エの中から一つ選び，記号で答えなさい。

ア Academic classes focus on a practical approach to French because all the students have studied it.

イ Students practice speaking aloud to introduce their imaginary friends in small groups.

ウ　In the activity, each student has to present her or his own imaginary friend four or five times.

エ　Students have to listen to their friends' presentations carefully to reproduce them.

(☆☆☆◎◎◎)

【2】次の1，2について，指示に従って答えなさい。

1　次の日本語を英語に直しなさい。

どんな真理でも，いったん発見されれば理解しやすい。重要なのは，それを発見することである。

2　生徒の学習意欲を高め，英語の授業で学んだ内容の定着を図る上で，効果的な家庭学習を行わせるには，教師はどのような工夫が必要ですか。あなたの考えを100語程度の英語で書きなさい。ただし，語数には，句読点や符号は含まないものとします。なお，解答の総語数を記入すること。

(☆☆☆◎◎◎)

【高等学校】

【1】次の英文を読んで，あとの問いに答えなさい。

When designing speaking tasks, it may be useful to distinguish between (1)'pedagogic' or 'language-focused' tasks, which are created specifically for certain types of language use, often to enable learning or assessment, and 'real-life' or 'target' tasks, which simulate language use outside the classroom (Nunan, 1989). For example, learner A is given a simple graph with a blue triangle, a red square and a black circle arranged diagonally across a page (or a ball, a hula hoop, a skipping rope and a water pistol at the four corners of a square, or whatever), and told to instruct learner B to draw the objects in the right configuration on an empty page, or learner B is given a drawing of a man's face and told to instruct learner A to draw it, possibly on a page that provides some of the basic lines such as the jaw line and the neck to help get the drawing started. The activity has an indirect relationship to real-life instruction-giving tasks, yet it is meaning-focused and communicative. It makes one of the learners instruct the other and both of them collaborate in checking that the instruction receiver is able to follow. If instruction-giving has been taught before the test, this may be a highly relevant activity to test. Topics can be varied by changing the picture or graph that the instruction-giver is talking from. To make the picture, the task designer can simply draw the figures, or cut pictures out of magazines and arrange them on a page.

'Real-life' or 'target' tasks replicate the essentials of non-test language use in the assessment situation. This is usually done through simulation or role-play. (2)Typical real-life tasks in formal tests put examinees in their professional role while the examiners act as customers, patients, guests, or other likely people who might interact with the examinee in the test language in occupational contexts.

The development of real-life test tasks requires careful analysis of the target language-use situations and, as McNamara (1996) points out, a careful balancing between the linguist's view of necessary language ability and the professional's view of appropriate professional communication. He distinguishes between performance testing in the strong and weak sense, such that strong performance testing replicates the 'real-life language-use event and also employs real-world criteria for judging task success, whereas proof of having enough language ability would be enough to gain a good score in a weak performance test. In (3)a simulation where a doctor should reassure a patient, being able to use appropriate language would suffice in a weak performance test, whereas the examiner in a strong performance test would have to judge whether he/she felt reassured in the situation. The decision about which criteria to use depends on the intended use of the test. The criteria in most language tests follow the weak performance testing logic, probably because both the testers and the examinees recognise that a language test is a language test. With formal tests the documentation should make clear which type of criteria are used, and in classroom assessment it would be helpful to discuss the differences between strong and weak performance criteria so that the learners understand how their performances are evaluated — in the test and outside it.

In learning-related assessment, simulations may also be undertaken in pairs or groups of four. Only a few tasks are suitable for this type of application, but when it is possible the advantage is an expanded role for the learners. Task design and discussions about relevant assessment criteria, practising for the test, the actual testing activity and the post-test reflection and evaluation blend together and serve (4)the general goal of supporting the participants' learning.

Role-plays in testing can also be less elaborate, as when examinees are asked to play the role of a passenger on a train and interact with a fellow passenger, go to a restaurant and order a meal, or buy something in a shop. These tasks are aimed at finding out how the examinees can cope with certain common language-use tasks and situations. Role cards may be used to provide cues for the participants, and these may be quite elaborate if one of the examinees plays the role of a service provider, such as a waiter. If the examinees are ready to play-act in this sense, the task may generate some fairly genuine social interaction, but some artificiality is unavoidable because the speakers are playing a role for the purposes of the test. This should be taken into account in assessing the performances.

(Sari Luoma, *Assessing Speaking* による。ただし，設問の都合で一部省略及び改変している。)

1　下線部(1)において，学習者が二人で協力して行うことは何か，本文に即して日本語で書きなさい。

2　下線部(2)において，試験官はどのような役割を演じるか，本文に即して日本語で書きなさい。

3　下線部(3)を“a strong performance test”の基準によって行う場合，

試験官が評価しなければならないことは何か，本文に即して日本語で書きなさい。

4　下線部(4)を達成するために必要なことは何か，本文に即して日本語で書きなさい。

5　本文の内容に即して，次の問いに英語で答えなさい。

(1)　According to the author, why do the criteria in most language tests follow the weak performance testing logic?

(2)　What do examiners have to find out through tasks such as role-plays?

6　本文の内容に合うものを，次のア～エの中から一つ選び，記号で答えなさい。

ア　The author quotes Nunan, showing that it is helpful to use a simple graph in assessing participants' performance.

イ　The task designers should draw their own figures or pictures, and shouldn't use magazines for the tasks.

ウ　The author quotes McNamara, who distinguishes between performance testing in the strong and weak sense.

エ　There are many tasks suitable for simulations undertaken in pairs or groups of four in learning-related assessment.

(☆☆☆◎◎◎)

【2】次の1，2について，指示に従って答えなさい。

1　次の日本語を英語に直しなさい。

どんな言語でも，練習しなくては上達しない。ことわざにもあるとおり，「習うより慣れろ」である。

2　「高等学校学習指導要領」(平成21年3月告示)の「第2章　第8節　外国語　第2款　各科目　第2　コミュニケーション英語Ⅰ　3　内容の取扱い」では，中学校におけるコミュニケーション能力の基礎を養うための総合的な指導を踏まえた上で指導することなど，中学校における指導との接続を求めています。あなたは，中学校における

指導との効果的な接続のために，高等学校における指導ではどのような点に配慮する必要があると考えますか。100語程度の英語で書きなさい。ただし，語数には，句読点や符号は含まないものとします。なお，解答の総語数を記入すること。

(☆☆☆◎◎◎)

解答・解説

【中高共通】

【1】1　No.1　(c)　　No.2　(b)　　2　No.1　(b)　　No.2　(d)　No.3　(a)　　3　No.1　(c)　　No.2　(a)　　No.3　(d)

4　No.1　Great. I'd (like you to hand them in at the end) of this class.

No.2　How unusual! The (biggest one is round on the top and has straight sides).

〈解説〉1　短い質問文に対して，答えを選ぶ形式。難度は高くないが，情報が質問文1文に集約されているので，1語も聞き逃さないよう注意する。　2　短い対話文と質問文を聞いて，答えを選ぶ最も一般的な形式。内容は日常的な会話。　3　200語程度の英文と質問文を聞いて，答えを選ぶ形式。2度放送文が流れるので，1度目は全体の流れを把握しながら，2度目は答えとなる箇所に注意しながら聞く。選択肢に目を通す，メモをとるなどは必須。　4　ディクテーションの問題である。No.1のhand them inの箇所は，単語の末尾の音と直後の単語の先頭の音が連結して違う発音になる「リエゾン(リンキング)」に絡めた出題である。もし聞き取れない場合は前後の文脈から「提出する」と推測して，正確に記述できるようにしたい。

【2】1　イ　　2　ウ　　3　イ　　4　エ　　5　イ　　6　ウ　　7　ウ　8　ア　　9　エ　　10　イ　　11　エ　　12　ア　　13　ア

14 イ　15 エ

〈解説〉1 Bの返答「ノートを使うことができる」からwrite on。
2 主節は現在の事実に反する仮定であるのに対し，if節は過去の事実に反する仮定。 3 figure out「わかる，理解する」。 4 継続用法の関係代名詞。spectacular technological improvementを指す。 5 「英語の表現を使うと」。独立不定詞。 6 「スティーブンソンは，エジンバラで生まれ，エジンバラ大学で教育を受けたのだが」。分詞句が主語の直後に置かれている。 7 so that構文。 8 count for a lot「大いに価値がある」。 9 simile「直喩」。一方「隠喩」はmetaphorである。
10 sell＋O＋short「Oを低く評価する」。 11 所持を表すon。
12 「チップを渡すことほどいつも煩わしいと思うことはない」。後続の文「最低1日に1度は…」からregularが適当。 13 demographic「人口統計の」。 14 the minutes「覚書き，メモ」。having以下は「前の会議の議事録を読み上げてもらうこと」。 15 knack「特技」。

【3】1 ① イ　② エ　③ ウ　2 (ア) ほとんどの人が，日常的な場面で使い，公式の場では使わないから。　(イ) 世界の隅々にまで広がった19世紀のアメリカの発明品であるから。 3 エ
4 どちらもはっきりと定義することが難しいものであるから。
5 (1) Yes, it does.　(2) Three.　6 ア

〈解説〉1 ① assent「同意」。 ② pervasive「普及力のある」。
③ punch line「(ジョークなどの)おち」。 2 下線部(1)の意味は，「OKは，ジーンズと同じくらいアメリカ的である」。理由は，第5段落3文目，4文目を訳せばよい。 3 anti-Stratfordians「反ストラットフォード派」。シェイクスピア作品は，ウィリアム・シェイクスピアが書いたものではないと考える人々。第7段落3文目の「ストラットフォード出身の一般人が，シェイクスピア劇や詩の高貴な文体を書いたはずがない」とシェイクスピアの存在すら否定する評論家の記述と，次の第8段落1文目の「OKがふざけた綴り間違いで始まった」とする記述から考える。 4 elusiveness「とらえどころのなさ」。第9段落2文

目以下の「OKには，正しい綴りや品詞が何かという問いに対する答えはなく，シェイクスピア劇の文に関してもはっきり説明をすることができない」という記述を参考にする。pin down「詳しい説明を求める，はっきりさせる」。　5　(1)　第1段落2文目「現代はOKに依存して動いていると言っても過言ではないだろう」。　(2)　第4段落2文目。blue jeans，Shakespeare，lightの3つ。　6　イ　college-educatedは誤り。ウ　borrowed OK from another languageが誤り。　エ　OKは定義があいまいとされるため，合致しない。

【中学校】

【1】1　(1)　To help to break the ice and create a more relaxed atmosphere in the class.　(2)　They give back a full description of the teacher's imaginary friend.　2　①　ウ　②　イ　③　ア　3　生徒が適切な方法で活動を行うことができるようにするため。　4　最後に人物像を聞いた生徒の説明を，最初に考えた生徒と一緒に再確認することで，説明される人物像が最初の人物像とどの程度異なるかを聞くこと。　5　目標とする言語でクラスメートに新しい友人の情報を伝えなければならないことが事前にわかるから。　6　エ

〈解説〉1　(1)　第2段落5文目に，「クラスビルディング活動を取り入れるのは，場を和ませるためとリラックスした雰囲気をつくるため」との記述がある。　(2)　第4段落1文目は「生徒自身の想像上の友人を創る前にすることは，教師が想像上の友人について述べたことを，そっくり生徒たちが返すこと」と示している。　2　①　aural「耳の，聴覚の」。　②　adore「～に目がない，大好きである」。　③　reinforce「強力にする，補強する」。　3　第3段落3文目By modeling以下を訳す。　4　下線部(2)のIt is really exciting to hear ….は，It～to構文であるから，面白いと考えることはto以下にある。　5　individual accountability「生徒一人ひとりの説明(責任)」。答えは第6段落3文目のbecause以下に示されている。　6　アはpractical approachが誤り。conceptに焦点が当てられている。イはsmall groupsが誤り。クラス全体の活動である。ウは誤

り。その活動は，パートナーから聞いた想像上の友人を，次のパートナーに伝えていくのであって，自分の想像上の友人を4回，5回と伝えるのではない。

【2】1　All truths are easy to understand once they are discovered. The point is to discover them.　　2　I think it's necessary for teachers to integrate an assignment into learning cycle, which means it's desirable that the assignment is connected with what students have learned in the lesson or what they're going to learn so that they can recognize it is an important part of their learning. Building vocabulary as a review and skimming the text as a preparation are good examples for this. Ideally, teachers should give an assignment corresponding to the learning level of each student and give each of them an appropriate feedback. That will get them motivated. (93 words)

〈解説〉1　onceは，接続詞で「いったん～すると」。The point is ～は「重要なことは～」。　2　模範解答では，家庭学習が，学校での学びにつながるものであることを生徒に認識させることや，課題の提示に工夫が求められることに言及している。

【高等学校】

【1】1　一方の学習者が他方に指示し，指示を受けた学習者が理解できたかを一緒に確かめること。　　2　店の客や患者など，ある職業的な設定の中で，評価する言語を使用して会話をする役割。　　3　評価者が患者としての立場で安心できたかということ。　　4　課題を設定し，適切な評価基準，テストまでの練習，実際のテスト活動，テスト後の振り返りや評価などについて議論すること。

5　(1)　Because both the testers and the examinees recognize that a language test is a language test.　　(2)　How the examinees can cope with certain common language-use tasks and situations.　　6　ウ

〈解説〉1　下線部(1)「教育上の，すなわち言語に焦点を当てたタスク」で学習者が協力して行うことは，第1段落4文目It makes以下に記述がある。　2　下線部(2)「公式なテストにおける典型的な実生活を模したタスク」で試験官が演じる役割は，下線部(2)を含む文のthe examiners以下に記述がある。　3　下線部(3)の意味は「医者が患者を安心させるシミュレーション」。weak performance testの基準では，適切な言葉を使うことができたかを評価する。一方，strong performance testで評価することは，下線部(3)を含む文のwhereas以下に記述がある。
4　第4段落3文目Task design以下に解答が記述されている。これらのことが渾然一体となって，学習者を支援するという目標を達成できるのである。　5　(1)　問いは「たいていの言語テストの評価基準は何故weak performance test論理に従うのか」。第3段落5文目のprobably because以下の記述をひろう。　(2)　問いは「試験官はロールプレイのようなタスクを通して，何を見出さなければならないか」。第5段落2文目finding out以下の記述をひろう。　6　本文では，simple graphだけでなくdrawingも同例として挙げているのでアは不適切。イは，「タスクに雑誌を使うべきでない」が第1段落7文目に合致しない。エは，「シミュレーションに適した活動がたくさんある」が第4段落2文目に合致しない。

【２】1　Whatever language it may be, you can't expect to be good at it without practice. The proverb goes, "Practice makes perfect."　2　In order to promote a smooth transition, consideration should be given so that students don't feel overburdened especially in the early stage due to the gap between JHS and HS. To take examples, HS students have to learn a huge quantity of vocabulary and read high volume of English sentences compared to JHS students. To avoid this kind of discontinuity, it's important that HS teachers should share the goals with JHS teachers and should get a complete view of the course of study for JHS so that HS students can acquire new items by reviewing the basic ones already introduced. (100 words)
〈解説〉1　模範解答は，複合関係詞を使って「それがどんな言語であっても」と表現している。You can't expect to be good at any languageも可。

as the proverb［saying］goes「ことわざにあるとおり」。　2　高等学校教員が中学校の指導内容を十分把握した上で段階的に指導することや，中学校教員と到達目標などを共有するなどが考えられる。

2017年度　実施問題

【中高共通】

【1】(放送による問題)　これはリスニング・テストです。放送の指示に従って答えなさい。

[トラック1]

ただいまから，試聴用の英文を約3分間流します。そのあとでチャイムが鳴りますから，そこでCDを止めてください。

[トラック2]

(問題)

ただいまから，リスニング・テストを行います。問題は1，2，3，4の四つです。聞いている間にメモを取っても構いません。答えはすべて解答用紙の所定の欄に記入しなさい。

では，1の問題から始めます。問題はNo. 1とNo. 2の2問です。

これから読まれる英文に対する応答として最もふさわしいものを，続いて読まれる(a)，(b)，(c)の中から一つ選び，記号で答えなさい。答えは，大文字，小文字どちらでも構いません。なお，英文と応答は1度しか読まれません。

では，始めます。

No. 1　Is this restaurant non-smoking? I hate the smell of cigarette smoke.

(a)　Yes, not at all.

(b)　Sure. Here you are.

(c)　Rest assured, it is.

No. 2 I've got my passport and visa. And is it necessary to have a certified polio vaccination?

(a) You'll have to ask the travel agency.

(b) You'll have to ask the firehouse.

(c) You'll have to ask the police station.

次に，2の問題に移ります。問題は，No. 1からNo. 3までの3問です。

これから，短い対話文を読みます。そのあとでクエスチョンと言って質問します。その答えとして最もふさわしいものを，続いて読まれる(a)，(b)，(c)，(d)の中から一つ選び，記号で答えなさい。答えは，大文字，小文字どちらでも構いません。なお，対話文・質問・答えの選択肢は1度しか読まれません。

では，始めます。

No. 1 W: I think we need to buy a new TV. This one's getting old.

M: Hmm, we've had this one six or seven years.

W: Actually, we bought it over ten years ago.

M: You're right. Time really flies.

Question: When did they buy the television set?

(a) Close to eight years ago.

(b) Exactly seven years ago.

(c) More than ten years ago.

(d) Neither of them can remember.

No. 2 W: Did you make the copies I asked for yet?

M: Gee. I haven't had time to.

W: Well, I absolutely need them this morning.

M: OK, I'll get John to do them for you right away then.

Question: What does the man say he is going to do next?

(a) Ask someone else to take care of the woman's request.

(b) Make copies for her as soon as he can.

(c) Apologize for not doing what the woman wanted.

(d) Come back to the office as he promised he would.

No. 3 M: Is it true you got a job in Chicago?

W: It sure is. I'm moving there at the end of the month.

M: Are you taking your car with you?

W: No reason to. The city is famous for its public transportation.

Question: What does the woman imply about Chicago?

(a) Its public transportation is terrible.

(b) A car isn't necessary to get around.

(c) Traffic jams are very common.

(d) There are many famous place to see.

次に3の問題に移ります。問題はNo. 1からNo. 3までの3問です。

これから，あるまとまりのある英文を読みます。そのあとで，クエスチョンと言って，その英文について三つの質問をします。その答えとして最もふさわしいものを，質問に続いて読まれる(a)，(b)，(c)，(d)の中から一つ選び，記号で答えなさい。答えは，大文字，小文字どちらでも構いません。なお，英文・質問・答えの選択肢は全体を通して2回読まれます。

では，始めます。

"What day is it?" We ask that all the time without any sense of amazement, but this ordinary question can trace its roots 5,000 years into the past.

Ancient Babylonians first created the week, dividing it into seven days. Each day was named for one of the seven known moving bodies in the sky: the sun, the moon, Mars, Mercury, Venus, Jupiter and Saturn. The Babylonians believed that each of these heavenly objects influenced people's lives on the days named for them. "Mars Day"was Tuesday. Because of the planet's red color, the Babylonians associated Mars with aggression and performed special ceremonies on Tuesdays to avoid the fearsome influence of this warlike planet. "Tews" was the English name for the god of war.

The month of March belongs to the red planet, too. We think of New Year's Day as January 1st, but it hasn't always been that way. The Roman god of war was known as Mars, a name we still use today for our neighboring red planet. From Roman times until recent centuries, March had the honor of beginning the new year because it was seen as a time of renewal, when the cold gave way to spring. Roman warriors set on expanding their empire couldn't help naming this month for their god of war because warmer temperatures and melting snow allowed them to start up their battles in full force again. March may "come in like a lion"today, but the month is far less bloody than it once was!

Question

No. 1 How was each day of the week named?

(a) It was named after our human body.
(b) It was named after nature on Earth.
(c) It was named after ancient Babylonians.
(d) It was named after a heavenly object.

No. 2 Why did the Babylonians hold special ceremonies on Tuesday?

(a) Because they feared the effect of Mars on them.
(b) Because they associated Mercury with aggression.
(c) Because they knew the color of Mars was red.
(d) Because they worshiped Mars as the god of the world.

No. 3 In Roman times what did they think of March?

(a) They thought it was the beginning of the year as we also do.

(b)　They thought it was bloody because more lions appeared in March when it got warmer.

(c)　They saw it as the beginning of the year because in March, new life came into existence and their battles started.

(d)　The month was named for Mars, and they believed it enabled them to win battles and build their empire.

次に4の問題に移ります。問題はNo. 1とNo. 2の2問です。

これから，英語による対話文を読みます。(　　)のところに入る英語を聞き取り，書きなさい。対話文はそれぞれ2回読まれます。

では，始めます。

No. 1　M: Did you get accepted into that university?

W: I haven't heard yet. (　　　　　　　　　　　　).

No. 2　M: What made you so angry, Lucy?

W: Charlie (　　　　　　　　　　　　) alone.

これで，リスニング・テストを終わります。次の問題に移ってください。

(☆☆☆◎◎◎)

【2】次の英文や対話文の中の(　　)に最も適するものを，下のア～エの中からそれぞれ一つずつ選び，記号で答えなさい。

1　I owe (　　) entirely to John that I have succeeded in my business.

ア　myself　　イ　it　　ウ　all　　エ　that

2　As the earth goes round the sun, (　　) does the moon go round the earth.

ア　nor　　イ it　　ウ　so　　エ　never

3 He had considerable difficulty ( ) the way to the station.

ア finding イ to find ウ find エ found

4 We reached the foot of the mountain, from the top of ( ) the whole city could be seen.

ア what イ that ウ which エ where

5 The first thing that ( ) me on my arrival in California was its vastness.

ア kicked イ smacked ウ spurred エ struck

6 She is a good speaker of English. ( ) a chance, she could have made a good speech in English.

ア Given イ Having given ウ Giving エ To give

7 A: Would you help me find the car keys? I'm ( ) for time. My friend will be at the station in fifteen minutes!

B: Here, on the table. You should be more careful.

ア troublesome イ late ウ prepared エ pressed

8 I'm always at my wits' ( ) when it comes to setting up a new computer.

ア final イ end ウ last エ goal

9 A ( ) is a shape with four straight sides of equal length and four right angles.

ア square イ rectangle ウ cube エ pentagon

10 I was impressed that you were switching from Japanese to English without ( ) a beat. You're perfectly bilingual!

ア missing イ losing ウ running エ erring

11 The scholars have decided to ( ) deeper into the strange phenomenon so as to solve the problem.

ア analyze イ delve ウ observe エ resolve

12 The literary work will be published with ( ) next month. It will be very useful to those who study the author.

ア anomaly イ annunciation ウ annotations

エ anonymity

13 (　　) levels in the region were below normal, so residents were advised to conserve water.

ア Proliferation　イ Profligate　ウ Precedence

エ Precipitation

14 Cost cutting measures are planned to (　　) up performance in the company.

ア cow　イ sheep　ウ beef　エ lamb

15 A: Do you know the (　　) president of the United States?

B: Yes, of course. Barack Obama.

ア incumbent　イ arable　ウ perpendicular　エ succinct

(☆☆☆◎◎◎)

【中学校】

【１】次の英文を読んで，あとの問いに答えなさい。

The Eternal Youth of People and Dogs

We play less as we age than we did as youngsters. Almost all juvenile mammals play, so much so that play defines youth more than any other activity. Young lambs ①leap up into the air from a standstill, twisting sideways at the top of their jump. Watching a group of them alternately rise and fall in the air is like watching popcorn pop. Pronghorn antelope yearlings spar with their horns in mock fights. Cats of all forms, from kittens to tiger cubs, box around anything they can get their paws on, from leaves to butterflies to crumpled paper. Young laboratory rats chase and pounce on one another and engage in a behavior that for all the world looks like tickling. Two-to three-year-old chimps do little but eat and play. Sometimes they play solitarily by swinging in trees and spinning in circles, but more often they play together, chasing, leaping onto one another, play fighting, and wrestling.

(a) But Peter Pan species, like humans and dogs, retain their playful natures into adulthood. I don't want to oversimplify this: adult animals like wolves and chimpanzees still play, but not at the high levels seen in dogs and humans. This tendency to continue ②exuberant play into adulthood is one of the factors that leads most scientists to consider dogs and humans as "paedomorphic," or juvenilized versions of their more "grown-up" relatives. (1)Paedomorphism is the retention of juvenile characteristics at sexual maturity, characteristics that usually fade away as an animal matures. In these animals the normal developmental process is delayed for so long that in some ways they never grow up. Almost every animal, no matter how simple, has different characteristics early in its development than it has later on when mature. Sometimes these characteristics are physical—for instance, some insects have vastly different physical forms as juveniles than they do as adults. We all are familiar with caterpillars changing into butterflies. "Juvenilized" insects have evolved so that they never morph into their ancestral adult form; they become adults while looking like juveniles. But sometimes these characteristics are behavioral. Often there is a link between anatomy, physiology, and behavior, and animals that not only look like the young of their juvenile ancestors sometimes act like them, too, even when they're grown-up. Paedomorphism is a fascinating evolutionary phenomenon to which I'm afraid I can't do justice here in this brief discussion. What matters in our inquiry about humans and dogs is how changes in the process of development can create adult animals who, like most juvenile mammals, remain remarkably playful even as they age.

Changes in developmental processes have much to teach us about how and why dogs can be so different from wolves and yet still be of the same species. (2)A Russian scientist named Dmitry Belyaev was interested in how the process of domestication resulted in animals who are less aggressive than their ancestors. Borrowing a group of foxes from Russian fur farms, Belyaev selectively bred only the most ③docile of foxes. He had to choose carefully, because most of the foxes with which he was working didn't take kindly to handling. Out of each litter, he only bred the foxes that were least likely to try to flee or bite and that were the most likely to lick the outstretched hand of the experimenter and to approach voluntarily. In just ten generations, 18 percent of the foxes born were what he classified as the "domesticated elite" —eager to establish contact with strangers, whimpering, and licking the experimenters'faces like puppy dogs. By the twentieth generation, 35 percent of them were eager to be petted rather than trying to flee or bite as most adult foxes would.

What makes this study so interesting, and so important to science, is that when the researcher selected for just one trait, that of docility, changes occurred in a multitude of other aspects of the foxes' behavior, anatomy, and physiology. The floppy ears of young canid pups stayed with the foxes into adulthood. The adult "domesticated elite" continued to act like pups even as they aged, showing less fear of unfamiliar things at a later age than the normal population of foxes; and reacting submissively to strangers by raising their paws, whining, and doing full-body wags as young pups do. Amazingly they developed patches of white in their fur, like so many of our domesticated animals.

(Patricia B. McConnell, *The Other End of the Leash*による。ただし，設問の都合で一部省略および改変している。)

1　本文の内容に即して，次の問いに英語で答えなさい。

(1)　Do the characteristics of almost every animal, whether they are physical or behavioral, become different into adulthood?

(2)　In Belyaev's research, what were 18 percent of the foxes born in just ten generations considered as?

2　下線部①～③の語を別の語で言い換えたとき，最も意味の近いものを，次のア～エの中からそれぞれ一つずつ選び，記号で答えなさい。

①　ア　jog　　イ　joke　　ウ　juggle　　エ　jump

②　ア　energetic　　イ　divine　　ウ　emotional　　エ　fortunate

③　ア　mischievous　　イ　negotiable　　ウ　obedient
　エ　premature

3　本文中の空欄(　a　)に入る英文として最も適切なものを，次のア～エの中から一つ選び，記号で答えなさい。

ア　Most mammals become playful because they are too busy getting along with other animals.

イ　As most animals age, the frequency of their play decreases until it ceases altogether.

ウ　Our species hardly shows its playful nature before reaching adulthood.

エ　Humans and dogs play as much as they did when they were young even when they mature.

4　下線部(1)について，筆者が重要であると考えているのはどのようなことか，本文に即して日本語で答えなさい。

5　下線部(2)が行った研究について，筆者が興味深く重要であると考えているのはどのようなことか，本文に即して日本語で答えなさい。

6　本文中に合うものを，次のア～カの中から二つ選び，記号で答えなさい。

ア　Play is an activity that never defines the age of mammals compared to any other activity.

イ　Sometimes two-to three-year-old chimps play solitarily, but more often they play together.

ウ　Juvenilized insects have evolved so that they can change into their ancestral adult form.

エ　For his research, Belyaev chose the foxes that were the most likely to try to flee or bite.

オ　By the twentieth generation, 35 percent of the foxes became more aggressive than their ancestors.

カ　In Belyaev's research, the adult foxes showed less fear of unfamiliar things at a later age.

(☆☆☆◎◎◎◎)

【2】次の英文を読んで，あとの問いに答えなさい。

Ana Paula Ferreira de Carvalho, a teacher working in Brazil with 14-16-year-old students, decided to pursue an issue－learner perceptions of teacher/teaching quality.

The question that I set out to investigate was: 'Why do learners seem to like some teachers better than others?' In other words, from the learners' point of view, what makes a good teacher?

I have always ①admired teachers who are loved and respected by their learners. Although I think my relationship with the learners is quite satisfactory, there seems to be something missing and (1)I thought I could find out more about it by doing research.

I decided to do the research in classes 701 and 702, so that I could compare the results. We had already worked on adjectives and we started preparing cards with many different adjectives which could describe general qualities of teachers and students, such as creative, patient, sensitive, friendly, educated, organised, tolerant, polite, and so on. We ended up with a list of 20 words. Next, we made cards with the opposite adjectives, which gave me the opportunity to work on prefixes and ②suffixes. In the end, we had a list of 40 words, one for each student.

I then asked them to walk around the class and find a partner to form a pair of adjective and opposite adjective. The cards were exposed on the board and in the next step we worked on giving definitions to those adjectives. We used the dictionary and many students were surprised to find out the exact meaning of words such as educated and patient.

Next I asked them to work in groups of four and produce posters. Five groups would produce the 'Good teachers' posters and the other five would produce the 'Bad teachers' posters. I asked them to choose (2)five adjectives to describe the good and the bad teacher, in order of the most to the least important quality. They would also have to draw a picture to represent their idea of a good and a bad teacher.

It was also important that I had already written down the qualities according to my point of view so that I could compare the results afterwards. And I wrote down: 'A good teacher is educated, organised, polite, creative, tolerant' 'A bad teacher is rude, uneducated, disorganized, boring, old-fashioned'.

The results were very interesting. All the groups in both classes 701 and 702 seem to think that the most important qualities in a teacher are those related to being friendly, sensitive, polite, patient, tolerant－qualities that reflect teachers' ability to interact with the group. They don't seem to pay that much attention to teachers' education or organisation, which were the first qualities in my personal list. Their drawings were also very clarifying: candlelight, open books, lamps, the sun, flowers were the images of the good teachers. Witches, skeletons, broken lamps, storms, coffins were the images of the bad teachers.

I came to the conclusion that perhaps my excessive focus on teaching contents and not giving them many opportunities to have group discussions of matters which are not related to those contents might pull them away a little bit. I realised that they need friends and those teachers who are more open to that kind of relationship are closer to their students. I don't know if I am prepared to change my behaviour, but I definitely have a feeling that I learned something new.

Also, to my surprise, they seemed to have reflected upon the qualities that I have and since then, they have been a lot closer to me than they used to be. That image of the 'very serious teacher who is all work and no play' seems to have ③vanished and I am happy with it.

(Dick Allwright and Judith Hanks, *The Developing Language Learner* による。ただし，設問の都合で一部省略および改変している。)

1　本文の内容に即して，次の問いに英語で答えなさい。

(1)　Why did Ana do the research in two classes?

(2) What were the important qualities of a good teacher in Ana's personal list?

2　下線部①～③の英語の定義として最も適切なものを，次のア～エの中からそれぞれ一つずつ選び，記号で答えなさい。

①　ア　to agree unwillingly that something is true or that someone else is right

イ　to get used to a new situation by changing the way you behave

ウ　to tell someone what you think they should do when you know more than they do

エ　to respect someone because they have done something that you think is good

②　ア　a group of letters added to the beginning of a word to make a new word

イ　a group of letters added to the beginning or end of a word to change its meaning

ウ　a letter or letters added to the end of a word to form a new word

エ　a letter or letters added to the middle of a word to change its meaning

③　ア　to make someone suffer because they have done something wrong

イ　to disappear suddenly, especially in a way that cannot be easily explained

ウ　to complete the last part, of something that you are doing

エ　to order someone to leave a place, especially a country, as a punishment

3 下線部(1)について，筆者が明らかにしようとしたことを，具体的に日本語で説明しなさい。

4　ポスターを作るにあたって，筆者が下線部(2)を使って生徒にさせようとしたことは何か，日本語で答えなさい。

5　筆者は，結論としてどのようなことに気づき，そのことがどのような変化をもたらしたのか，日本語で簡潔に書きなさい。

6　本文の内容に合うものを，次のア～エから一つ選び，記号で答えなさい。

ア　Ana worried about the relations among the students and she decided to do research.

イ　The students had already worked on adjectives and they knew the definitions from the dictionary.

ウ　The students made 20 pairs of adjectives and put them on the board before producing posters.

エ　Ana asked each group of the students to draw pictures of both good teachers and bad teachers.

(☆☆☆◎◎◎◎)

【3】次の問いに答えなさい。

1　次の日本語を英語に直しなさい。

自分にできることを，自分が持っているものを用いて，今いる場所でやりなさい。

2　「旅行」を題材とし「一般動詞の過去形」を学習する単元のまとめとして，授業において言語活動を行います。あなたは，どのような活動を取り入れますか。また，その活動を行う上で，どのような点に配慮する必要がありますか。あなたの考えを100語程度の英語で書きなさい。ただし，語数には，カンマやピリオド等の句読点，疑問符や引用符等の符号は含まないものとします。なお，解答の総語数を記入すること。

(☆☆☆◎◎◎)

【高等学校】

【1】次の英文を読んで，あとの問いに答えなさい。

Any language teacher knows that letters, sounds, and words are symbols or signs that denote, that is, refer to objects and events in the real world, as in: 'the word *tree* is a linguistic symbol' . When we say that 'language is a symbolic system', we mean that it is made of linguistic signs that are related to one another in systematic and conventional ways. Non-linguistic signs include, for example, a flag as a national symbol, or a green light as a symbol for 'go ahead'. Even though for monolingual speakers linguistic signs have become so attached to their referents that they seem to be part of the object itself, for multilinguals or newcomers to a language, (1)<u>the fact that the same object is called tree in one language, *Baum* or *arbre* in another</u>, makes it evident that the linguistic sign as symbolic form is quite arbitrary, even though it is used in non-arbitrary ways.

We may focus on two aspects of symbols. On the one hand, symbols are conventional in nature, they refer to and represent the social and psychological reality of a speech community. As signs shared by a social community, symbols derive their meaning from (2)<u>the force of social convention</u>. Learners of a foreign language have to adhere to the grammatical and lexical conventions of the symbolic system they are learning and to the social conventions of its use. By conforming to these conventions they are given the symbolic power to enter a historical speech community and be accepted as members of that community. However, such membership has its price: grammaticality, social acceptability, and cultural appropriateness put limits on what an individual may say or write.

On the other hand, (3)<u>the use of symbols</u> triggers subjective resonances both in the users and in the receivers. It reproduces a speaker's sense of self and enables him or her to act upon the symbolic order of the speech community. Because each speaker's experiences are different, each speaker inflects conventional symbolic forms with personal, often idiosyncratic, meaning. For non-native speakers, the power that comes from being able to sound like or even to pass for someone else, to put one's own experience into someone else's words, to speak English but to feel Persian or speak German with an

American sensibility, creates new symbolic power relations that enable learners to break with conventions and to bring about other symbolic realities. The social and cultural meanings given to events by a given speech community can generate for speakers who don't belong to that community a new sense of self. For example, I am writing this in Paris, where I hear on French TV President Bush addressing the American people and commemorating September 11, 2001. The American president speaks in English but I hear him in French through the French telecaster's translation. For the first time, I see and hear the 9/11 events through the eyes and the language of someone else－an astonishing metamorphosis: September 11 becomes a historical rather than an ideological event, Bush's words cease to address me, as a fellow American; they address 'them', the Americans, commemorating 'their' traumatic event on the evening news. The French language frees me to hear the American president with French ears, that is, with empathy but with the distance afforded by a different position in space and time. In a second, (4)my view of reality and of my own position has changed, as it does when I look at a European map of the world where the world revolves not around North America, but around Europe. French words, French maps are all symbols that mediate for me a different reality and a different subject position.

These new subject positions are not just social or psychological realities, but, rather, they are symbolic, that is, created through the language user's engagement with and manipulation of symbols of a very concrete, material kind, such as vowels and consonants, nouns and verbs, sounds and accents, as well as maps and televised images. The word 'symbolic', when applied to entities such as 'symbolic reality', 'symbolic self', or 'symbolic power', refers not only to the *representation* of people and objects in the world but to the *construction* of perceptions, attitudes, beliefs, aspirations, values through the use of symbolic forms.

(Claire Kramsch, *The Multilingual Subject*による。ただし，設問

の都合で一部省略している。)

1　本文の内容に即して，次の問いに英語で答えなさい。

(1)　According to the author, do non-linguistic signs include such symbols as a flag and a green light?

(2)　What can generate a new sense of self for speakers who don't belong to the speech community?

2　多言語話者やその言語の初心者にとって，下線部(1)によって明らかになるのはどのようなことか，本文に即して日本語で答えなさい。

3　下線部(2)の内容を説明したものとして最も適切なものを，次のア～エの中から一つ選び，記号で答えなさい。

ア　symbols that learners of a foreign language have to refer to and represent as the reality of a speech community

イ　linguistic signs attached by monolingual speakers as referents so that they seem to be the part of the object itself

ウ　the grammatical and lexical usage of the symbolic system learners of a foreign language have to conform to

エ　the power that prevents an individual from being able to put one's own experience into someone else's words

4　下線部(3)によって可能になるのは，どのようなことか，本文に即して日本語で答えなさい。

5　下線部(4)について，筆者の「現実や自身の位置についての見方が変わる」のはなぜか，その理由を本文に即して日本語で答えなさい。

6　本文の内容に合うものを，次のア～エの中から一つ選び，記号で答えなさい。

ア　Any language teacher knows that symbols or signs don't always indicate objects and events in the real world.

イ　Learners of a foreign language should believe that they can finally be accepted as members of the speech community.

ウ　For non-native speakers, words of a foreign language are all symbols that can be used for different meanings.

エ　The word 'symbolic' refers to the construction of perceptions, beliefs, or values through the use of symbolic forms.

(☆☆☆☆◎◎◎◎)

【2】次の問いに答えなさい。

1　次の日本語を英語に直しなさい。

簡単なことを完璧にこなす根気強い人でなければ，難しいことを難なくこなす能力を身につけられないものだ。

2　次のグラフは，「平成27年度　英語教育実施状況調査(高等学校)の結果概要」における平成27年12月1日現在でのICT機器の活用について表したものです。このグラフからどのようなことが読み取れますか。また，読み取ったことを踏まえ，あなたは，授業においてどのようなICT機器をどのように活用しますか。100語程度の英語で書きなさい。ただし，語数には，カンマやピリオド等の句読点，疑問符や引用符等の符号は含まないものとします。なお，解答の総語数を記入すること。

英語の授業におけるＩＣＴ機器の活用

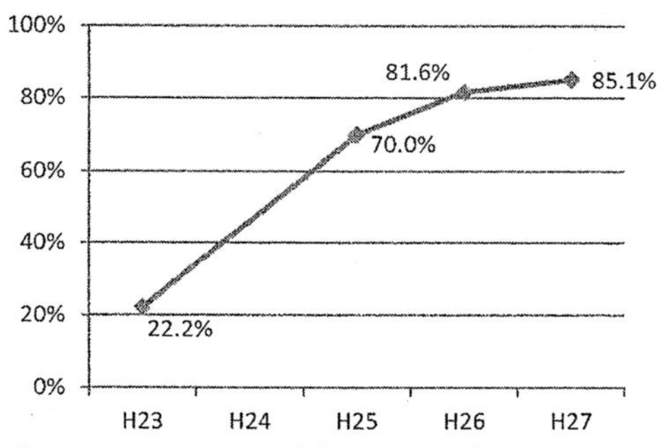

注１：H23、H25、H26は実績値、H27は計画値。

注２：H23 の数値は「『国際共通語としての英語力向上のための５つの提言と具体的施策』に係る状況調査」の結果に基づく。

(☆☆☆☆◎◎◎)

解答・解説

【中高共通】

【1】1　No. 1　(c)　No. 2　(a)　2　No. 1　(c)　No. 2　(a)
No. 3　(b)　3　No. 1　(d)　No. 2　(a)　No. 3　(c)
4　No. 1　Keep your fingers crossed for me　No. 2　walked away as if to tell me to leave him

〈解説〉1　No. 1　rest assuredで「安心する」という意味。　No. 2　パスポートとビザを取得するにあたりポリオワクチンを接種する必要があるか，という質問に対する答えなので，尋ねるのに適切な場所は旅行代理店となる。　2　No. 1　女性の2つ目の発言のover ten yearsを(c)ではmore than ten yearsに言い換えている。　No. 2　女性の1つ目の発言にDid you make the copies I asked for yet?とあり，女性が男性にコピーを取るように頼んであったことがわかる。男性の発言でI'll get John to do them for you …とあるので，男性が自分でしないでジョンにコピーを取ることを頼むことがわかる。get John to do themをask someone else to take care of the woman's requestに言い換えている。　No. 3　女性はシカゴで仕事についたが，車をもっていかないという。その理由としてThe city is famous for its public transportation.とあり，「シカゴは公共輸送機関で有名」だから「あちこち移動するのに車は必要ない」と考える。
3　No. 1　第2段落2文目の「それぞれの曜日は空にある7つの見慣れた動体の1つに由来する」から判断する。moving bodies in the skyが(d)ではheavenly objectと言い換えられている。　No. 2　曜日の名前は天体に由来し，第2段落3文目以降に「それぞれの曜日にその天体が人に影響を与えるとバビロニア人たちは信じていた。彼らは赤い惑星のMarsから攻撃を連想し，Tews(英語で戦争の神を意味する)の日ということで，Mars DayをTuesdayにした」とあることから判断する。
No. 3　第3段落3文目に，「ローマ人の戦争の神はMarsとして知られていた」とある。ローマ時代から最近まで，3月は寒さが春に替わる再生の時で，新年の始まりと思われていた。そして5文目に「帝国を拡大するローマ戦士たちは，気温が温暖で，雪が解けるので全力で戦いを始めることができるため，この月を戦争の神MarsにちなんでMarchと名づけないではいられなかった」とあることから判断する。renewalを(c)ではnew life came into existenceと言い換えている。

4　No. 1　Keep yourは「キーピュァ」のように聞こえる。keep one's fingers crossedで「幸運を祈る」という意味。　No. 2　walked awayは「ゥオークタゥエイ」のように聞こえる。as，if，to，tell，me，to，leave，him，aloneは，つづりの短い単語が連続して素早く言われるので，as if to tell meとto leave him aloneのように意味のまとまりを意識して聞き取る。

【2】1　イ　2　ウ　3　ア　4　ウ　5　エ　6　ア　7　エ　8　イ　9　ア　10　ア　11　イ　12　ウ　13　エ　14　ウ　15　ア

〈解説〉1　itは形式目的語で，that節以降が真主語。owe ～ to …「～を…に負っている」。　2　as「～するように」とso「そのように」が呼応している。英文は「地球が太陽の周りを回っているように，そのように月も地球の周りを回っている」の意。　3　have difficulty (in) doingで「～(do)するのが困難である」。　4　… the mountain, which the whole city could be seen from the top of.のfrom the top ofが関係代名詞whichの前にきている。「町全体が頂上から見られる山の麓に私たちは着いた」となる。　5　strike ～「～の心を打つ」，on one's arrival「～が到着したとき」。　6　If having been given (a chance)「機会を与えられたら」を省略したもの。　7　pressed for timeで「時間に追われている」という意味。　8　at one's wit's end「途方に暮れて」，when it comes to「～ということになると」という意味。　9　a shape以下の「等しい長さの4本の真っすぐな辺と4つの直角をもつ形」から判断する。

10　without missing a beat「調子を崩さずに」。　11　delve into ～「～を探求する」。　12　ア「特異」，イ「告知すること」，ウ「注釈」，エ

「匿名」。with annotationsで「注釈付きで」。　13　ア「増殖」，イ「道楽者」，ウ「先行」，エ「降水」。　14　beef upで「強化する」という意味。　15　ア「現職の」，イ「耕作に適した」，ウ「垂直な」，エ「簡潔な」。

【中学校】

【1】1　(1)　Yes, they do.　(2)　They were considered as the “domesticated elite.”　2　①　エ　②　ア　③　ウ　3　イ　4　発達の過程における変化が，成長した後も遊び好きのままの動物を，どのようにして作り出すのかということ。　5　研究者が狐を選ぶ際に基準としたたった一つの資質が，狐の他の多くの側面に変化をもたらしたということ。　6　イ，カ

〈解説〉1　(1)　質問は「ほとんどすべての動物の特徴は，それが肉体面であっても，行動面であっても，成体になるにつれ異なってくるか」。第2段落6文目に「ほとんどすべての動物はどんなに単純(な作り)であっても，その発達の初期は，あとで成熟したときとは異なる特徴を有している」から判断する。　(2)　質問は「Belyaevの研究で，たった10世代の間に生まれたキツネの18%は何とみなされているか」。第3段落6文目に「たった10世代の間に生まれたキツネの18%は，彼が分類したdomesticated elite(家畜化されたエリート)だった」とあることから判断する。　2　①　leapは「跳ぶ」という意味。　②　exuberantは「活発な，元気に満ちた」という意味。　③　docileは「従順な」という意味。　3　空欄aの直後に「しかし」とあり，「人や犬などピーターパンのような種族は，遊び好きな性質を残したまま大人になる」と続くので，本来は年を取って大人になれば遊ばなくなると考え，イ「ほとんどの動物は年を取ると，遊ぶ頻度が減り，まったく遊ばなくなる」が入る。　4　第2段落4文目にpaedomorphismの説明として「幼形保有は，動物が成熟するにつれ，ふつうは少しずつ消えていく幼年期の特徴を，成熟期に保有していること」とある。同段落3文目には「活発な遊びを成体期まで続ける傾向は，犬や人が，それらよりもっ

と成熟した近縁種の幼形進化した，あるいは幼若化した形であると科学者に思わせる要素の1つである」とあり，犬や人が幼形保有している動物だと考えている。同段落最後の文に「人や犬について私たちが探求するとき大切なことは」とあり，近縁種が幼形進化した(幼形保有したまま進化した)人や犬を探求するとは，幼形保有を探求することだと考え，その探求で重要なことは「発達の過程における変化が，年を取ってさえ，ほとんどの幼年期の哺乳類のように著しく遊び好きなままでいる成体動物を，どうやって作り上げることを可能にするのかということだ」とあることから判断する。 5 第3段落2文目に「ロシア人科学者のDmitry Belyaevは，祖先ほど攻撃的でない動物を，家畜化の過程を通して，どのように生み出すのかに興味があった」とあり，それ以降に狐を使った研究内容が述べられている。それを受けて第4段落1文目に「この研究を科学にとってとても興味深く，重要なものとしているのは」とあり，それ以降に「研究者がたった1つの資質，つまり従順さを求めて選んだ時に，狐の行動や生体構造，生理機能といった他の多くの側面に変化をもたらした」と，筆者が興味深く，重要なものと考えていることが述べられている。 6 イは「2～3歳のチンパンジーは1人で遊ぶこともあるが，それよりも一緒に遊ぶことのほうが多い」という意味。第1段落9文目と一致する。カは「Belyaevの研究で，成体の狐は年を取ってから見慣れないものへの恐怖心が少なくなっていることを示した」という意味。第3・4段落で狐を使った研究内容が述べられていて，第4段落3文目の「成体の家畜化されたエリートは，年を取ってさえ子犬のようにふるまい続け，正常な(集団の)狐よりも，年を取ってから見慣れないものへの恐怖心が少なくなっていることを示した」と一致する。

【2】1 (1) Because she thought she could compare the results.

(2) They were educated, organized, polite, creative, and tolerant.

2 ① エ ② ウ ③ イ 3 生徒が考えるよい教師の要素は何かということ。 4 よい教師と悪い教師を描写するために，重要なものから順に選ぶこと。　5　教えることに集中するだけでなく，生徒に自由に話し合わせることで生徒との距離が近くなるということに気づき，以前より生徒との関係が親密になった。　6　ウ

〈解説〉1　(1)　第3段落1文目後半，so that「～のために(目的)」以降に述べられている。　(2)　第6段落2文目にある「よい教師は教養があり，きちんとして，礼儀正しく，創造的で，寛容である」という資質を，筆者であるAnaは書き留めたことから判断する。　2　①　admireは「称賛する，敬服する」という意味で，エ「よいと思うことをしたことで，その人を尊敬すること」と一致する。　②　suffixは「接尾辞」という意味で，ウ「新しい単語を作るために語尾に付け加えられた文字」と一致する。　③　vanishは「消える」という意味で，イ「特にあっけなく，説明できない方法で突然消える」と一致する。　3　第1段落で「学習者から見て何がよい教師を作る(育てる)のか」という論題(question)が述べられ，第2段落で筆者は学習者に愛され，尊敬される教師を敬服し，よい教師だと思うが，自分には何かが足りないと思っている。調査することによって，それ(論題。学習者から見て何がよい教師を作るのか)についてもっと明らかにすることができると思った，と話が続いていく。　4　下線部の直後に「最も重要な資質から重要でない資質の順によい教師と悪い教師を描写するために」と理由が述べられている。　5　第8段落最初に「私は～の結論に達した」とあり，「教える内容に過度に集中し，生徒にその内容とは関係のない事柄を話し合う(自由に話し合う)機会をあまりたくさん与えなかったので，生徒を少し遠ざけたかもしれない」という結論が述べられている。そこから気づいたことは，2文目のI realised ～「私は～に気づいた」以降に，「生徒たちは友だちが必要」，つまり自由に話し合うことができる人が必要だと気づき，そういう関係(友だちのような関係)にオープンな先生は生徒たちとより親密になるという変化が述べられている。　6　第3段落3文目以降に，結局20語の(形容詞の)リストを作り，それぞれの語に接頭辞や接尾辞をつけて反対の意味の語を作り，合計40枚のカードをそれぞれ生徒に渡したとある。第4段落では生徒がパ

ートナーを1人見つけ，「形容詞」と「その反対の意味の形容詞」のペアーを作るので，カードは20組だと考える。2文目にその20組のカードは黒板上に示されたとあることから判断する。

【3】1　Do what you can do, with what you have, where you are.　　2　First I put the students in small groups and make them talk about memorable trips freely － when, where and with whom they went, how they enjoyed the trips, etc. － using the past tense. Secondly, they ask each other about their trips and write down the content. After the group works, some students represent the group and present how their trips were before the whole classes. Lastly, I take question and answer time a while. Through these communicative activities, the students can learn how to use not only the positive form of the past tense but the negative and the interrogative forms. (101 words)

〈解説〉1　「自分ができること」はwhat you can do,「自分が持っているもの」はwhat you haveにする。「～を用いて」は「～で」と手段を表すwithにする。「今いる場所で」はwhere you are。whereは関係副詞でat the place where you areのこと。whereの中に前置詞atと先行詞のthe placeが含まれている。　2　「一般動詞の過去形」を学習する単元のまとめの授業を考える。その際，「旅行」を題材とするという指定があるので，まず生徒たちに自分が経験した旅行について小グループに分かれて自由に述べさせることから始めるとよい。ある程度まとまったら，クラス全員の前で発表させ，感想を言い合ったり，質問をしたりする。これらの言語活動を通して一般動詞の過去形を生徒に定着させることができる。

【高等学校】

【1】1　(1)　Yes, they do.　　(2)　The social and cultural meanings given to events by the speech community can.　　2　象徴的な形としての言語記号は，たとえ非恣意的に使われているとしても，きわめて恣意的であるということ。　　3　ウ　　4　話し手が言語共同体の象徴的な秩序

に作用すること。　5　フランス語によって，英語をフランス語の感覚で，共感しつつも異なる時間と空間から距離感を持って聞くことができるから。　6　エ

〈解説〉1　(1)　第1段落3文目に「非言語記号にはたとえば，国の表象としての旗や，「進め」を意味する表象としての青信号が含まれる」とあることから判断する。　(2)　第3段落5文目に「ある言語共同体によって出来事に付与された社会的で文化的な意味は，その共同体に属していない話し手のために，新しい自己意識を生み出す」とあることから判断する。　2　the fact that ～ makes it evident that ～は，itが形式目的語で真目的語はthat節以下なので，明らかになるものがthat節以下に言われる。　3　下線部(2)を含む1文は「社会共同体で共有される記号として，表象は「社会的慣習の圧力」から意味を得る」の意。この文の直後に「外国語の学習者は，彼らが学ぶ記号体系の文法的慣習と語彙的慣習，そしてそれを使用する際の社会的慣習を忠実に守らなければならない」とあり，社会共同体と記号を共有し，文法や語彙の慣習に従い，それらを使用するときの社会的慣習に従わなければならない(社会的慣習の圧力)ことで，歴史ある言語共同体に参加する象徴的な力をもらい，その共同体の一員として受け入れられるとあることから，ウ「外国語の学習者が従わなければならない記号体系の文法的用法と語法」と一致する。　4　表象を使うことで可能になることが問われているので，第3段落2文目のand以降に「(それ(表象を使うこと)は)話し手が言語共同体の象徴的な秩序に作用することを可能にする」とあることから判断する。　5　下線部(4)の直前の文で「フランス語は私を解放してくれて，フランス語の耳で，つまり共感しつつも，空間と時間において(アメリカではなくフランスという)異なる位置から与えられた距離感で，アメリカ大統領の話を聞けるようにする」とあり，共感しつつも異なる距離感で聞くことで見方が変わると考える。
6　第4段落2文目に「symbolicという語は～だけでなく，記号形式を使って知覚や態度，信念，願望，価値観を創出することを意味として含んでいる」とあることから判断する。

【2】1　Only those who have the patience to do simple things perfectly will acquire the skill to do difficult things easily.　2　In order to help students improve their communicational skills, ICT equipment has now been used in English classes by more than 80% of the high schools surveyed, which is four times more than five years ago. I will use iPad to have students make a video introducing a typical day of a Japanese high school student to foreign people. In groups of three or four students, they take pictures of some parts of their daily lives, like morning rush hours, school life, club activities, weekend, etc. Then they make English narrations and choose background music for each picture and compile a video with all of them combined. They present the video in front of the class. (116 words)

〈解説〉1　「～人だけが～能力を身につけるだろう」と言い換え，主語と動詞と目的語から成るonly those … will acquire the skill …. を作る。それからthoseのあとに「簡単なことを完璧にするための根気強さを持っている(人)」として，those who have the patience to do simple things perfectlyとし，the skillのあとに「難しいことを簡単にする(難なくこなす)ための(能力)」として，the skill to do difficult things easilyとする。　2　アニメなど動きのあるコンテンツで，生徒と双方向で学習する。生徒1人ひとりの能力に応じてレベルを設定する。ネイティブの発音を聞き取れる。教室以外の他の場所，他学校，あるいは海外の人ともコミュニケーションができる。生徒の家庭学習に関わることができるなどの利点を生かした活動を書くとよい。

2016年度　実施問題

【中高共通】

【1】(放送による問題)　これはリスニング・テストです。放送の指示に従って答えなさい。

[トラック1]

[試聴用英文(約3分間)]

ただいまから，試聴用の英文を約3分間流します。そのあとでチャイムが鳴りますから，そこでCDを止めてください。

(試聴用の英文)

〈チャイム連続音〉

(空白1分間)

[トラック2]

(問題)

〈チャイム連続音〉

ただいまから，リスニング・テストを行います。問題は1，2，3，4の四つです。聞いている間にメモを取っても構いません。

(間2秒)

では，1の問題から始めます。問題はNo.1とNo.2の2問です。

これから読まれる英文に対する応答として最も ふさわしいものを，続いて読まれる(a)，(b)，(c)の中から一つ選び，記号で答えなさい。答えは，大文字，小文字どちらでも構いません。なお，英文と応答は1度しか読まれません。

(間2秒)

では，始めます。

No.1　This office is so hot today.

(a)　No, not for me. Thanks.

(b)　Yes, he's in the office today.

(c) Maybe we can open a window.

(間5秒)

No.2 How did your lecture go yesterday?

(a) He was out yesterday.

(b) It couldn't have been better.

(c) He went there by bike.

(間7秒)

〈チャイム〉

次に，2の問題に移ります。問題は，No.1からNo.3までの3問です。

これから，短い対話文を読みます。そのあとでクエスチョンと言って質問します。その答えとして最もふさわしいものを，続いて読まれる(a)，(b)，(c)，(d)の中から一つ選び，記号で答えなさい。答えは，大文字，小文字どちらでも構いません。なお，対話文・質問・答えの選択肢は1度しか読まれません。

(間2秒)

では，始めます。

No.1

W: The order for your office party Thursday afternoon should be ready on Thursday morning.

M: Great, but I'd like to pick it up on Wednesday if that's OK. I'll be busy with clients on Thursday morning.

W: I'd advise against that-the food won't stay fresh. We could deliver the food to your office on Thursday morning, if you'd like. It's really much better if it's fresh.

M: That would he a great help. Thank you.

Question: What does the woman offer to do for the man?

(a) Give him a discount

(b) Introduce him to a customer

(c) Take him to a restaurant

(d) Deliver an order to his office

(間4秒)

No.2 (効果音)

M: Hello. This is the George Hotel. How can I help you?

W: Hello, this is Jenny Brown. Could you please connect me to Agnes Lam's room?

M: Just a moment please... I'm sorry, I can't find anyone by that name in our records. Are you sure she's staying here?

W: Yes, I'm sure. I was just talking to her a minute ago. Oh, wait, I made a mistake. It's Agnes Lim, not Agnes Lam.

M: Oh, yes, I see her name. Let me connect you to her room.

Question: What is the problem?

(a) Agnes Lam is not in her room.

(b) The office is closed.

(c) The caller gave the wrong name.

(d) The man has lost his list.

(間4秒)

No.3 (効果音)

W: Hello. Thank you for calling World Communications.

M: Hi, I'd like to make a person-to-person call to Paris, France. How much will that be?

W: It's \$3.00 for the first five minutes and 40¢ for each additional minute.
Question: How much will the man pay for a fifteen-minute call?

(a) He will pay \$7.00.
(b) He will pay \$4.40.
(c) He will pay \$12.00.
(d) He will pay \$21.00

(間7秒)

〈チャイム〉
次に3の問題に移ります。問題は，No.1からNo.3までの3問です。
これから，あるまとまりのある英文を読みます。そのあとで，クエスチョンと言って，その英文について三つの質問をします。その答えとして最もふさわしいものを，質問に続いて読まれる(a)，(b)，(c)，(d)の中から一つ選び，記号で答えなさい。答えは，大文字，小文字どちらでも構いません。なお，英文・質問・答えの選択肢は全体を通して2回読まれます。

(間2秒)

では，始めます。

As anybody who interacts with an infant notices, you speak very differently to a young child than you do to another adult. You raise the pitch of your voice, you speak more slowly, you have long pauses, the utterances are shorter. There're a number of things you do with the melody of your voice, as well as with the linguistic structure of speech, that are very, very different. Why does simplified speech help the child? An obvious answer is that the child doesn't know language, and so you're simplifying the grammar of the language in order to make it easier for a baby to understand, to decode language, and sort of get a grip on it for the first time.

I've worked in a number of European languages as well as American English, and found that in all these languages people behave in very much the same way. So it was of considerable interest to me to extend this work to languages that are very different from English, and cultures that are very different from American and western European culture. Japan is an ideal place to begin that cross-cultural collaboration, because it's a society that is industrialized and has many things in common with European culture; however, its attitudes toward child rearing, its attitudes toward the expression of emotion are very different from ours; and obviously the language, in its history and structure, is very different from the Indo-European languages.

(間3秒)

Question

No.1　What do you usually do when you speak to a child?

(a)　Use simple expressions

(b)　Speak more loudly

(c)　Pitch a slow ball

(d)　Speak in a deep voice

(間3秒)

No.2　Why is simplified speech useful for the child?

(a)　Because he knows nothing about language.

(b)　Because it enables him to understand language.

(c)　Because he is simplifying the grammar of the language.

(d)　Because even a baby knows language.

(間3秒)

No.3 What is the reason that Japan is an ideal place to begin cross-cultural collaboration?

(a) Japan is an industrialized society.

(b) Japanese culture is similar to American and western European cultures.

(c) The Japanese language comes from the Indo-European languages.

(d) There are both similarities and differences in some respects between Japan and Europe.

(間3秒)

くりかえします。

〈チャイム〉

次に4の問題に移ります。問題はNo.1とNo.2の2問です。

これから，英語による対話文を読みます。(　　)のところに入る英語を聞き取り，書きなさい。対話文はそれぞれ2回読まれます。

(間2秒)

では，始めます。

No.1 M: Do you know why Emily was angry? She said nothing at all yesterday.

W: Her parents went to Spain on business. (　　).

(間10秒)

くりかえします。

No.2　M: Where do you want to put the piano?
W: The best place (　　) the bed.

(間10秒)
くりかえします。

〈チャイム連続音〉

これで，リスニング・テストを終わります。次の問題に移ってください。

(☆☆☆☆◎◎◎)

【2】次の英文や対話文の中の(　　)に最も適するものを，下のア～エの中からそれぞれ一つずつ選び，記号で答えなさい。

1　A: I set my watch three minutes forward yesterday, but it is five minutes slow again.
B: You bought it just a week ago. You should bring it to the shop you bought it at and have it (　　).

ア　repair　イ　repairing　ウ　repaired
エ　to be repaired

2　The study of language has along history, (　　) over thousands of years.

ア　extends　イ　extended　ウ　extend　エ　extending

3　When he went for a walk after dinner, (　　) his wife said happened once a week, he saw a bear near the road.

ア　it　イ　that　ウ　which　エ　what

4　(　　) we miss the last train, what will we do?

ア　Suppose　イ　Consider　ウ　Think　エ　Propose

5　I've known Makoto since we were little. We are on first-name (　　).

ア　relatives　イ　friends　ウ　callings　エ　terms

6 In spite of bad weather, ( ) people came to the concert. The big hall was filled with fans.

ア quite a few イ as many ウ quite a little

エ a many number of

7 I didn't know what to say when asked the way to the station in English. I wished then I ( ) English.

ア know イ knew ウ had been knowing

エ have known

8 A: What is that big book titled "Thesaurus"?

B: You can use this dictionary mainly when you want to know ( ).

ア antonyms イ onomatopoeias ウ metonymies

エ synonyms

9 The novel written by the famous writer ( ) on quickly with young people.

ア went イ caught ウ ran エ came

10 Would you keep the children ( ) until I come back? I'll be back before noon.

ア company イ look ウ neighborhood エ care

11 In Japan attending senior high school is not ( ), but nowadays almost all students go there after graduating from junior high school.

ア compliant イ compulsory ウ comparative

エ complacent

12 The lecturer talked so fast that I couldn't ( ) in what he said.

ア figure イ follow ウ take エ make

13 Please put on something ( ) so that we can find you easily in the crowd.

ア vulnerable イ rampant ウ precarious

エ conspicuous

14 Our company is planning to ( ) in on a promising market to make move profits.

ア　zero　　イ　one　　ウ　two　　エ　three

15　The idea that plants could communicate was once considered (　　) because it wasn't scientifically proved.

ア　forensic　　イ　fastidious　　ウ　fallacious

エ　ferocious

(☆☆☆◎◎◎)

【3】次の英文を読んで，あとの問いに答えなさい。

From October 1966 through December 1967, my wife and I lived among the *Betsileo people of Madagascar and studied their economy and social life. Soon after our arrival, we met two well-educated schoolteachers who were interested in our research. The woman's father was a congressman who became a cabinet minister during our stay. Our schoolteacher friends told us that their family came from a historically important and typical Betsileo village called *Ivato, which they invited us to visit with them.

We had traveled to many other villages, where we were often displeased with our reception. As we drove up, children would run away screaming. Women would hurry inside. Men would ①retreat to doorways, where they lurked bashfully. Eventually someone would ②summon the courage to ask what we wanted. This behavior expressed the Betsileo's great fear of the *mpakafo*. Believed to cut out and devour his victim's heart and liver, the *mpakafo* is the Malagasy vampire. These cannibals are said to have fair skin and to be very tall. Because I have light skin and stand six feet four inches tall, I was a natural suspect. The fact that such creatures were not known to travel with their wives helped convince the Betsileo that (1)I wasn't really a *mpakafo*.

When we visited Ivato, we found that its people were different. They were friendly and hospitable. Our very first day there, we did a brief census and found out who lived in which households. We learned people's names and their relationships to our schoolteacher friends and to each other. We met an excellent informant who knew all about the local history. In a few afternoons, I learned much more than I had in the other villages in several sessions.

Ivatans were willing to talk because I had powerful sponsors, village natives who had made it in the outside world, people the Ivatans knew would protect them. The schoolteachers vouched for us, but even more significant was the cabinet minister, who was like a grandfather and benefactor to everyone in town. The Ivatans had no reason to fear me because their more influential native son had asked them to answer my questions.

Once we moved to Ivato, the elders established a pattern of visiting us every evening. They came to talk, attracted by the ③inquisitive foreigners but also by the wine, cigarettes, and food we offered. I asked questions about their customs and beliefs. I eventually developed interview schedules about various subjects, including rice production. I mimeographed these forms to use in Ivato and in two other villages I was studying loss intensively. Never have I interviewed as easily as I did in Ivato. So enthusiastic were the Ivatans about my questions that even people from neighboring villages came to join the study. Since these people knew nothing about the social scientist's techniques, I couldn't discourage them by saying that they weren't in my sample. Instead, I agreed to visit each village, where I filled out the interview schedule in just one house. Then I told the other villagers that the household head had done such a good job of teaching me about their village I wouldn't need to ask questions in the other households.

As our stay drew to an end, the elders of Ivato began to lament, saying, "We'll miss you. When you leave, there won't be any more cigarettes, any more wine, or any more questions." They wondered $_{(2)}$what it would be like for us back in the United States. They knew that I had an automobile and that I regularly purchased things, including the wine, cigarettes, and food I shared with them. I could afford to buy products they would never have. They commented, "When you go back to your country, you'll need a lot of money for things like cars, clothes, and food. We don't need to buy those things. We make almost everything we use. We don't need as much money as you, because we produce for ourselves."

The Betsileo are not unusual among people whom anthropologists have studied. Strange as it may seem to an American consumer, who may believe that he or she can never have enough money, some rice farmers actually believe that they have all they need. The lesson from the Betsileo is that scarcity, which economists view as universal, is variable. Although shortages do arise in nonindustrial societies, (3) the concept of scarcity is much less developed in stable subsistence-oriented societies than in the societies characterized by industrialism, particularly as the reliance on consumer goods increases.

(注)　Betsileo:　ベツィレウ族　　Ivato:　イヴァト(地名)

(C.D. Kottak, *Anthropology:The Exploration of Humasn Diversity*による。ただし，設問の都合で一部省略および改変している。)

1　下線部①～③の語を別の語で言い換えたとき，最も意味の近いものを，次のア～エの中からそれぞれ一つずつ選び，記号で答えなさい。

①　ア　refuse　　イ　reveal　　ウ　revolt　　エ　retire

②　ア　dismiss　　イ　muster　　ウ　occupy　　エ　order

③　ア　boring　　イ　indifferent　　ウ　curious　　エ　lively

2　下線部(1)のように，ベツィレウ族の人々が納得したのはなぜか，本文に即して日本語で答えなさい。

3　イヴァトの人々が，下線部(2)のように考えたのはなぜか，本文に即して日本語で答えなさい。

4　下線部(3)を日本語に直しなさい。

5　本文の内容に即して，次の問いに英語で答えなさい。

(I)　How were the people in Ivato when the author and his wife first visited it?

(2)　Does the author think that the Betsileo are a notable example for those who have studied anthropology?

6　本文の内容に合うものを次のア～オの中から一つ選び，記号で答えなさい。

ア　Soon after the author and his wife arrived in Madagascar, they met a congressman of the country.

イ　The author traveled to many other villages and often received a warm welcome there.

ウ　Ivatans were glad to talk with the author because he promised to be a powerful sponsor for them.

エ　The author filled out his interview schedule in just one house in each village which he had agreed to visit.

オ　According to the author, economists' view that scarcity depends on the society is universal.

(☆☆☆◎◎◎)

【中学校】

【1】次の英文を読んで，あとの問いに答えなさい。

(1)Cheryl, a teacher from Hobart, Tasmania, wanted to develop a teaching program that would help her students to individualize their learning of English for specific purposes (ESP). She chose this focus because she had become increasingly aware of the frustration experienced by students who were unable to describe their vocational skills, experiences, and recreational interests because of a limited range of vocabulary. She realized that it did not seem to matter how ①competent a student was in general English, vocabulary in ESP was consistently lacking.

With her post-beginner class she adopted a teaching approach which allowed her students to develop vocabulary on a topic of their choice. First, the students chose an area of specific vocabulary they wanted to develop through independent study. Next, Cheryl ensured that the students could get access to resources and made it clear that she was available to support them. She provided them with visual and reference materials, dictionaries, technical books, ESP textbooks, newspapers and journals, a variety of CD-ROMs, and computers with Internet access. Cheryl saw her role as helping the students to establish realistic, short-term, and achievable goals. She wanted the students to take responsibility for their own learning and establish self-monitoring strategies for assessing which words were ②appropriate and useful.

Cheryl then offered the students three classroom sessions with her. In these sessions, she drew attention to things such as vocabulary definitions and categories, verbs and phrases, and words and ③clauses in context. She encouraged the students to go outside the classroom for their projects, so they also made use of resources in the community. For example, one student spoke to a music student about how to read music, two students audited a tourism lecture at the local technical college, and another student spoke to a salesman in a car yard.

The ESP interests of the students were very varied and were based on their personal or career interests. They included Genetics, Biology, Travel and Tourism, Cards, Graphics in Computers, Guitars and Music, Soccer Clubs and Sponsorship, Journalism, Magnetism and Energy in Physics, Bangkok, the Structure and Operation of Import/Export Companies, and Enzymes In Humans.

Finally, Cheryl scheduled (2)a fourth classroom session for students, to present their work to others in the class. The presentations were an opportunity for them to display their new vocabulary. The students showed a great deal of inventiveness in the way they did their presentations: a song written and sung in English; an explanation of the computerized Galileo system of international travel and hotel reservations; a simulated bus tour of Bangkok; a car salesman giving a sales pitch; and a description of how to get a hot tip for a newspaper story.

To collect data, Cheryl monitored the students' responses to the course through discussions with individual students and her own observations. She also used a questionnaire to survey the students on where they got their new vocabulary. In order of importance and frequency these were books, the Internet, people, newspapers, brochures, visits, CD-ROMs, and other resources, such as video.

Cheryl argued that her new teaching approach means that the students become more confident in taking responsibility for ESP vocabulary development once they have been given (3)a starting point and strategies. She concluded that ESP requires setting up opportunities, offering support, and, above all, trusting the students to use their time effectively.

(J.C. Richards, T.S.C.Farrell, *Professional Development for Language Teachers*による。ただし，設問の都合で一部省略および改変している。)

1 下線部①～③の英語の説明として最もよくあてはまるものを，次のア～エの中からそれぞれ一つずつ選び，記号で答えなさい。

① ア determined or able to be more successful than other people or business

イ able to exist or be used together without causing problems

ウ so interesting or exciting that you have to pay attention

エ having enough skill or knowledge to do something to a satisfactory standard

② ア showing support or agreement for something

イ correct or right for a particular time, situation, or purpose

ウ special or important enough to mention

エ to take something for yourself, when you have no right to do this

③ ア a group of words that contains a subject and a verb, but which is usually only part of a sentence

イ a group of words which does not have a main verb, used to form part of a sentence

ウ a group of words which begins with a capital letter and ends with a period

エ a group of words that has a special meaning that is different from the ordinary meaning of each separate word

2　下線部(1)で，Cherylがこのように考えたのは，どのような理由からか，本文に即して日本語で説明しなさい。

3　下線部(2)で，生徒は何を目的に，どのようにプレゼンテーションを行ったか，本文に即して日本語で説明しなさい。

4　下線部(3)は具体的にどのようなことか，本文に即して日本語で書きなさい。

5　本文の内容に即して，次の質問に英語で答えなさい。

(1)　In order for students to use resources in the community, what did Cheryl do?

(2)　According to Cheryl's conclusion, what does ESP require most?

6　本文の内容に合うものを，次のア～オの中から二つ選び，記号で答えなさい。

ア　Cheryl prepared various resources for students to access and supported them.

イ　In the third classroom session, students all showed their vocabulary to each other so that they could learn.

ウ　In the program, students established their own goals and took responsibility for their own learning.

エ　The interests of the students were similar because they wanted the same career.

オ　Cheryl used a questionnaire to know what students thought about the program.

(☆☆☆☆◎◎◎)

【2】次の1，2について，指示に従って答えなさい。

1　次の日本語を英語に直しなさい。

自分の無知に気づけば気づくほど，より一層学びたくなる。

2　「中学校学習指導要領」(平成20年3月告示)では，「2　内容(1)言語活動」の「イ　話すこと」において，「(オ)与えられたテーマについて簡単なスピーチをすること。」が示されています。授業において，生徒のスピーチをどのような手順で評価すべきですか。あなたの考えを100語程度の英語で書きなさい。ただし，語数には，カンマやピリオド等の句読点，疑問符や引用符の符号等は含まないものとします。なお，解答の総語数を記入すること。

(☆☆☆◎◎◎)

【高等学校】

【1】次の英文を読んで，あとの問いに答えなさい。

Evaluation can be of two kinds: micro or macro. In a *micro-evaluation the implementation of specific tasks is studied. It involves a consideration of what transpires when a specific task is performed in a specific instructional context. In a *macro-evaluation whole courses based on tasks are investigated. Both types of evaluation can be directed at 'accountability' (i.e. the extent to which the task/course achieves its goals) or 'improvement' (i.e. how the task/course can be improved).

In Ellis (1997) I distinguished three different approaches for conducting a micro-evaluation of a task; a student-based evaluation, a response-based evaluation (where the evaluator seeks to determine whether the task elicited the performance and outcomes intended), and a learning-based evaluation (where the evaluator investigates whether the task has resulted in any learning). Each of these approaches requires different types of data. A student-based evaluation (①). A response-based evaluation (②) that results from the outcome of the task. A learning-based evaluation ideally (③) have occurred. However, it might also be possible to demonstrate learning microgenetically through the detailed analysis of learners' performance of the task.

Micro-evaluations of tasks are rarely published. However, over the years I have asked students in my masters-level classes at various institutions to carry out micro-evaluations of tasks (Ellis, 2011). I will report on one of these here.

Freeman (2007) set out to evaluate a dictogloss task. This required students to listen to a listening text nine sentences long on the subject of obesity. They listened three times. On the first occasion they were asked to answer a multiple-choice question designed to establish whether they had understood the general content of the text. On the second occasion, the students were told to note down the key content words while on the third occasion different students were required to focus and take notes on the use of different linguistic forms (i.e. relative clauses, passive verb forms and transition signals). The students then worked in groups of three to reconstruct the text and write it out. Freeman's evaluation was designed to establish both accountability and to provide information about how to improve the task. To this end she collected a variety of data—the notes the students made during the third listening (i.e. the extent to which they noticed and noted the target forms they were directed to attend to), the reconstructed text, a questionnaire to elicit the students' opinions of the task, a transcript of the discussion that took place while the students were reconstructing, notes made by observers of the lesson and a summative reflective report by the teacher.

The analyses of these data sets demonstrated that the students were successful in noticing and noting the target structures, that they attempted to use the target forms in their reconstructed text, that they engaged in a number of language-related episodes as they discussed their reconstruction (most of which led to correct language use), and that they reported the task had enabled them to communicate freely and that the interactions they engaged in during the discussion helped them with grammar. Freeman concluded that the students were largely successful in achieving the outcome of the task (the reconstruction of the text), that the task was successful in inducing noticing of the target forms, also encouraged attendance to other aspects of language, and led to active engagement (although not equally for all students). By and large then she felt that (1)<u>the task had achieved its objectives</u>. However, she also identified a number of ways in which it could be improved. For example, she suggested that allowing the student to share the notes they had taken reduced the amount and quality of the interaction and that a better procedure would be to have asked the students to put away their notes before they started to reconstruct the text. Another suggestion was to assign the task of scribe of the reconstructed text to the least proficient of the students to encourage greater participation by this student.

(2)<u>Micro-evaluations</u> are designed to inform practice rather than theory. They are local in nature. They can be seen as a form of practitioner-research. They help teachers to examine the assumptions that lie behind the design of a task and the procedures used to implement it. They require them to go beyond impressionistic evaluation by examining empirically whether a task works in the way they intended and how it can be improved for future use.

(R.R. Ellis, *Language Teaching Research & Language Pedagogy*による。ただし，設問の都合で一部省略および改変している。)

1　本文中の空欄(　①　)～(　③　)にあてはまる最も適切な英語を，それぞれ次のア～エの中から一つずつ選び，記号で答えなさい。ただし，同じ記号は二回以上使わないこと。

ア　can provide an opportunity for extended multiparty interaction where there is a focus on linguistic form

イ　requires some kind of pre-and post-test to determine when any changes in learners' ability to use the second language

ウ　can be conducted using self-report instruments such as questionnaires, interviews and focus group discussions

エ　requires observation/recording of learners' performance of a task and also the analysis of any product

2　Freemanが下線部(1)のように考えた理由としてあてはまらないものを，次のア～エの中から一つ選び，記号で答えなさい。

ア　Students were largely successful in achieving the reconstruction of the text in the dictogloss task.

イ　The task was successful in inducing noticing of the target structures and forms.

ウ　Allowing the student to share the notes reduced the amount and quality of the interaction.

エ　The task encouraged attendance to other aspects of language and led to active engagement.

3　教師が下線部(2)を行うことによる利点は何か，筆者が挙げている二つの利点を本文に即してそれぞれ日本語で書きなさい。ただし，解答の順序は問わない。

4　本文の内容に即して，次の問いに英語で答えなさい。

(1)　What was the topic of the text that the students were required to listen to in Freeman's dictogloss task?

(2)　What did Freeman do to examine whether her evaluation was designed appropriately in terms of accountability and improvement?

5　本文の内容に合うものを次のア～オの中から一つ選び，記号で答えなさい。

ア　Both micro-evaluation and macro-evaluation can be directed at how the task/course can be improved.

イ　Over the years the author has asked high school students to carry out many kinds of tasks in their class.

ウ　The author thinks it might be impossible to demonstrate learning through the detailed analysis of the task.

エ　On the second occasion of the task, the students had to work in groups of three to reconstruct the text.

オ　The interactions the students engaged in during the discussion helped them note down the key content words.

(☆☆☆☆◎◎◎)

【2】次の1，2について，指示に従って答えなさい。

1　次の日本語を英語に直しなさい。

自分の無知に気づけば気づくほど，より一層学びたくなる。

2 「高等学校学習指導要領解説外国語編・英語編」(平成22年5月)では，4技能の総合的な指導を通して，これらの技能を統合的に活用できるコミュニケーション能力の育成を目指すことが求められています。4技能を統合的に活用するとはどういうことですか。また，あなたはどのような活動を授業に取り入れますか。あなたの考えを100語程度の英語で書きなさい。ただし，語数には，カンマやピリオド等の句読点，疑問符や引用符等の符号は含まないものとします。なお，解答の総語数を記入すること。

(☆☆☆◎◎◎)

解答・解説

【中高共通】

【1】1 No.1 (c) No.2 (b) 2 No.1 (d) No.2 (c) No.3 (a) 3 No.1 (a) No.2 (b) No.3 (d)

4 No.1 She must have been so lonely No.2 for it would be in the corner across from

〈解説〉1 No.1 最初に読まれた英文は「今日オフィスはとても暑い」なので，応答としては(c)「窓を開けてもいいよ」が適当。

No.2 最初に読まれた英文は「昨日講義はどうだった」なので，応答としては(b)「それ(講義)はよりよくなったはずがない」すなわち「この上なく最高だった」が適当。 2 No.1 「木曜の午前に注文品が準備できる」という女性の最初のセリフから，女性が店員で男性が客だとわかる。パーティーは木曜の午後で，男性は忙しいので水曜に取りに行く(pick up)というが，食べ物の鮮度が保てないので，木曜の午前に配達する(deliver)という会話の流れ。聞き取りに際してはなるべく早く会話が行われている場所や状況を把握し，出来事の順を曜日や時間とともに覚える習慣をつけよう。 No.2 電話での会話を聞き取る問題では，最初に電話をかける人(caller)と受ける人(receiver)がどんな組織に属しているのか，あるいは誰の友達なのかなど素性や関係性がいわれるので，聞き逃さないこと。女性の2つ目のセリフにI made a mistake.とあり，以下にどんな間違いをして問題になっているかが述べられている。　No.3　電話をかける人と受ける人の素性や関係が初めにいわれ，そのあとに電話をかけている人が要件を言うので，しっかり把握する。男性の最初のセリフにI'd like to make a person-to-person call. How much will that be?「指名電話をかけたいが料金はいくらか」と，要件が言われている。最初の5分は3ドルで，その後1分ごとに40セントなので，15分では，3ドル(最初の5分)＋4ドル(40セント×残りの10分＝4ドル)＝7ドルとなる。　3　英文・質問・答えの選択肢は2度ずつ読まれるので，最初に話の流れを追い，質問文は特に注意して聞き取る。2度目には質問の答えを探しながら聞き取って答えを特定する。　No.1　第1段落2文目に「声の調子を上げる」，「ゆっくり話す」など違う話し方の例がいろいろ言われ，それらをまとめて4文目にWhy does simplified speech help the child?「どうして単純化された話し方が子どもの役に立つのか」とあることから判断する。(c)のpitchは「(音の)調子」以外にも「投げる」という意味がある。(d)の deep voiceは「太い声，低い声」のこと。　No.2　the childを代名詞heで受けている。単純化された話し方が子どもの役に立つ理由として，第1段落5文目のAn obvious answer「明白な答え」以降に，「子どもは言葉を知らないので，赤ん坊が理解し，言葉を解読し，最初にある程度把握することを簡単にするために言葉の文法を単純化する」とあるので，(b)「話し方を単純化して子どもが言葉を理解できるようにする」が正解。(c)のgrammar「文法」については本文で述べられていない。

No.3　日本語が異文化間の共同作業を始めるのに理想的な場所である理由は，第2段落3文目のbecause以下に書かれている。「日本は産業化して，ヨーロッパ文化と共通点が多い社会だが，子育てや感情表現のやり方が異なり，また言葉(日本語)は，その歴史や構造がインド＝ヨーロッパ語族とは非常に異なる」という部分から判断する。

4　No.1　男性の発言にwhy Emily was angry?とあり過去の出来事を話題にしているので，must have been「～だったに違いない」と過去の出来事を推量している。haveの[h]音は小さく弱く言われたり，言われなかったりして，must haveは[t]と[æ]音がくっついて「マスタブ」のように聞こえ，have beenの[v]音と[b]音は類似音なので[v]音が消えて「マスタビーン」のように聞こえる。　No.2　for it would beはforの[r]音とitの[t]音がくっつき，wouldの[d]音とbeの[e]音が続いて「フォリット(ゥ)ウビ」のように聞こえるので，wouldを聞き逃さないように注意しよう。「ピアノにとって一番いい場所はベッドの向かいの(部屋の)隅」という意味。

【2】1　ウ　　2　エ　　3　ウ　　4　ア　　5　エ　　6　ア　　7　イ
8　エ　　9　イ　　10　ア　　11　イ　　12　ウ　　13　エ
14　ア　　15　ウ

〈解説〉1　時計が遅れるので，買ったところに持って行って，修理してもらうほうがいいという内容。使役動詞(have)以降でitはmy watchを指す。私の腕時計は「修理する」のではなく「修理される」と考え，repairedと過去分詞にする。　2　extendは「ずっと続く」という意味。文中のコンマ(,)＋doingは付帯状況の分詞構文であることが多い。「語学の学習には長い歴史があり，(そして)何千年以上もずっと続いている」。　3　関係代名詞はふつう直前の名詞を修飾するが，コンマ(,)＋whichは前の文の一部を先行詞にすることがある。「彼は夕食のあと散歩をした」という文の一部が先行詞で，それを「週に1度行われると彼の妻は言っていた」という関係代名詞節が後ろから修飾している。問題文を直訳すると「彼が夕食のあと散歩したとき，それは週に1度行われると彼の妻は言っていたのだが，彼は道路の近くでクマを見た」。　4　(　)＋S＋V ～, S＋V ….という文の構造なので，接続詞ifと同じような使われ方をするsupposeが正解。Suppose that S＋V ～, S＋V ….で「もし～なら，…」という意味。　5　on ～ termsで「～の関係で」という意味。on first-name termsで「ごく親しい関係で(ファーストネームで呼び合う間柄で)」という意味。　6　a fewは「2，3の」という意味だが，quite a fewで「かなり多くの」という意味。英文は「悪天候にも関わらず，かなりの人がコンサートにやって来た。大きいホールはファンで埋まった」。ウのquite a littleは不可算名詞に使い，「多量の，かなり多くの」という意味。エはa large number ofなら「多くの」という意味で正解。　7　wishを使った仮定法の文。1文目I didn't know ～ English.には「(その時)私は英語で駅への道を聞かれたとき，何と言ったらよいかわからなかった」と残念に思った過去の事実がある。この事実に反して，「英語を知っていたらよかったのに」と願望するのでI wish以下は仮定法過去の文にする。たとえば「1週間前に，英語がわからなくて道案内ができなかったことを，昨日すまなく思った」のなら，すまなく思ったことよりももっと前に英語がわからなかったので，I was sorry I hadn't known English.「(1週間前に)英語を知らなかったことを(昨日)すまなく思った」と，時制がずれるときは I wished I had known English.と仮定法過去完了にする。　8　thesaurus「類義語辞典」の意味を問われているので，エの「類義語」が正解。アは「対義語」という意味で原形はantonym，イは「擬音(声)語」という意味で原形はonomatopoeia，ウは「換喩」という意味で原形はmetonymy。
9　catch onで「流行する」という意味。　10　keep ～ companyで「～と一緒にいる」という意味。　11「高校に通うことは～ではないが，今日ほとんどの学生が中学を卒業するとそこへ行く」とあり，義務教育のことを述べているのでイ「義務の」が正解。ア「従順な」，ウ「比較による」，エ「自己満足の」。　12「講師はとても速く話したので私は彼の言うことを理解できなかった」という意味。空欄の直後にinがあるのでウのtake in「理解する」が正解。アはfigure outなら正解。イはinがなくfollowだけなら正解。エはmake outなら正解。　13　空欄直後のso thatは目的を表し，以下に「私たちがあなたを人ごみの中で容易に見つけられるようにするために」とあるので，「目立つものを着てください」と考え，エconspicuous「目立った」にする。ア「傷つきやすい」，イ「はびこっている」，ウ「不安定な」。　14　空欄の直後にin onがあるので，zero in on「～に専念する」にする。英文は「我々の会社はもっと利益を出すために有望な市場に専念する計画でいる」の意味。　15　because以降は「それは科学的に証明されていなかったので」。前半は「植物はコミュニケーションできるという考えは，以前は(　　)だと思われていた」となるので，ウ「誤った推論に基づく」が入る。ア「犯罪学の」，イ「気難しい」，エ「残忍な」。

【3】1　①　エ　　②　イ　　③　ウ　　2　人を食べるような化け物が，妻を連れて旅をするとは思っていなかったから。　　3　自国に戻れば，筆者が物を買うのにたくさんのお金が必要になると思ったから。　4　不足という考え方は，安定した必要最小限の生活を営む社会では，産業主義で特徴づけられた社会ほど進んでいない。　　5　(1)　They were friendly and hospitable.　　(2)　No, he doesn't.　　6　エ

〈解説〉1　①　retreatは文脈から戸口へ「退く，逃げる」という意味。ア「断る」，イ「明らかにする」，ウ「そむく」，エ「退く」。

②　summonは文脈から勇気を「奮い立たせる」という意味。ア「解散させる」，イ「(勇気などを)奮い起こす」，ウ「占有する」，エ「命令する」。　③　inquisitiveは文脈から「好奇心の強い」という意味。ア「退屈な」，イ「無関心な」，ウ「好奇心が強い」，エ「活発な」。

2　筆者は肌の色が淡く背が高いので，人を食べる*mpakafo*と特徴が似ていた。しかし，第2段落の最後の文に「そのような化け物(*mpakafo*)は妻と旅をしないことが周知の事実」とあり，妻とともにやって来て，一緒に生活しているので，ベツィレウ族の人々は納得したのである。

3　下線部(2)は「私たちがアメリカに戻ると，どのようになるのだろうか，と彼ら(イヴァトの長老たち)は思った」とあり，実際にどう思っていたか第6段落6文目のThey commented以下に，「あなたたちが自分の国(アメリカ)に戻ると，車や衣類や食料などを買う金がたくさん必要だろう」とコメントしていることから判断する。　4　第6段落7文目以降に「私たちはそれらのもの(車や衣類や食料など)を買う必要はない。私たちは使うものはほとんどすべて作る。私たちは自分たち

で作るので，あなたたちほど金は必要ない」とあり，これをもっと大きな視点から述べた英文である。下線部の英文はin stable subsistence-oriented societies「安定した必要最小限の生活を営む社会」とin the societies characterized by industrialism「産業主義で特徴づけられた社会」を比較している。more developedではなくless developedなので「より進んでいない」という意味になる。muchは比較級を強めて「はるかに」。
5　(1)　問いは「筆者とその妻が初めて訪れたとき，イヴァトの人たち(イヴァト村に住むベツィレウ族)はどうだったか」。第3段落1，2文目「イヴァトを訪れたとき，そこの人々は違っているとわかった。彼らは友好的で親切にもてなしてくれた」とあることから判断する。
(2)　問いは「ベツィレウ族は文化人類学を学んだ人々にとって注目に値する例だと筆者は思っているか」。第7段落1文目に「ベツィレウ族は文化人類学者たちが研究した人たちの中で珍しい部族ではない」とあり，ほかの例とあまり変わらないことが言われている。
6　ア　英文は「筆者と彼の妻がマダガスカルに到着するとすぐにその国の国会議員に会った」。第1段落2文目に「到着するとすぐに私たちの研究に関心をもっている2人の教養のある学校の先生に会った」とあり，一致しない。　イ　英文は「筆者はほかの多くの村へ行き，そこで温かい歓迎を受けた」。第2段落1文目に「私たちはほかの多くの村へ行き，そこの接待にしばしば不快な思いをした」とあり，一致しない。　ウ　英文は「筆者が強力なスポンサーになることを約束したので，イヴァト村に住むベツィレウ族は喜んで筆者と話をしてくれた」。第4段落1文目に「私(筆者)にはイヴァト村に住むベツィレウ族が自分たちを守ってくれる，外の世界で成功した村出身者の有力なスポンサーがいたので，彼らは喜んで話してくれた」とあり，一致しない。
エ　英文は「筆者が訪問に同意したそれぞれの村の1世帯だけで，(研究対象への)インタビューを行った」。これは第5段落の最後から2文目の内容と一致する。　オ　英文は「筆者によると，不足(という考え)は社会によって決まるという経済学者の考えは普遍的である」。第7段落3文目に「ベツィレウ族から得た教訓は，経済学者は不足(という考え)を普遍的なものだと考えているが，定まらないものであるということだ」とあり，一致しない。

【中学校】

【1】1 ① エ ② イ ③ ア 2 生徒が使える語彙は限定されており，職業上の技能や経験，娯楽における興味を表現することができずにフラストレーションを経験していると感じたから。
3 新しい語彙を紹介することを目的に，創意工夫あふれるプレゼンテーションを行った。 4 生徒が，個別の学習を通じて伸ばしたい特定の語彙の分野を選択したこと。 5 (1) She encouraged the students to go outside the classroom for their projects. (2) It requires trusting the students to use their time effectively. 6 ア，ウ

〈解説〉1 ① competentは生徒が英語全般で「能力のある」という意味なので，エ「満足のいく基準まで行動をするための十分な技術や知識をもっている」が正解。ア「ほかの人や企業よりも成功すると決めているかあるいはその能力のある」，イ「問題を引き起こすことなく一緒に存在できるか使われることができる」，ウ「とてもおもしろく刺激的なので注目しなければならない」。 ② appropriateは特殊目的のための英語学習においてという文脈において「適切で」役に立つ単語，という意味になるので，イ「特定の時間や状況，目的に対し正しかったり，適切である」が正解。ア「あることに対し支持や同意を示すこと」，ウ「言及するのに十分特別であったり重要な」，エ「あることを行う権利がないが独り占めすること」。 ③ clausesは「(主語と動詞からなる意味のまとまりである)節」という意味なので，ア「主語と動詞を含むが，通常は文の一部である語のグループ」が正解。イ「本動詞はなく，文の一部を形成するために使われる語のグループ」，
ウ「大文字で始まり，ピリオドで終わる語のグループ」，エ「それぞれの語の通常の意味とは違う特別な意味をもつ語のグループ」。
2 Cherylが彼女の生徒が特殊目的のための英語学習を個人化する(個人の要望に合わせて作る)ことに役立つ指導プログラムを開発したいと

考えた理由は，続く文のbecause以下に述べられているので，日本語を適切に用いてまとめる。　3　下線部(2)以下の文には「クラスでほかの生徒に課題の発表を行う4番目の教室のセッション」とあり，直後のThe presentations ～以降にプレゼンテーションをdisplay their new vocabulary「新しい語彙を表示する」とshowed a great deal of inventiveness「たくさんの創意工夫を示した」のように行ったとある。
4　第7段落1文目に「彼女(Cheryl)の新しい指導方法では，生徒が出発点と戦略を与えられれば特殊目的のための英語に合う語彙を伸ばす責任を持つことでもっと自信が出る」とある。第1段落で，Cherylは特殊目的のための英語の学習を個人化する(個人の要望に合わせて作る)ことに役立つ指導プログラムを開発したがっていたとある。第2段落1文目で「Cherylは自分のクラスで，生徒が自分で選択した話題の語彙を伸ばすことを可能にする指導方法を採用した」とあり，続く2文目で「「最初に」生徒は個別の学習を通して伸ばしたい特定の語彙の分野を選択した」とあるので，これが出発点(a starting point)になる。
5　(1)　質問は「生徒が地域社会の中にある補助教材を使うためにCherylは何をしたか」。第3段落3文目に「彼女は生徒に学習課題のために教室から外に出るよう仕向け，そうすることで生徒は地域社会の中にある補助教材も使用した」とあることから判断する。
(2)　質問は「Cherylの結論によると，ESPは何を一番必要とするか」。第7段落2文目にShe concluded that とあり後半にand, above all「そしてとりわけ」とあるのでこれ以降が一番必要なことだと考える。
6　ア　英文は「Cherylは生徒がアクセスできるいろいろな補助教材を用意し，彼らをサポートした」。第2段落3文目に「生徒が補助教材にアクセスできるようにした」とあり，4文目に具体的な補助教材が書かれているので，一致する。　イ　英文は「3番目の教室のセッションでは生徒はみんなお互いが学べるように語彙を示した」。第5段落1文目に「生徒が彼らの課題(特殊目的のための英語用に集めた語彙)をクラスのほかの生徒に発表する4番目の教室のセッション」とあり，3番目ではないので一致しない。　ウ　英文は「プログラムでは，生徒は自分の目標を設定し，自分の学習に責任を持った」。第2段落6文目に「Cherylは生徒に自分の学習に責任を持ってもらい，どの単語が適切で役に立つか評価するための自己監視方法を確立することを望んでいた」とあり，一致する。　エ　英文は「生徒は同じ職業をのぞむので，興味は似ている」。第4段落1文目に「特殊目的のための英語の関心は生徒によって違い，個人的あるいは職業的な関心に基づいていた」とあり，一致しない。　オ　英文は「Cherylは生徒がプログラムについて何を思っているのか知るためにアンケートを使用した」。第6段落の2文目に「Cherylはまた生徒たちが新しい語彙をどこで手に入れたか調査するためにアンケートも使用した」とあり，アンケートの目的が一致しない。

【2】1　The more I realize I don't know, the more I want to learn.

2　First evaluate the attitude of students. Check if they are afraid of the mistakes they make while speaking English and they speak clearly with appropriate volume of voice to make themselves understood well. Secondly evaluate their pronunciation and usage of grammar and words. Students should pay attention to pronouncing individual sounds and linking words and using the proper rhythm and intonation. And form grammatically correct sentences and use fillers to make their speech easy to understand. Finally evaluate the content of speech. Well-organized content helps students to express their ideas and opinions effectively in English. They should also have knowledge of cultural background of the topic given.　(107語)

〈解説〉1 「自分の無知にたくさん気がつけば気がつくほど，よりたくさん学びたくなる」と考え，the＋比較級，the＋比較級の文にする。自分の無知は「私は(ものを)知らない」と考え，I don't knowにする。前半はThe more I realize (that) I don't knowで表せる。「より一層学ぶ」は「もっとたくさん学ぶ」と考え the more I want to learn.で表せる。

2 「中学校学習指導要領解説外国語編」(平成20年7月)では，「与えられたテーマについて簡単なスピーチをすること」について，「学校や日常生活などで体験したことや自分の夢など，生徒の学習段階や興味・関心に合わせて，適切なテーマを与えることが大切である。また，絵や実物を示して聞き手の理解を容易にするなどの工夫をさせることも考えられる」としている。このことを踏まえながら作成する。また，「評価規準の作成，評価方法等の工夫改善のための参考資料(中学校外国語)」(平成23年7月　国立教育政策研究所教育課程研究センター)などを参照しながら，評価の手順についての理解を深めておきたい。

【高等学校】

【1】1 ① ウ　② エ　③ イ　2 ウ　3 利点1 タスクの背後にある仮説やそれを実行するのに使われる手順を考察することができる。　利点2 タスクが意図したように働いているかどうか，またさらにその後にどのように改善できるかを経験的に考察することができる。　4 (1) It was obesity.　(2) She collected a variety of data.　5 ア

〈解説〉1 第2段落2文目に「それぞれの取り組みにはそれぞれ異なるデータが必要である」とあり，空欄にどういうデータが必要なのか言われる。 ①「生徒を中心とした評価」に必要なデータとして，生徒自らが参加して答える(自己申告する)と考え，ウ「アンケートや面接，フォーカスグループによる議論などの自己申告の手段を用いて行われることが可能だ」が正解。 ②「応答を中心とした評価」は第2段落1文目のresponse-based evaluationに続く(　)内に「評価者は意図したパフォーマンスや結果をタスクが引き出したかどうか決めようとする」とあるので，その引き出されたもの(応答)を観察・記録したものがデータだと考え，エ「学習者のタスクのパフォーマンスを観察・記録すること，また(タスクの結果から生じる)成果物の分析を必要とする」が正解。 ③「知識中心の評価」は，第2段落1文目のlearning-based evaluationに続く(　)内に「評価者はタスクが結果として知識になったかどうかを調べる」とあるので，知識が身に付いたかどうかタスクの前と後にテストをしてその結果がデータだと考え，イ「第二言語を

使用する学習者の能力にいつ何か変化が起こるかを判定するために事前・事後テストを必要とする」が正解。　2　ア　英文は「生徒はおおむね英文復元練習のタスクでテキストの再構築をすることに成功した」。第5段落2文目のFreemanが結論づけたものの最初にthe students were largely successful in achieving the outcome of the task (the reconstruction of the text)があり一致する。　イ　英文は「目標の言語構造と言語形式を気づかせることに成功した」。第5段落2文目のFreemanの結論の2つ目にthe task was successful in inducing noticing of the target formsとあり，一致する。　ウ　英文は「書き取ったものを(他の)生徒と共有させることで交流の質と量を減らした」。これは第5段落5文目にあるFreemanの知見である。　エ　英文は「そのタスクは言語の他の側面への注目を促し，積極的に関わるようになった」。第5段落2文目の結論の最後にalso encouraged attendance to other aspects of language, and led to active engagementとあり，一致する。　3　第6段落4文目に「ミクロ的評価は教師が，タスクの(設計の)背後にある仮説やそれを実行するのに使われる手順を考察するのに役立つ」とあり，教師にとっての利点と考えられる。また5文目に「ミクロ的評価は，タスクが意図したように働いているかどうか，また将来使うために改善できるかどうか経験的に考察することによって，教師が印象に基づく評価を超えることを必要とする」とあり，教師が自分の印象ではなく，データに基づいて生徒を評価できるので利点だと考えられる。

4　(1)　問いは「Freemanの英文復元練習のタスクで生徒が聞き取るよう求められているテキストのトピックは何だったか」。第4段落2文目に「これ(英文復元練習のタスク)は生徒が肥満という主題の9文からなるリスニングテキストを聞き取ることを求める」とあり，obesity「肥満」であることがわかる。　(2)「アカウンタビリティ(タスクやコースがどのくらい目標を達成するかという程度)と改善という点で，Freemanの評価が適切に作られているかどうか考察するために彼女は何をしたか」。第4段落8文目に「この目的(アカウンタビリティを作り，タスクの改善のしかたに関する情報を提供することの両方)のために彼女(Freeman)はさまざまなデータを集めた」とあることから判断する。
5　ア　英文は「ミクロ的評価とマクロ的評価の両方の評価はタスクやコースがいかに改善されるかに対して行われる」。これは第4段落7文目の内容と一致する。　イ　英文は「何年もの間，筆者は高校生に授業で様々なタスクを行うように求めてきた」。この記述はない。　ウ　英文は「タスクを詳細に分析することを通して，学んだことを示すことは不可能かも知れないと筆者は考えている」。この記述はない。　エ　英文は「タスクの2回目に生徒はテキストを再構築するために3人のグループで作業しなければならなかった」。第4段落5文目に「生徒はそれから(テキストを3回聞いたあと)テキストを再構築するために3人のグループで作業した」とあり，テキストを3回聞いたあとにするので，一致しない。　オ　英文は「生徒たちが議論のなかで行う交流が重要語句を書き取ることに役立つ」。第5段落5文目に「生徒が書き取ったものを共有させることで交流の量や質を減少させた」とあるが，交流が重要語句を書き取ることに役立つという記述はない。

【２】1　The more I realize I don’t know, the more I want to learn.
2　Integrating the four skills of English in teaching means to develop students’ abilities such as listening, speaking, reading and writing, so that they can communicate through speaking and writing, the knowledge acquired through listening and reading, combined with their experiences and ideas. In class, I have students do dictogloss activities. I prepare and read the short, topic-based text to the students and have them listen and take notes. And then I have students form groups of two to four and share their notes. After reading the text a final time, they make a final written version of the text as close to the original as possible.　(106語)
〈解説〉1「自分の無知にたくさん気がつけば気がつくほど，よりたくさん学びたくなる」と考え，the＋比較級，the＋比較級の文にする。自分の無知は「私は(ものを)知らない」と考え，I don’t knowにする。前半はThe more I realize (that) I don’t knowで表せる。「より一層学ぶ」は

「もっとたくさん学ぶ」と考え the more I want to learn.で表せる。

2　現実の言語の使用場面では,「聞くこと」,「話すこと」,「読むこと」,「書くこと」の4技能は，おのずと有機的な関連をもっている。そのため，自然で円滑なコミュニケーションを反映して，4技能を有機的に結び付けバランスよく指導することで，社会生活において外国語を活用できるようにすることが求められる。学習指導要領に関する英作文の問題については，自分で様々な指導場面を想定し，どのような根拠に基づき指導し，具体的にどのような手順で行っていくかを英文でまとめる練習を重ねるとよいだろう。

2015年度　実施問題

【中高共通】

【1】(放送による問題)これはリスニング・テストです。放送の指示に従って答えなさい。

[トラック1]

[試聴用英文(約3分間)]

ただいまから，試聴用の英文を約3分間流します。そのあとでチャイムが鳴りますから，そこでCDを止めてください。

(試聴用の英文)

＜チャイム連続音＞

(空白1分間)

[トラック2]

(問題)

＜チャイム連続音＞

ただいまから，リスニング・テストを行います。問題は1，2，3，4の四つです。聞いている間にメモを取っても構いません。

(間2秒)

では，1の問題から始めます。問題はNo.1とNo.2の2問です。

これから読まれる英文に対する応答として最も ふさわしいものを，続いて読まれる(a)，(b)，(c)の中から一つ選び，記号で答えなさい。なお，英文と応答は1度しか読まれません。

(間2秒)

では，始めます。

No.1　Did you hear that Kate will be transferred to Boston?

(a)　Yes, she likes traveling very much.

(b)　Yes, she told me about it yesterday.

(c) No, she has been there twice.

(間5秒)

No.2 How will Mike get to the meeting tomorrow?

(a) He went there by train.

(b) He will drop in at his office.

(c) He said he would drive there.

(間7秒)

＜チャイム＞

次に，2の問題に移ります。問題は，No.1からNo.3までの3問です。

これから，短い対話文を読みます。そのあとでクエスチョンと言って質問します。その答えとして最もふさわしいものを，続いて読まれる(a)，(b)，(c)，(d)の中から一つ選び，記号で答えなさい。なお，対話文・質問・答えの選択肢は1度しか読まれません。

(間2秒)

では，始めます。

No.1

W: My boss gave me a new assignment in Europe, so I'm leaving for Milan on the 13th.

M: Are you packed and ready to go?

W: Oh, I usually get around to packing my bags the day before I go. It's better for me that way. I'm always changing my mind about what to bring. Actually, I'm still waiting to find out about my accommodations.

M: Good luck!

Question : When will the woman pack her bags?

(a) On the 12th.

(b) On the 13th.

(c) On the 29th.

(d) On the 30th.

(間4秒)

No.2

Yoko : I've decided what to do during my vacation. I usually travel to China and Korea, but this year I decided to go to India.

Sara : That's wonderful, Yoko. I was thinking about spending my vacation in Hawaii. But I would love to visit India. Is it expensive to go there?

Yoko : No, not at all, Sara. Why don't we go together?

Sara : That sounds great. I'll contact the travel agency and see if it's not too late to book the trip.

Question : What will Sara most likely do next?

(a) She will fly to Hawaii with Yoko.

(b) She will buy a ticket to Korea.

(c) She will call the travel agent.

(d) She will go to a bookshop.

(間4秒)

No. 3

M: I'd like to return this book and borrow another one today.

W: I can't lend you any books today. As you know, if you keep a book beyond its due date, your borrowing privileges are suspended.

M: I'm sorry, but I had to go to my friend's party yesterday. I'd like you to make an exception to the rule. It's only one day late and I really need to borrow this book.

W: No, we can't make any exceptions. Your borrowing privileges have been suspended for five days.

Question: Who is the man talking to?

(a) He is talking to a bookstore clerk.

(b) He is talking to a businessperson.

(c) He is talking to a rental shop owner.

(d) He is talking to a librarian.

(間7秒)

＜チャイム＞

次に3の問題に移ります。問題は，No.1からNo.3までの3問です。

これから，あるまとまりのある英文を読みます。そのあとで，クエスチョンと言って，その英文について三つの質問をします。その答えとして最もふさわしいものを，質問に続いて読まれる(a)，(b)，(c)，(d)の中から一つ選び，記号で答えなさい。なお，英文・質問・答えの選択肢は全体を通して2回読まれます。

(間12秒)

では，始めます。

The World Heritage Committee of UNESCO decided to inscribe Mount Fuji on the U.N. agency's prestigious World Heritage list in June 2013.

The 3,776-meter volcano straddling Yamanashi and Shizuoka prefectures was approved by the 21-member panel of UNESCO during its 37th session in Cambodia's capital.

Japan's highest and most celebrated peak, a shrine, five major lakes, waterfalls, and a pine grove were designated "cultural" rather than "natural" sites and registered under the title "Mt. Fuji: Object of Worship, Wellspring of Art."

Japan asked UNESCO to register Mount Fuji in January 2012 because it has been viewed as a religious site, depicted in many paintings and helped nurture Japan's unique culture.

The UNESCO panel dubbed ICOMOS, the International Council on Monuments and Sites, recommended in April that Mount Fuji be listed but without the pine grove, which is a distant 45 km away.

However, the panel had a change of heart.

Residents and officials had earlier attempted to register Mount Fuji as a natural World Heritage site but were thwarted by the illegal dumping of garbage and the fact that the peak lacks global uniqueness as a volcanic mountain.

It was dropped from consideration in 2003.

In 2012, Japan formally asked UNESCO to add Mount Fuji to the list of cultural World Heritage sites in consideration of its religious significance and repeated depictions in works of art.

ICOMOS then recommended Mount Fuji for registration in April, noting that it is a national symbol of Japan, blends religious and artistic traditions, and has an influence that "clearly goes beyond Japan."

(間3秒)

Question

No.1　When did Japan ask UNESCO to register Mount Fuji as a cultural World Heritage site?

(a)　In January 2012.

(b)　In April 2012.

(c) In March 2013.

(d) In June 2013.

(間3秒)

No. 2 Why wasn't Mount Fuji registered as a natural World Heritage site in 2003?

(a) Because it didn't have religious significance and repeated depictions in works of art.

(b) Because residents and officials didn't make enough effort to register Mount Fuji.

(c) Because it was considered as a cultural World Heritage site rather than a natural site.

(d) Because garbage was dumped there illegally and the peak lacked uniqueness as a volcanic mountain.

(間3秒)

No. 3 Why did ICOMOS recommend Mount Fuji for registration this time?

(a) Because it viewed Mount Fuji as Japan's highest and most beautiful mountain.

(b) Because it noted that Mount Fuji has both religious and artistic traditions.

(c) Because it regarded Mount Fuji as a symbol of Japan and the world.

(d) Because it found that many people went to Mount Fuji to clean it.

(間3秒)

くりかえします。

〈略〉

(間6秒)

＜チャイム＞

次に4の問題に移ります。問題はNo.1とNo.2の2問です。これから，英語による対話文を読みます。(　　)のところに入る英語を聞き取り，書きなさい。対話文はそれぞれ2回読まれます。

(間2秒)

では，始めます。

No.1
W: What's wrong, Mark?
M: To tell the truth, (I have a sharp pain in my neck) now.

(間10秒)

くりかえします。
〈略〉

(間10秒)

No. 2
M: Why don't you go to the basketball game next Saturday, Susan? The basketball players are so nice and cool!
W: Well, they move so fast and (I always end it too difficult to follow them).

(間10秒)

くりかえします。
〈略〉

(間10秒)

<チャイム連続音>

これで，リスニング・テストを終わります。次の問題に移ってください。

(☆☆◎◎◎)

【2】次の英文や対話文の中の(　　)に最も適するものを，下のア～エからそれぞれ一つずつ選び，記号で答えなさい。

1　What do you say to (　　) the British Museum while we stay in London?
　ア　visit　　イ visiting　　ウ　being visiting　　エ　having visited

2　There are some cases (　　) the rule doesn't hold.
　ア　which　　イ　where　　ウ　whose　　エ　whom

3　The room was a complete mess but she (　　) making it look as good as new.
　ア　set about　　イ　came about　　ウ　blew about
　エ　had about

4　The fossils (　　) near my house are recognized as being the direct ancestors of modern humans.
　ア　finding　　イ　are found　　ウ　found　　エ　to find

5　A: Do you know the (　　) form of "phenomenon"?
　B: Sure. It's "phenomena."
　ア　singular　　イ　monotonous　　ウ　plural　　エ　numerous

6　A: Did everything go all right at the conference?

B: Yes, the whole thing worked like a (　　).

ア　luck　　イ　fortune　　ウ　happiness　　エ　dream

7　Who do you think (　　) yesterday?

ア　it was that I met　　イ　was it that I met　　ウ　was he who I met

エ　he was who I have met

8　She (　　) me into going jogging every day before work.

ア　stopped　　イ　talked　　ウ　made　　エ　had

9　It is said that corn is the most predominant crop used for biofuels in the U.S. (　　) rapeseed being the most common in the U.K. and Europe.

ア　by　　イ　on　　ウ　with　　エ　at

10　This species of animal is on the (　　) of extinction.

ア　verge　　イ　account　　ウ　step　　エ　extent

11　A: Did you manage to get that car you wanted for a lower price?

B: Yes, the dealer (　　) 10% off the price because I offered to pay cash.

ア　kicked　　イ　punched　　ウ　knocked　　エ　hit

12　(　　) is the branch of linguistics that deals with the system of sound of a particular language.

ア　Morphology　　イ　Stylistics　　ウ　Etymology

エ　Phonetics

13　I'm afraid a Japanese driver's license is not (　　) here. You can't drive a car.

ア　ominous　　イ　valid　　ウ　incessant　　エ　profound

14　The baseball game was called off because of the (　　) weather.

ア　inclement　　イ　immaculate　　ウ　mundane　　エ　docile

15　It is important to be wary of any emails (　　) personal information.

ア　solidifying　　イ　solacing　　ウ　sojourning　　エ　soliciting

(☆☆◎◎◎)

【3】次の英文を読んで，あとの問いに答えなさい。

The great conservationist Rachel Carson, who summed up what was known about the blue part of the planet in her 1951 book, *The Sea Around Us,* was unaware that continents move around at a stately geological pace or that the greatest mountain chains, deepest valleys, broadest plains, and most of life on Earth are in the ocean. Nor did she appreciate that technological advances developed for wartime applications were being mobilized to find, catch, and market ocean wildlife on an unprecedented scale, reaching distant, deep parts of the ocean no hook or net or trawl had ever touched before.

"Eventually man ... found his way back to the sea," she wrote. "And yet he has returned to his mother sea only on her terms. He cannot control or change the ocean as, in his brief tenancy of earth, he has subdued and plundered the continents."

In her lifetime－1907 to 1964－she did not, could not, know about the most significant discovery concerning the ocean: it is not too big to fail. Fifty years ago, we could not see limits to what we could put into the ocean or what we could take out. Fifty years into the future, it will be too late to do what is possible right now. We are in a "sweet spot" in time. (1) Never again will there be a better time to take actions that can ensure an enduring place for ourselves within the living systems that sustain us. We are at an unprecedented, pivotal point in history, when the decisions we make in the next ten years will (　①　) the direction of the next ten thousand.

[　　　　　　　　　　A　　　　　　　　　　]

(2) "If I could be anywhere... anywhere right now, I would want to be here," croons the singer-songwriter Jackson Browne in a lilting tune he composed in 2010. Why here?　Why now?　Where would you choose, given the power to live on Mars, slip into the future, or glide back decades, centuries, or even millions or billions of years from our "here on Earth" and the twenty-first century's now?

[　　　　　　　　　　B　　　　　　　　　　]

Why not escape to Mars?　Or leap back or forward in time?

Before the middle of this century, a few astronauts likely will be setting up housekeeping on the red planet, but they will have to take along a life-support system. Water is scarce, and it is the single nonnegotiable thing all life requires. The atmosphere on Mars is about 95 percent carbon dioxide and therefore (②) to humans (much like Earth's atmosphere in her early years), the temperature averages around -55 degrees centigrade (-67 degrees Fahrenheit). Food, shelter, clothing?　Better pack them along and, somehow, find water. Perversely, at the same time some are doing their utmost to make the red planet more like the blue one, a process called "terraforming," we seem to be doing all we can to (3)<u>"Marsiform" Earth</u>. Human actions here on the blue planet have caused the abundance and diversity of life, along with the potable fresh water supply, to decrease, while carbon dioxide is increasing.

[　　　　　　　　　　　　　C　　　　　　　　　　　　　]

Earthlings take for granted that the world is blue, embraced by an ocean that harbors most of the life on the planet, contains 97 percent of the water, drives climate and weather, stabilizes temperature, generates most of the oxygen in the atmosphere, absorbs much of the carbon dioxide, and otherwise tends to hold the planet steady－a friendly place in a universe of inhospitable options.

[　　　　　　　　　　　　　D　　　　　　　　　　　　　]

Owing to more than 2 billion years of microbial *photosynthetic activity in the sea and several hundred million years of land-based photosynthesis, Earth's atmosphere now is just right for humans－roughly 21 percent of oxygen, 79 percent nitrogen, with trace gases, including just enough carbon dioxide to drive photosynthesis and the continuous production of oxygen and food. Even today, one kind of inconspicuous but enormously abundant sea-dwelling blue-green bacteria, *Prochlorococcus, (③) 20 percent of the oxygen in the atmosphere, thereby supplying one in every five breaths we take. With other planktonic species, as well as seagrasses, mangroves, kelps, and thousands of other kinds of algae, ocean organisms do the heavy lifting in terms of taking up carbon dioxide and water via photosynthesis, producing sugar that drives great ocean food chains, and yielding atmospheric oxygen along the way. As much as 70 percent of the air we breathe is produced by underwater life.

[E]

Should you choose to go back a billion years on Earth, you would find a planet a lot like Mars except for the abundance of water. Life would be mostly microbial. No trees; no flowers or moss or ferns; no bees or bats or birds－a bleak place compared to the great diversity of life that gradually developed, each and every organism doing its part to shape the barren land and seascapes into an increasingly rich and complex living tapestry.

(注) photosynthetic：光合成の　*Prochlorococcus*：プロクロロコッカス(植物プランクトンの一種)

(S.A. Earle, *The Sweet Spot in Time*による。ただし，設問の都合で一部省略および改変している。)

1 下線部(1)を日本語に直しなさい。

2 空欄(①)～(③)について，最もよくあてはまる語句を，次のア～エの中からそれぞれ一つずつ選び，記号で答えなさい.

(①)：ア desert　イ determine　ウ differ　エ digest

(②)：ア lethal　イ secure　ウ essential　エ strict

(③)：ア invented by　イ assimilates into　ウ got rid of　エ churns out

3 次の段落を本文中に入れるとしたら，[A]～[E]のどの位置に入れるのが最も適当か。一つ選び，記号で答えなさい。

Some might say anywhere *but* here and now!　The world today is at war or on the brink of war. Weapons devised by humans can, in a single stroke, eliminate more people than existed on Earth in 1800. Poverty and hunger haunt hundreds of millions. The world economy is deeply troubled. Diseases are rampant. The natural systems that make life on Earth possible are in sharp decline on land, in the atmosphere above, and in the seas below. Earth's natural fabric of life is in shreds, with consequences that threaten our own existence.

4 下線部(2)の歌の一節について，筆者の意見は賛成か，反対か。「賛成」または「反対」のいずれかを記し，その理由を本文に即して日本語で答えなさい。

5 下線部(3)とは，だれが何をどのようにすることか，本文に即して日本語で具体的に説明しなさい。

6 本文の内容と主旨が一致していないものを，次のア～オから一つ選び，記号で答えなさい。

ア Little did Rachel Carson know that technology developed for wartime weapons would also be applied for fishery today.

イ Fifty years ago we were not sure about the important fact that the ocean is not an infinite storehouse for humans.

ウ A life support system will be less important for humans on Mars when the red planet is inhabited in the near future.

エ It is taken as a matter of course that the ocean plays an important role for the environment and the climate of Earth.

オ Underwater flora takes up carbon dioxide through photosynthesis and produces atmospheric oxygen in return.

(☆☆☆◎◎◎)

【中学校】

【1】次の英文を読んで，あとの問いに答えなさい。

*CLIL teachers will have to consider how to actively involve learners to enable them to think through and articulate their own learning. This in turn implies that learners need to be made aware of their own learning through developing metacognitive skills such as 'learning to learn'. Interactive classrooms are typified by group work, student questioning and problem solving. If in a CLIL classroom students are required to cooperate with each other in order to make use of each other's areas of strength and ①compensate for weaknesses, then they must learn how to operate collaboratively and work effectively in groups. Leaving these skills to develop by chance is not an option. Instead, we need to support students in developing life skills such as dealing with the unexpected, observational skills, and constructing knowledge which is built on their interaction with the world, yet purposefully guided by values and convictions (van Lier, 1996).

Therefore, for CLIL teaching to support effective learning, it has to take into account not only the knowledge and skills base, but also cognitive ②engagement by the students. For example, the Queensland School Reform Longitudinal Study(1998-2000) reported on the need to (1)'shift teachers' attention and focus beyond basic skills to key aspects of higher-order thinking ... towards more productive pedagogies' (Department of Education, Queensland, 2002: 1). Evidence showed that, to raise achievement levels, learners had to be intellectually challenged in order to transform information and ideas, to solve problems, to gain understanding and to discover new meaning. (2) Effective content learning has to take account not only of the defined knowledge and skills within the curriculum, but also how to apply these through creative thinking, problem solving and cognitive challenge. Young people not only need a knowledge base which is continually growing and changing, they also need to know how to use it throughout life. They need to know how to think, to reason, to make informed choices and to respond creatively to challenges and opportunities. They need to be skilled in problem solving and higher-order, creative thinking, in order to construct a framework through which to interpret meaning and understanding: "If learning is to be retained and to be readily available for use, then learners must make their own construction of knowledge－make it their own－and must learn to take responsibility for the management of their own learning" Nisbet, 1991:27).

So what is a thinking curriculum for CLIL? If the previous arguments about the importance of cognitive engagement are central to the CLIL classroom, it is not enough to consider content learning without integrating the development of a range of thinking and problem-solving skills. Since the publication of Bloom's taxonomy outlining six different thinking processes in 1956, the categorisation of different types of thinking has been the subject of great debate (McGuinness, 1999). In 2001, Anderson and Krathwohl published an updated version of Bloom's taxonomy by adding a 'knowledge' dimension to Bloom's 'cognitive process' dimension. This ③transparent connecting of thinking processes to knowledge construction resonates with conceptualizing content learning in the CLIL setting. The cognitive process dimension consists of lower-order thinking (remembering, understanding and applying) and higher-order thinking (analysing, evaluating and creating), both of which are integral to effective learning. The knowledge dimension provides a framework for exploring the demands of different types of knowledge: conceptual, procedural and metacognitive.

Other theorists have subsequently continued to develop the idea of taxonomies for different types of thinking (Marzano, 2000). However, the important point is not the choice of taxonomy, but rather the transparent identification of the cognitive and knowledge processes associated with the CLIL content. This is essential not only to ensure that all learners have access to developing these processes, but crucially that they also have the language needed to do so.

(注)　CLIL : Content and Language Integrated Learning　内容言語統合型学習

(D. Coyle, P. Hood, D. Marsh, *CLIL Content and Language Integrated Learning*による。ただし，設問の都合で一部省略および改変している。)

1　下線部①～③の英語の定義として最もよくあてはまるものを，次のア～エの中からそれぞれ一つずつ選び，記号で答えなさい。

①　ア　to reduce something and fit it into a smaller space or amount of time

イ　to provide something good to balance or reduce the bad effects of damage, loss, etc.

ウ　to examine people or things to see how they are similar and how they are different

エ　to produce a book, list, report, etc. by bringing together different items, articles, etc.

② ア　the final part of a word, constituting a grammatical inflection

イ　the gradual acquisition of the norms of a culture or group

ウ　the surrounding or conditions in which a person, animal, or plant lives

エ　the action of being involved with something in an attempt to understand it

③ ア　being plain and easy to recognize, understand, perceive or detect

イ　going beyond the limits of human knowledge, experience or reason

ウ　denoting, or dealing with states of consciousness beyond the limits of personal identity

エ　operating in or between many different countries, without being based in any particular one

2　筆者は，CLILでは，認知の過程には六つの思考力の段階があるとしている。それらはどのように二つに分類されるか，本文に即して日本語で説明しなさい。

3　下線部(1)によれば，2の思考力に配慮し，教員はどのような順序で単元を構成していくべきか，日本語で説明しなさい。

4　下線部(2)を日本語に直しなさい。

5　本文の内容に即して，次の質問に英語で答えなさい。

(1)　Instead of leaving skills such as operating collaboratively to develop unexpectedly, what do we need to do?

(2)　What provides a framework for exploring conceptual, procedural and metacognitive knowledge ?

6　本文の内容に合うものを，次のア～オから二つ選び，記号で答えなさい。

ア　Considering how to actively involve learners to enable them to think through and articulate their own learning should be needed for CLIL teachers.

イ　In order to transform information and ideas, to solve problems, to gain understanding and to discover new meaning, learners didn't have to be intellectually challenged.

ウ　Young people have to know how to think, to reason, to make informed choices and to respond creatively to challenges and opportunities.

エ　It is enough to consider content learning without integrating the development of a range of thinking and problem-solving skills in the CLIL classroom.

オ　The transparent identification of the cognitive and knowledge processes including the CLIL content is less important than the choice of taxonomy.

(☆☆☆◎◎◎)

【2】次の1，2について，指示に従って答えなさい.

1　次の日本語を英語に直しなさい。

教育とは，世界を変えるために用いることができる，最も強力な武器である。

2　平成23年6月に「外国語能力の向上に関する検討会」がとりまとめた「国際共通語としての英語力向上のための5つの提言と具体的施策」において，各中・高等学校が，学習指導要領に基づき，生徒に求められる英語力を達成するための学習到達目標を「CAN-DOリスト」の形で設定することが求められました。「CAN-DOリスト」とはどのようなものか説明し，それをどのように活用するか，100語程度の英語で書きなさい。ただし，語数には，カンマやピリオド等の句読点，疑問符や引用符等の記号は含まないものとします。なお，解答の総語数を記入すること。

(☆☆☆☆◎◎◎)

【高等学校】

【1】次の英文を読んで，あとの問いに答えなさい。

Swain's (1985) output hypothesis has been influential in clarifying the role of speaking and writing in second language learning. As its name suggests, the output hypothesis was initially formulated as a reaction to Krashen's (1985) input hypothesis and the inadequacy of the input hypothesis in explaining the effects of immersion education. "Put most simply, the output hypothesis claims that the act of producing language (speaking and writing) constitutes, under certain circumstances, part of the process of second language learning" (Swain, 2005). The opportunities that output provides for learning, however, are not exactly the same as those provided by input. Swain (1995) suggests three functions for output : ①the noticing/triggering function, ②the hypothesis testing function, and ③the metalinguistic (reflective) function.

The noticing/triggering function occurs when learners are attempting to produce the second language and they consciously notice gaps in their knowledge. That is, they do not know how to say what they want to say. Izumi's (2002) research indicates that the effect on acquisition of noticing a gap through output was significantly greater than the effect of noticing through input. This effect can be explained in two ways. First, (1) productive learning involves having to search for and produce a word form, whereas receptive learning involves having to find a meaning for a word form. Productive learning typically results in more and stronger knowledge than receptive learning (Griffin and Harley, 1996). Second, generative use involves meeting or using previously met language items in ways that they have not been used or met before and produces deeper learning than the simple retrieval of previously met items (Joe, 1998). Izumi (2002) suggests that the grammatical encoding that is required by output forces learners to integrate the new items into a more cohesive structure. Decoding items from input does not require this same kind of integration. That is, (2)<u>output sets up learning conditions that are qualitatively different from those of input.</u> This is not to say that input is inferior, simply that it is different and thus an important part of a balanced set of opportunities for learning. The full effect of the noticing/triggering function is not complete until learners have had the chance to make up for the lack that they have noticed. This can occur in several ways. First, having noticed a gap during output, the learners then notice items in input that they did not notice before. If learners notice that there is something they do not know when writing, they later "(3)<u>read like a writer</u>" giving attention to how others say what they wanted to say. This is often referred to as moving from semantic to syntactic processing. This is similar to an amateur guitar player not just enjoying a performance by a top-class guitarist, but also analysing the techniques and chord voicings he or she uses in the hope of copying these later. Second, having noticed a gap during output, learners may successfully fill that gap through a lucky guess, trial and error, the use of analogy, first language transfer, or problem solving. Webb (2002) found that learners were able to demonstrate aspects of vocabulary knowledge of previously unknown words even though they had not had the opportunity to learn those aspects of knowledge, but (4)<u>which they were able to work out through analogy and first language parallels.</u> Third, having noticed a gap during output, learners may deliberately seek to find the item by reference to outside sources like teachers, peers, or dictionaries.

Swain's second function of output is the hypothesis-testing function. This involves the learner trying out something and then confirming or modifying it on the basis of perceived success and feedback. This hypothesis-testing function is particularly important in interaction when learners negotiate with each other or a teacher to clarify meaning. The feedback provided in negotiation can improve not only the comprehensibility of input, but can also be a way for learners to improve their output (Mackey, 2007). Similarly, a large body of research shows that feedback from the teacher during communicative classroom interaction has significant effects on learning (Leeman, 2007). However, there are many ways of giving feedback and not all are equally effective. Feedback need not be immediate, as in the case of feedback on writing.

(I. S. P. Nation and J. Newton, *Teaching ESL/EFL Listening and Speaking*による。ただし，設問の都合で一部省略および改変している。)

1 外国語学習における下線部(1)の活動として，当てはまらない活動事例はどれか。次のア～エから一つ選び，記号で答えなさい。

ア The learners read a text and then have to produce their own written version of it without looking back at the original. The learning benefits of this exercise can be increased if the learners are required to fill in an information transfer diagram after reading the text.

イ The learners listen to a short text read twice to them while they take notes. The learners work in groups to reconstruct an approximation of the text from their notes. The teacher facilitates class comparisons of versions from different groups and then encourages a discussion so that learners can pay attention to the points of usage that emerge.

ウ The learners read their incomplete work to each other to get comments and suggestions on how to improve and continue it. The learners can work in groups and read each other's compositions. They make suggestions for revising before the teacher marks the compositions.

エ The teacher works with learners, using the first language to explain the meaning of a text, sentence by sentence. The use of translation makes sure that learners understand, and when the learners do some of the translation themselves, it allows the teacher to check whether they understand.

2　次は，下線部(2)で述べられている筆者の主張の一部を，短くまとめたものです。(　X　)，(　Y　)に入る言葉をそれぞれ10字以内の日本語で書きなさい。ただし，句読点も字数に含めること。

input中心の学習環境では，学習する項目の(　X　)だけで十分だが，output中心の学習環境では，学習した項目を(　Y　)ような，より深い学習を生み出す。

3　下線部(3)とはどのようなことか，アマチュアのギター奏者の例を用いながら，本文に即して日本語で答えなさい。

4　下線部(4)について，whichの内容を明らかにして日本語に直しなさい。

5　本文の内容に即して，次の質問に英語で答えなさい。

(1)　What do the learners do after they first noticed a gap during output?

(2)　What interaction is the hypothesis-testing function particularly important in?

6　本文の内容に合うものを次のア～オから一つ選び，記号で答えなさい。

ア　The output hypothesis was initially formulated as an advocate to Krashen's input hypothesis and suggested in order to explain how adequate the input hypothesis was in explaining the effects of immersion education.

イ　When learners consciously notice that they do not know how to say what they want to say in the second language, the effect on acquisition of noticing a gap through output was significantly greater than that through input.

ウ　Noticing/triggering function is realized only when learners have had the chance to notice a gap through input, and it is the reason that input is as important a part of a balanced set of opportunities for learning as output.

エ　Techniques such as lucky guess, trial and error, the use of analogy, first language transfer, or problem solving are useful in feedback when learners seek to fill the gap through output and demonstrate aspects of vocabulary.

オ　If the adequate feedback is not provided from the other learners or teachers as soon as the learner realized the gap through output about what they want to try out in the second language, feedback is less effective for the learner.

(☆☆☆☆☆◎◎◎◎◎)

【2】次の1，2について，指示に従って答えなさい。

1　次の日本語を英語に直しなさい。

教育とは，世界を変えるために用いることができる，最も強力な武器である。

2　「高等学校学習指導要領」(平成21年3月告示)では，「英語表現Ⅱ」の目標として，「事実や意見などを多様な観点から考察し，論理の展開や表現を工夫しながら伝える能力を伸ばすこと」を掲げています。もしあなたが，「英語表現Ⅱ」の時間にディスカッションの指導をするとしたら，どのように行いますか。学習指導要領の趣旨を踏まえ，100語程度の英語で書きなさい。ただし，語数には，カンマやピリオド等の句読点，疑問符や引用符等の記号は含まないものとします。なお，解答の総語数を記入すること。

(☆☆☆☆◎◎◎)

解答・解説

【中高共通】

【1】1　No.1　(b)　No.2　(c)　2　No.1　(a)　No.2　(c)　No.3　(d)　3　No.1　(a)　No.2　(d)　No.3　(b)　4　No.1　To tell the truth, (I have a sharp pain in my neck) now.　No.2　Well, they move so fast that (I always find it too difficult to follow them).

〈解説〉1 No.1　Did you hear that Kate will be transferred to Boston?「ケイトがボストンに転勤する予定であることをご存知ですか。」に対する返答としては，「はい，きのう彼女は私にそれを話しました」の(b)が正答。　No.2　How will Mike get to the meeting tomorrow?「マイクは明日の会議にどうやって行くのですか。」に対する応答としては，「彼は車で行くつもりだと言っていました。」の(c)が正答。　2 No.1　質問文は，When will the woman pack her bags?「女性はいつ荷物を詰めるつもりですか。」女性がミランに発つのは13日であると1文目に述べられているが，荷物を詰めるのはthe day before I go「私が行く前の日」とあるので(a)が正答。　No.2　質問文は，What will Sara most likely do next?「サラが次に最もしそうなことは何ですか。」サラは最後の発言でI'll contact the travel agencyと述べているので，それを言い換えている(c)が正答。　No.3　質問文はWho is the man talking to?「その男性が話しかけているのは誰ですか。」男性は本を返却して新しい本を借りるための交渉をしているので，正答は(d)である。　3 No.1　質問文はWhen did Japan ask UNESCO to register Mount Fuji as a cultural World Heritage site?「日本がユネスコに富士山を世界文化遺産に登録するように頼んだのはいつですか。」本文に述べられている通り，正答は(a)である。　No.2　Why wasn't Mount Fuji registered as a natural World Heritage site in 2003?「なぜ富士山は2003年に世界自然遺産に登録されなかったのですか。」本文のthe illegal dumping of garbage and the fact that the peak lacks global uniqueness as a volcanic mountainの言い換えである(d)が正答。　No.3　最後の1文から(b)が適当。　4　書き取り問題。難しい単語は出てこない。問題文は2回読まれるので，1回目に聞きのがしてもあわてず，2回目にその箇所に集中して聴き取れば問題ない。

【2】1　イ　2　イ　3　ア　4　ウ　5　ウ　6　エ　7　ア　8　イ　9　ウ　10　ア　11　ウ　12　エ　13　イ　14　ア　15　エ

〈解説〉1　what do you say to ～ingは親しい間柄で勧誘を表すくだけた表現。　2　casesを先行詞とする関係詞はwhereである。holdはこの場合は自動詞で「適用できる，当てはまる」の意。　3　set about A「Aに取りかかる」　4　この文の動詞はbe動詞areなので，空欄部は過去分詞を用いたfossilsの修飾である。　5　phenomenaはphenomenonの複数形(plural)である。　6　like a dream「素晴らしく，見事に」　7　do you thinkが間接疑問文と共に用いられる際の語順は「what＋do you think＋主語＋動詞」となるので正答はアである。　8　talk A into B「AにBをするように説得する」　9　独立分詞構文と共に用いて付帯状況を表すのはwithである。　10　on the verge of extinction「絶滅寸前にある」　11　knock 10% off the price「その値段から1割引する」
12　phonetics「音声学」　13　valid「有効な」　14　inclement weather「荒れ模様の天気」　15　solicit「(金銭・援助・情報など)を求める」

【3】1　私たちを支える生態系の中で，私たちの永続的な場所を確保する行動を起こす好機は今をおいて他にはない。　2　①　イ
②　ア　　③　エ　　3　B　　4　賛成　　理由…現在の地球は，すべての生命体それぞれが，不毛の土地や海を豊富で複雑な自然環境に作り替えるための役割を果たしながら少しずつ発展してきたものであり，将来の地球は，人間が住むのに適さない環境になると考えているから。　　5　人間が，火星のように，地球上の二酸化炭素を増大させ，水や豊富で豊かな生命を減少させていくこと。
6　ウ

〈解説〉1925年から出版されているアメリカ合衆国の文芸雑誌Virginia Quarterly Review (VQR) に所収されている*The Sweet Spot in Time*からの出題である。VQRはインターネット上で過去の記事を含めて公開されているので，日頃から英語学習に活用するとよいだろう。　1　文頭のNever againによって倒置が起こっている。There will never again be a better time.「よりよい時は2度と来ないだろう。」がこの文の主要な構造である。a better time以下はa better timeを修飾する。2度用いられて

いるthatはいずれも従属節の主語を導く関係代名詞である。
2　①　desert「去る」，determine「決定する」，differ「異なる」，digest「消化する」，「この先10年の間に我々が決めることが，その先10000年の方向を(　①　)だろう」という文脈なので，イのdetermineが正解。
②　lethal「破滅的な」，secure「安全な」，essential「不可欠な」，strict「厳しい」，「火星の大気は95％が二酸化炭素なので，人間にとっては(　②　)。」となるので，アのlethalが入る。　③　invent「発明する」，assimilate A into B「AをBに取り込む」，get rid of「取り除く」，churns out「大量生産する」，「海中の植物プランクトンの一種であるプロクロロコッカスが大気中の酸素の20％を(　③　)。」なので，エが正解となる。　3　本文中に挿入する段落の1文目に着目する。前の段落の最後の文との対応関係を考えると，容易にBを選択することができるだろう。Bの直前の段落が疑問文で終わっており，さらに次の段落が新たな疑問文で始まっているので，読んでいて少し違和感を覚えれば理想的である。この手の問題は，あらかじめ設問に目を通しておくと解答に余計な時間をかけなくて済むだろう。　4　選択肢の正答は「賛成」であるが，記述の箇所は比較的自由に解答することができるだろう。「今できることは過去にはできなかったことであり，未来にはできなくなる」という主旨が書けていれば良いだろう。　5　この問題では，採点の基準として，「誰が」，「何を」，「どのようにする」という3つの要素が含まれていることが重要となるだろう。それに注意すれば正答は難しくはないだろう。　6　ア　第1段落2文目，Nor did she appreciate that ～ をLittle did Rachel Carson know that ～と言い換えている。　イ　第3段落2文目のFifty years ago, we could not see limits to ～ could take out.と主旨が一致する。　エ　第7段落冒頭のEarthlings take for granted ～ embraced by an ocean ～. のtake for grantedをis taken as a matter of courseと言い換えて，同様の主旨を述べている。　オ　第8段落で，海中の植物が光合成をして酸素を生み出していると述べている。
ウ　第6段落に「火星に住むにはlife-support systemが必要だ」と述べられているので，主旨が逆である。

【中学校】

【1】1 ① イ　② エ　③ ア　2 記憶，理解，応用からなる低次の思考力と，分析，評価，創造からなる高次の思考力。　3 単元の前半では，低次の思考力を中心に展開し，後半では，高次の思考力を駆使するタスクに取り組ませるべきだ。　4 効果的な内容学習は，カリキュラムの中で限定された知識や技能だけではなく，創造的な思考，問題解決や認識力をためす課題を通して知識や技能をどのように活用していくのかということを考慮しなければならない。

5 (1) We need to support students in developing life skills.　(2) The knowledge dimension does.　6 ア，ウ

〈解説〉CLIL(クリル：内容言語統合型学習)に関する文章である。CLILは雑誌でも特集が組まれるなど，近年日本においても注目されているものである。英語科の教員採用試験を受験するうえで必須の知識である。クリルに関する知識があるか否かで本文の読みやすさ，取り組みやすさが大きく左右されるだろう。まずは，解答前に本文以外の情報を頭に入れておくことが重要である。語注として，CLIL: Content and Language Integrated Learningが挙げられているのはかなり良心的であると言えるだろう。出典は2010年に出版されたCLILである。　1 語義に関する問題である。語義は日頃から英英辞典を用いて理解する習慣をつけておくとよい。　① すぐ後の，for weakness，～ how to operate collaboratively and work effectively in groups に注目。compensate「埋め合わせる」　② engagement「取り組み」の意。直前のcognitiveに注目すると，エの「何かを理解しようとして起こす行動」が適切。　③ transparent「明白な」の意から，ア「理解したり，感じたりするのが，明白で簡単なこと」が正解。　2 第3段落第6文で述べている。設問の「6つの思考力の段階」とは，記憶，理解，応用，分析，評価，創造である。これを高次のものと低次のものとに2分して述べる。　3 「低次から高次へ」という大枠を崩さなければ，比較的自由に解答してもよいだろう。　4 並列の関係を理解すればスムーズに構文をとることができるだろう。主部はEffective content learning

であり，全体としてはnot only A, but also BのAおよびBが長くなっているものである。
5 (1) 第1段落のInstead以下をもとに解答する。 (2) 第3段落の最後の文をもとに解答する。 6 イは第2段落第3文，エは第3段落第2文，オは第4段落第2文のそれぞれの内容と一致しない。

【2】1 Education is the most powerful weapon which you can use to change the world. 2 解答省略。

〈解説〉英作文の問題では，知っている単語，構文を駆使して背伸びしすぎない無難な英文を書くことを心がけよう。非英語母語話者にとって，直感の働かない外国語を誤りなく正確に書くことは非常に困難であり，微妙なニュアンスの差異による違和感などを見過ごしてしまう場合が多い。英作文では，見たことのない英文は書かないことが鉄則である。その意味で，英文を多く見ることは英作文をするうえで最も重要なトレーニングである。重要な文法や語法が含まれる英文等の例文暗記がよいだろう。 1 和文英訳では，あまり意訳しすぎず，求められていると思われる文法事項を駆使することができれば理想的である。この問題では，「教育は武器である。」が大枠であり，これに修飾語を付け加えていくことが基本的な作業であろう。模範解答では関係代名詞のwhichが用いられているが，to不定詞などによる修飾でも問題ないだろう。 2 設問にある5つの提言は有名なものなので，是非とも本文に目を通しておきたい。こうした文部科学省の重要な資料は基本的にインターネット上に公開されているので容易に入手できるだろう。また，提言で言及されているCAN-DOリストとは端的に言うと英語を用いてできる能力を「～ができる」という具体的な形で表したリストであるが，近年大きな注目を集めている概念なので関連書籍には是非目を通しておきたい。

【高等学校】

【1】1　エ　　2　X　意味を解読する　　Y　規則化して活用する

3　トップクラスのギター奏者の演奏を，のちに自分でコピーすることを考えて分析しながら聞くように，のちに実際に自分が書くことを考えながら読むということ。　4　学習者はもともと知らない語句の語彙的な知識を類推や母国語との対比などで理解することができた。　5　(1)　They notice items in input that they did not notice before. (2)　In interaction when learners negotiate to clarify meaning.

6　イ

〈解説〉本文を読む前に本文以外の情報を頭に入れておこう。この文章の出典は*Teaching ESL/EFL Listening and Speaking*であり，口頭でのインプットやアウトプットに関する話題が展開される。うっかり本文から読み始めてしまっても，1文目から登場する，日本の英語教育においても有名なSwainのアウトプット仮説や，Krashenのインプット仮説などから，その後の内容をイメージして読むことが重要であろう。この二人の論者について知らないのであれば，大学等で用いられる第二言語習得論の教科書で勉強すべきだろう。　1　当てはまるものではなく，当てはまらないものを選ぶ点に注意しなければならない。正答のエのみが明らかにproductiveではなく，容易に選択することができるだろう。　2　下線部を含む段落で下線部より前に述べられてきたことをもとに短く解答する。　X　第2段落第5文の後半に出てくるreceptive learning とはinput中心の学習環境を指している。　Y　第2段落第8文のintegrate the new items into a more cohesive structure.の部分を要約すればよい。「解読」の代わりに「理解」，「規則化」の代わりに「統合」など，様々な別解が考えられる。　3　下線部の後に述べられているguitar playerに関する記述について触れることが必須である。下線部の「作家のように読む」と，「アマチュア・ギタリストが自分でコピーするためにプロのギターを聴く」という例とを対比させるように解答する。　4　関係代名詞whichが指すのはaspects of vocabulary knowledge of previously unknown words「もともと知らない語句の語彙的な知識」である。　5　(1)　第2段落第14文のFirst, having noticed a gap during output, the learners then notice items in input that they did not notice before.をもとに解答する。　(2)　第3段落第3文のThis hypothesis-testing function is particularly important in interaction when learners negotiate with each other or a teacher to clarify meaning.をもとに解答する。　6　第2段落第3文のthat以下に，選択肢イと同様の主旨が述べられている。

【2】1　Education is the most powerful weapon which you can use to change the world.　　2　解答省略。

〈解説〉英作文の問題では，知っている単語，構文を駆使して背伸びしすぎない無難な英文を書くことを心がけよう。非英語母語話者にとって，直感の働かない外国語を誤りなく正確に書くことは非常に困難であり，微妙なニュアンスの差異による違和感などを見過ごしてしまう場合が多い。英作文では，見たことのない英文は書かないことが鉄則である。その意味で，英文を多く見ることは英作文をするうえで最も重要なトレーニングである。重要な文法や語法が含まれる英文等の例文暗記が良いだろう。　1　和文英訳では，あまり意訳しすぎず，求められていると思われる文法事項を駆使することができれば理想的である。この問題では，「教育は武器である。」が大枠であり，これに修飾語を付け加えていくことが基本的な作業であろう。模範解答では関係代名詞のwhichが用いられているが，to不定詞などによる修飾でも問題ないだろう。　2　「英語表現」という科目は2009(平成21)年に改訂された学習指導要領において新設されたものである。表現，つまりスピーキングとライティングを重視した科目であるとされるが，この学習指導要領では4技能の統合が強調されているので，スピーキングとライティングを統合した指導について述べることが一つの方針として考えられる。特に，設問にもある「論理の展開や表現を工夫」という点を考えると，表面的な会話の指導では片付けられないことは明らかだろう。

2014年度　実施問題

【中高共通】

【1】(放送による問題)これはリスニング・テストです。放送の指示に従って答えなさい。

[トラック1]

試聴用英文(約3分間)

ただいまから，試聴用の英文を約3分間流します。そのあとでチャイムが鳴りますから，そこでCDを止めてください。

(試聴用の英文)

<チャイム連続音>

(空白1分間)

[トラック2]

(問題)

〈チャイム連続音〉

ただいまから，リスニング・テストを行います。問題は1，2，3，4の四つです。聞いている間にメモを取っても構いません。答えはすべて解答用紙の所定の欄に記入しなさい。

(間2秒)

では，1の問題から始めます。問題はNo.1とNo.2の2問です。

これから読まれる英文に対する応答として最もふさわしいものを，続いて読まれる(a)，(b)，(c)の中から一つ選び，記号で答えなさい。なお，英文と応答は1度しか読まれません。

(間2秒)

では，始めます。

No.1　Do you think anyone would mind if I opened the window?

(a)　That was Mr. Green.

(b)　Yes, I think it did.

(c) No. Go ahead.

(間5秒)

No.2 I read in the newspaper this morning that a 13-year-old girl is studying science at Harvard University.

(a) Do you want to be a scientist?

(b) Wow. She must be a genius.

(c) How did you know that?

(間7秒)

〈チャイム〉

次に，2の問題に移ります。問題は，No.1からNo.3までの3問です。

これから，短い対話文を読みます。そのあとでクェスチョンと言って質問します。その答えとして最もふさわしいものを，続いて読まれる(a)，(b)，(c)，(d)の中から一つ選び，記号で答えなさい。なお，対話文・質問・答えの選択肢は1度しか読まれません。

(間2秒)

では，始めます。

No.1

W : Dad, I have a question. Some of my friends are getting scooters, and I'd like to get one, too. What do you think? Is it OK with you and Mom?

M : I'm not sure what your mother will say, but I'd say absolutely not.

W : But Dad! I'll be using my own money.

M : It's not a matter of money. You cannot even ride a bike very well. I don't want you to get hurt.

Question : What is her father's opinion?

(a) He thinks it's too expensive for his daughter to buy a scooter.

(b) He thinks it's too noisy for his daughter to ride a scooter.

(c) He thinks it's very useful to ride a scooter.

(d) He thinks it's not safe for his daughter to ride a scooter.

(間4秒)

No.2

W : Can I help you?

M : Yes. I'm looking for something for my mother. She likes plain colors, but all I can find here are these bold-colored clothes. I need to buy the present today. Her birthday is tomorrow.

W : Well, we haven't put out our spring collection yet, but I may be able to pull some things from the back for you.

M : That would be nice. Thank you.

Question : What problem does the man have?

(a) He cannot find a gift for his mother.

(b) He has forgotten about his mother's birthday.

(c) He doesn't know what his mother likes.

(d) He doesn't have any money on him.

(間4秒)

No.3

M : Shouldn't David be here by now? His train arrived over an hour ago.

W : Oh, I forgot to tell you. He called and said he decided to take a later train.

M : I wish you had told me that earlier. I could have grabbed a bite to eat before he comes. We have a long meeting tonight to prepare for the presentation tomorrow.

W : Don't worry. I've taken care of that for you. I ordered sandwiches which should be arriving soon.

Question : What does the woman say she has done for the man?

(a) Prepared a presentation.

(b) Told David about her schedule.

(c) Arranged for refreshments.

(d) Made some sandwiches.

(間7秒)

〈チャイム〉

次に3の問題に移ります。問題は，No.1からNo.3までの3問です。

これから，あるまとまりのある英文を読みます。そのあとで，クエスチョンと言って，その英文について三つの質問をします。その答えとして最もふさわしいものを，質問に続いて読まれる(a)，(b)，(c)，(d)の中から一つ選び，記号で答えなさい。なお，英文・質問・答えの選択肢は全体を通して2回読まれます。

(間2秒)

では，始めます。

After the recent disaster in Tohoku, a lot of people volunteered in the disaster area. Many people from abroad came over to help in the recovery of the disaster area. I also visited the area and brought food, clothing and other supplies that they would need. I learned lots of things through the experience.

Of course it is really important to help people in the affected area, but I heard that there were some problems. In such a big disaster, you can't have streams of people just coming into the area and trying to do something without proper organization. There are lots of military up there, lots of police from all over the country, firefighters, many, many people. So organizing and managing them is a big job.

I saw people from abroad while I stayed there. There was a man from Australia who was helped by Japanese volunteers when there was a disaster in his country. He came to Tohoku to return the favor. I found that volunteering is, in a way, a personal thing, but it also is a kind of diplomacy. A lot of studies need to be done, and if we look into the jobs of volunteer workers, it will be a great way for us to share cultures, each other's thoughts and to bring the world closer.

There are some companies that organize volunteer opportunities for their employees. I know that some of the universities are looking into things they can do in the future. And as far as giving credits, it would definitely be valuable. In companies in the West and some in Asia, if you've volunteered, it's a kind of plus in your resume when you go in for a job interview, because it apparently gives you the skills of leadership and of teamwork, even before you start your job. I think that's a very good idea.

(間3秒)

Question

No.1 What did the speaker learn from her experience of volunteering in the disaster area?

(a) Organizing people is one of the most important things in volunteering.

(b) A lot of people went into the area but there were not enough jobs.

(c) A lot of people from military and police organized volunteer works.

(d) It is easy to organize and manage volunteers in the disaster area.

(間3秒)

No.2 Is the experience of volunteering a kind of plus to get a job?

(a) Yes. Companies need experiences of working in a disaster area like Tohoku.

(b) Yes. Companies think that you acquire skills of leadership and teamwork through it.

(c) No. It is not necessary to have opportunities of volunteering.

(d) No. It is important in Western companies but not so important in those in Asia.

(間3秒)

No. 3 What did the speaker say about volunteering?

(a) It is only a personal thing and you should do it for your own benefit.

(b) We should not study about volunteering before going abroad.

(c) We have to go to Australia because they had a disaster.

(d) It is a good way to develop closer relationships between countries.

(間3秒)

くりかえします。

(間6秒)

〈チャイム〉

次に4の問題に移ります。問題はNo.1とNo.2の2問です。これから，英語による対話文を読みます。(　　)のところに入る英語を聞き取り，書きなさい。対話文はそれぞれ2回読まれます。

(間2秒)

では，始めます。

No.1

W : You look very tired these days. Are you OK?

M : There are mice living in my attic. (The noise is keeping me awake all night).

(間10秒)

くりかえします。

(間10秒)

No.2

W : why did you decide to move to Italy?

M : Well, (the summers there are really beautiful).

(間10秒)

くりかえします。

(間10秒)

〈チャイム連続音〉

これで，リスニング・テスト終わります。次の問題に移ってください。

(☆☆☆◎◎◎)

【２】次の英文や対話文の中の(　　)に最も適するものを，下のア～エからそれぞれ一つずつ選び，記号で答えなさい。

1　The stock price of the company (　　) depending on changes in the price of gold.

ア　accumulates　　イ　compensates　　ウ　generates

エ　fluctuates

2　(　　) is the study that deals with the methods of education.

ア　Anthropology　　イ　Pedagogy　　ウ　Psychology

エ　Linguistics

3　The Civil Rights Movement tried to eradicate (　　) on the basis of race, gender and religion.

ア　liberation　　イ　discrimination　　ウ　assumption

エ　inauguration

4　Efficient business people work hard even when they are not under pressure to (　　) a deadline.

ア　miss　　イ　cross　　ウ　meet　　エ　put on

5　I'm sorry to (　　) you, but you have a phone call from your grandfather.

ア　interrupt　　イ　resist　　ウ　mean　　エ　count

6　The horizontal axis indicates the age groups and the (　　) axis shows the number of children they raise.

ア　superficial　　イ　synthetic　　ウ　vertical　　エ　primary

7　He made a wonderful speech and got a (　　) of applause.

ア　round　　イ　set　　ウ　seat　　エ　bond

8　"Tanka" is a 17-(　　) traditional short poem in Japan.

ア　rhyme　　イ　consonant　　ウ　molecule　　エ　syllable

9　A : What do you recommend as a (　　) for a 5-year-old boy?

B : Well, how about this new toy aircraft?

ア　sovereign　　イ　souvenir　　ウ　subsidy　　エ　segment

10　It's high time you (　　). You look very lazy and untidy.

ア　have cut your hair　　イ　had cut your hair

ウ　have your hair cut　　エ　had your hair cut

11　This pumpkin is twice (　　) a normal Japanese one.

ア　the size of　　イ　a size of　　ウ　size as　　エ　the size as

12　A : Can I speak to Bill, please?

B : He's (　　) right now. Would you like to leave a message?

ア　made up　　イ　tied up　　ウ　set up　　エ　taken up

13　A : I'm in favor of changing the marketing strategy.

B： I couldn't agree (　　).

ア　more　　イ　with　　ウ　on　　エ　up

14　A： I (　　) at my first interview, and I lost my confidence.

B： Don't worry. You'll get used to being interviewed soon.

ア　took over　　イ　brushed up　　ウ　messed up　　エ　came out

15　A： Was Tomoko that good at giving a speech in English when she was in high school?

B： Must have been, or she (　　) the first prize winner in the speech contest at that time.

ア　would be　　イ　wouldn't be　　ウ　would have been

エ　wouldn't have been

(☆☆◎◎◎)

【3】次の英文を読んで，あとの問いに答えなさい。

In many countries around the world, it is common for the state to ask its citizens if they will volunteer to be organ donors. Now, organ donation is one of those issues that elicit strong feelings from many people. On the one hand, it's an opportunity to turn one person's loss into another person's salvation. But on the other hand, it's more than a little unsettling to be making plans for your organs that don't involve you. It's not surprising, therefore, that different people make different decisions, nor (1)<u>(that / it / vary / of / surprising / is / rates / organ donation)</u> considerably from country to country. It might surprise you to learn, however, how much cross-national variation there is. In a study conducted a few years ago, two psychologists, Eric Johnson and Dan Goldstein, found that rates at which citizens consented to donate their organs varied across different European countries, from as low as 4.25 percent to as high as 99.98 percent. What was even more striking about these differences is that they weren't scattered all over the spectrum, but rather were clustered into two distinct groups — one group that had organ-donation rates in the single digits and teens, and one group that had rates in the high nineties — with almost nothing in between.

What could explain (2)<u>such a huge difference</u>? That's the question I put to a classroom of bright Columbia undergraduates not long after the study was published. (①), what I asked them to consider was two anonymous countries, A and B. In country A, roughly 12 percent of citizens agree to be organ donors, while in country B 99.9 percent do. So what did they think was different about these two countries that could account for the choices of their citizens? Being smart and creative students, they came up with lots of possibilities. Perhaps one country was secular while the other was highly religious. Perhaps one had more advanced medical care, and better success rates at organ transplants, than the other. Perhaps the rate of accidental death was higher in one than another, resulting in more available organs. Or perhaps one had a highly socialist culture, emphasizing the importance of community, while the other prized the rights of individuals.

All were good explanations. But then came the (3)<u>curveball</u>. Country A was in fact Germany, and country B was ... Austria. My poor students were stumped — what on earth could be so different about Germany and Austria? But they weren't giving up yet. Maybe there was some difference in the legal or education systems that they didn't know about? Or perhaps there had been some important event or media campaign in Austria that had galvanized support for organ donation. Was it something to do with World War II? Or maybe Austrians and Germans are more different than they seem. My students didn't know what the reason for the difference was, but they were sure it was something big — you don't see extreme differences like that by accident. Well, no — but you can get differences like that for reasons that you'd never expect. And for all their creativity, my students never pegged (4)<u>the real reason</u>, which is absurdly simple : In Austria, the default choice is to be an organ donor, whereas in Germany the default is not to be. The difference in policies seems trivial — it's just the difference between having to mail in a simple form and not having to — but it's enough to push the donor rate from

12 percent to 99.9 percent. And what was true for Austria and Germany was true across all of Europe — all the countries with very high rates of organ donation had opt-out policies, while the countries with low rates were all opt-in.

Understanding the influence of default settings on the choices we make is important, (　②　) our beliefs about what people choose and why they choose it affect virtually all our explanations of social, economic, and political outcomes. Read the ※op-ed section of any newspaper, watch any ※pundit on TV, or listen to any late-night talk radio, and you will be bombarded with theories of why we choose this over that. And although we often decry these experts, the broader truth is that all of us are equally willing to espouse our own theory of human choice. (　③　), virtually every argument of social consequence is either explicitly or implicitly an argument about why people make the choices they make. And, of course, how they can be encouraged, educated, legislated, or coerced into making different ones.

(注)　op-ed : opposite editorialの略　　pundit : (皮肉的に)学者先生

(Duncan J. Watts, *Everything Is Obvious* による。ただし，設問の都合で一部省略及び改変している。)

1　本文中の空欄(　①　)～(　③　)に最もよくあてはまる語句を，次のア～オの中から一つずつ選び，記号で答えなさい。ただし，文頭に来る語も小文字で示されています。また，同じ記号は二回以上使わないこと。

ア　because　　イ　actually　　ウ　obviously　　エ　hopefully

オ　indeed

2　下線部(1)について，正しい英文となるように，(　　)内の語句を並べかえなさい。

3　下線部(2)は，具体的にどのようなことを述べているのか，日本語で答えなさい。

4　下線部(3)を別の語で言い換えたとき，最も近い意味の語をア～エから一つ選び，記号で答えなさい。

ア irritation　イ anger　ウ disappointment

エ astonishment

5 下線部(4)の内容を，本文に即して日本語で説明しなさい。

6 本文の内容に合うものを，次のア～カから二つ選び記号で答えなさい。

ア Organ donation has always been controversial in that one person's loss never leads to another person's salvation.

イ All the possibilities students thought out have something to do with the cultural conditions of the countries.

ウ At last, students could not answer the question they were asked about the difference between country A and B.

エ Students were surprised because they didn't know a fact that media campaign in Austria had galvanized support for organ donation.

オ People tend to adopt the idea that their own theory of human choice was made up by those with the special skill or knowledge of a particular subject.

カ Default settings play an important role in influencing our choices we make.

(☆☆☆◎◎◎)

【中学校】

【1】次の英文を読んで，あとの問いに答えなさい。

Skilled performers often have to cope with the challenges of *open* environments — situations where information critical to successful performance changes in unpredictable ways, moment by moment. In order to meet such challenges a person must be able to focus and refocus attention at the moment in order to keep up with changing circumstances. In many non-linguistic areas of complex performance, it is easy to recognize that (1)<u>such abilities</u> can be crucial to success. For example, skilled driving, hockey playing, and chess playing are all examples (2)<u>(is to / in / a change / bring</u>

about / the goal / where) an environment that is itself in a dynamic state (e.g., getting a car safely through a busy intersection, placing a ※puck in a well-defended goal, or overcoming a chess opponent's strategic defense moves).

A similar case can be made for ※L2 communication. Fluent speakers must be able to package information into appropriate language as thoughts come to mind, and they must do so in a relatively smooth manner or risk ※losing the floor. Moreover, in packaging thoughts into language, speakers often have to take into account feedback from the ※interlocutor about whether the message is being properly understood. (3)This requires the ability to flexibly redirect the focus of attention in order to recruit the appropriate linguistic resources for formulating the message. In this sense, attention-based processing is a complementary aspect of the L2 cognitive fluency, complementary to the automatic aspects of processing. L2 cognitive fluency needs to include both efficient processing (fast and stable) and flexibility of attention control.

There are many different ways of thinking about attention and how it might play a role in L2 fluency. There is no universally accepted definition of attention. Nevertheless, there are common themes found throughout the literature that will serve the present discussion well. Cohen, Aston-Jones, and Gilzenrat(2004), for example, provide a useful global summary of what attention is, describing it as "the emergent property of the cognitive system that allows it to successfully process some sources of information to the exclusion of others, in the service of achieving some goals to the exclusion of others." Appropriate topics for attention research usually include the study of mechanisms involved in (①staying on task), in(②task sharing), in (③task switching), in preparing for an upcoming task, and other forms of cognitive control.

(注)　puck：パック(アイスホッケー用のゴム製の平円盤)
L2：第2言語(母語を学んだ後に学ぶ言語)
lose the floor：　発言権を失う　　interlocutor：　対話の相手
(Norman Segalowitz, *Cognitive Bases of Second Language Fluency*に

よる。ただし，設問の都合で一部省略及び改変している。)

1　下線部(1)について，such abilitiesとはどのような能力を指しているか，車の運転を例にとり，本文に即して日本語で説明しなさい。

2　下線部(2)について，意味が通るように，(　　)内の語句を並べかえなさい。

3　下線部(3)について，thisは何を指しているか，日本語で説明しなさい。

4　下線部①～③の英語の説明として最もよくあてはまるものを，次のア～ウの中から一つずつ選び，記号で答えなさい。

ア　switching focus from one task to another

イ　allocating cognitive resources to sustain processing on a particular target

ウ　overseeing the sharing of resources in situations where more than one task is being performed

5　本文の内容に即して，次の質問に英語で答えなさい。

(1)　What are *open* environments?

(2)　What does L2 cognitive fluency need to include?

6　本文の内容に合うものを，次のア～エから一つ選び，記号で答えなさい。

ア　A person must be able to focus and refocus attention at the moment in order to fight against successful performance.

イ　Attention-based processing is independent of the automatic aspects of processing.

ウ　Although there is no universally accepted definition of attention, there are common themes found throughout the literature that will satisfy the present discussion well.

エ　Cohen, Aston-Jones, and Gilzenrat(2004) provide a useful global summary of what cognitive fluency is.

(☆☆☆☆◎◎◎)

【2】次の1，2について，指示に従って答えなさい。

1　次の日本語を英語に直しなさい。'

真摯に勇気を持って人生と向き合えば，人間は経験を通じて成長する。このようにして人格が作られるのだ。

2　「中学校学習指導要領」(平成20年3月告示)では，「聞くこと」，「話すこと」，「読むこと」及び「書くこと」の4技能の総合的な指導を通して，これらの4技能を統合的に活用できるコミュニケーション能力を育成することが求められています。読むことを中心にして活動させる際に，他の技能をどのように関連づけて指導しますか。あなたの考えを100語程度の英語で書きなさい。ただし，語数には，カンマやピリオド等の句読点，疑問符や引用符等の符号は含まないものとします。なお，解答の総語数を記入すること。

(☆☆☆◎◎◎)

【高等学校】

【1】次の英文を読んで，あとの問いに答えなさい。

A difference between ※L1 and ※L2 reading is the sheer amount of exposure to print that a learner experiences. Most L2 readers have only very limited exposure to L2 print, (1)<u>(L2 classroom / of which / contexts / from / most / comes)</u>. L1 students may encounter millions of words of printed text in a year, every year, from early on in their schooling experience. Reading an hour a day in the L1 (including magazines, flyers, Web sources, e-mails, cereal boxes, TV captions, etc.) will expose an L1 learner to 3-4 million words per year (assuming 200 wpm × 365 days). One would be ①<u>hard-pressed</u> to make an argument that most L2 readers can achieve anywhere near this level of exposure to reading that L1 readers easily achieve as academically oriented learners. The most obvious L1-L2 difference is going to be the massive fluency practice with more frequent aspects of the language. ②<u>Automaticity</u> will emerge in L1 reading as a matter of course for processing the orthography, morphology, words, and syntax of the language. In L1 reading, many high-frequency words will be automatically recognized sight words. In addition, the extensive exposure will also mean continual practice in all of the reading skills and strategies as well as many opportunities to develop the types of metacognitive awareness that support critical comprehension abilities.

Readers often have different motivations for reading in the L2 when compared with reading in their L1s. In fact, one can say that every person will have a unique combination of motivations for reading, whether in the L1 or the L2. However, (2)there are clear situations in which reading in the L2 is going to be different from L1 reading in terms of purposes and goals(and motivation is driven by goals, purposes, and persistence). In many L1 settings, people read because they have certain types of expertise or skills that they are willing to develop, or they read for enjoyment, often reading for hours or exploring Web pages for extended periods of time (because reading is relatively effortless). In many cases, L1 readers carry out work-related tasks that involve extended periods of reading. In academic settings, students read in order to learn and be challenged by new ideas and information that they encounter. The extent of their motivation in academic reading is strongly associated with their academic goals more generally, their educational experiences, and their future ③aspirations.

L2 readers, in many contexts around the world, are reading texts that often are very difficult and at the upper edge of their linguistic resources. The reasons for reading, particularly in foreign-language classrooms, are often limited to developing language skills rather than building academic expertise. (3)The goals for reading are often (X) rather than (Y). L2 reading goals for students are also often constrained by the limited expectations of others in terms of outcome goals and purposes for reading. The context itself, commonly the foreign-language classroom, also suggests that L2 reading is not very important for larger academic goals and future aspirations. Even for academically oriented EFL and ESL students who recognize the need for

English, they also know that they read well in their L1s and that their future may rest more with their L1 literacy skills than their L2 literacy skills. Motivation in L2 reading is a relatively unexplored territory, but it should be clear from this comparison that L2 readers often (though not always) engage in L2 reading with different motivations for reading and very different expectations in terms of long-term outcomes.

(注)　L1：母語　　L2：第2言語(母語を学んだ後に学ぶ言語：second language)

(William Grabe, *Reading in a Second Language*による。ただし，設問の都合で一部省略及び改変している。)

1　下線部(1)について，正しい英文となるように，(　　)内の語句を並べかえなさい。

2　下線部①～③の語句とほぼ同じ意味になるものを，それぞれ次のア～エの中から一つずつ選び，記号で答えなさい。

①　ア　comfortable and consoling
　　イ　anxious and embarrassed
　　ウ　relaxed and not worried
　　エ　troubled and distressed

②　ア　interpreting the sentence with much effort
　　イ　taking in the language instinctively
　　ウ　deciphering the letters misguidedly
　　エ　pronouncing the words accurately

③　ア　ambition　　イ　surge　　ウ　contagion　　エ　desperation

3　下線部(2)を日本語に直しなさい。

4　下線部(3)の(　X　)，(　Y　)に入る語句として最も適切なものを，それぞれ次のア～オから一つずつ選び，記号で答えなさい。

ア　to make sure the purpose of L1 reading
イ　to reflect their own awareness of L1 and L2
ウ　to build new academic skills and knowledge bases

エ　to carry out language-learning assignments

オ　to draw connections between L1 and L2

5　本文の内容に合うものを，次のア～カから二つ選び，記号で答えなさい。

ア　The amount of the printed words that L2 learners encounter in a day is as much as that of L1 learners in their schooling experience.

イ　When it comes to the frequency of learners being exposed to the language, L1 words are easier than those of L2 to be recognized as simple sight words.

ウ　Whether in the L1 or the L2, motivations and the goals among the learners are often common.

エ　The work-related tasks of L1 learners that involve extended periods of reading is always connected with their academic goals or their educational experiences.

オ　Texts used in L2 reading are sometimes the latest linguistic resources available and very difficult for L2 learners.

カ　L2 reading is more important than L1 reading for L2 learners because they know that the expertise and skills through the foreign language classroom will be necessary for their future goals.

6　第三段落で筆者が述べていることに対し，高等学校の外国語の授業で扱う教材を選ぶ際に，どのような観点に留意する必要があるか，「高等学校学習指導要領」(平成21年3月告示)の内容をふまえて，日本語で答えなさい。

(☆☆☆◎◎◎)

【2】次の1，2について，指示に従って答えなさい。

1　次の日本語を英語に直しなさい。

　真摯に勇気を持って人生と向き合えば，人間は経験を通じて成長する。このようにして人格が作られるのだ。

2　「高等学校学習指導要領」(平成21年3月告示)では，「英語表現Ⅰ」

の学習内容として,「聞いたり読んだりしたこと,学んだことや経験したことに基づき,情報や考えなどをまとめ,発表する」活動を行うこととなっています。「発表する」活動を指導する際の留意点についてあなたの考えを100語程度の英語で書きなさい。ただし,語数には,カンマやピリオド等の句読点,疑問符や引用符等の符号は含まないものとします。なお,解答の総語数を記入すること。

(☆☆☆◎◎◎)

解答・解説

【中高共通】

【1】1　No.1　c　No.2　b　2　No.1　d　No.2　a　No.3　c　3　No.1　a　No.2　b　No.3　d　4　No.1　There are mice living in my attic. (The noise is keeping me awake all night).　No.2　Well, (the summers there are really beautiful).

〈解説〉1,2は会話とそれについての質問および答えを聞き,適切なものを選ぶ問題で1度しか読まれないが内容は初級会話レベルである。3は記事についての質問に対して適切な答えを選択する問題,4は対話の一部を書き取る問題で,それぞれ2度読まれる。内容は高校教科書程度で特に難しくはないが,リスニング全体の分量は比較的多いので,注意力が途切れないようTOEICや実用英語検定の問題集などで練習をしておくとよいだろう。

【2】1　エ　2　イ　3　イ　4　ウ　5　ア　6　ウ　7　ア　8　エ　9　イ　10　エ　11　ア　12　イ　13　ア　14　ウ　15　エ

〈解説〉1　stock price は「株価」。株価と言えば「変動する」のfluctuate,他にrise「上がる」,fall「下がる」などがピンと来る。他選択肢はア

「蓄積する」，イ「補う」，ウ「発生させる」。　2「教育法に関わる学問」であるからイの「教育学」。接頭辞 ped- は，「教育」，「学問」，「子供」などを表す。(例) pediatrician「小児科医」，pedantic「衒学的な」，など。接頭辞でも接尾辞でもないが，encyclopedia「百科事典」も同根。

3　Civil Rights Movement は，マイナリティによる運動全般を指すこともあり得るが，一般的には1950年代に始まった，合衆国黒人による公民権法成立を要求する運動(後に女性解放運動も巻き込み拡大していった)を指す。「人種，性および宗教に基づいた---を根絶する」であるから「差別」のイが適切。　4　be under pressure to meet a deadline で「締め切りに追われる」。meet のかわりに make でも可。「有能なビジネスマンは締め切りに追われていない時でもバリバリ仕事をする」

5　ア「邪魔する」，イ「拒否する」，ウ「意味する」，エ「数に入れる」で，you が目的語であること，I'm sorry to と言っていることなどから「邪魔する」が適切と判断できる。「お邪魔してすみませんがお祖父様から電話が入っています」　6　文前半 the horizontal axis「水平軸=X軸」とあり空欄後にも axis とあることから，対になる言葉 vertical「垂直の」が適切とわかる。「X軸は年齢層によるグループ，Y軸は彼らが育てる子供の数を示している」　7　round of applause で「一斉に湧き起こる拍手」を意味する成句。「彼は素晴らしいスピーチを行い嵐のような拍手を浴びた」　8「短歌は17音節による日本の伝統的な短い詩である」(正しくは「俳句」を意味していると思われるが，筆者が短歌と混同したのだろう) 日本語は「ひと文字一音節」であるが，英語では「文字」は母音，子音ひとつでも文字であって必ずしも音節を形成しない。俳句における文字はリズムの形成という重要な要素があるため，ここでは「音節」としなければ意味が通らない。

9　ア「統治者」，イ「記念の物，みやげ」，ウ「補助金」，エ「部分，節」　「5歳の男の子向けに」と言っているので「おみやげ」が適切。

10　[It's high time S 過去形]で，「もうとっくに～しているべき時間だ」という意味の強意表現。「今の時間だと，[もうすでに～した]という状態のはずなのに」という意味合いである。「もうとっくに散髪していなきゃいけない時なのに。だらしなくてみっともないよ」　had your hair cut の had は使役動詞で「～してもらう」なので,「髪を切った状態にしてもらう⇒(床屋に行って)散髪する」となる。　11　twice the size of ～ で「～の2倍の大きさがある」。意味は, twice as large as ～ と同じ。比較の標準となっているのは a normal Japanese one である。「このかぼちゃは普通の日本のものの2倍の大きさだ」　12　後の文に「ご伝言を残されますか？」とあるので Bill は何かの事情で今電話に出られないと理解でき,「(忙しく)手が離せない」のイがあてはまる。
13　[could not 動詞+比較級]で,「これ以上～になりえない」すなわち「最高に～だ」, という意味になる。(例) I couldn't be happier.「最高に幸せだ」　問題文の場合, 形容詞比較級は選択肢でアの more だけであり, また他選択肢はすべて, 後ろに名詞が来るべき前置詞で文法的にも無理があるため, 自動的にこれが正解,「これ以上同意できないくらいだ⇒まったく同感」という意味。選択肢にless があれば「まったく同感できないね」で, これでも正解になる。　14　文後半に「自信をなくしました」とあるので, interview で失敗したと想像でき, ウの messed up「混乱した, めちゃくちゃになった」があてはまる。
15「トモコは高校で英語のスピーチがそんなに得意だったのか？」との質問に対し, Must have been. と答えているので, 時制をそろえると, ウかエ。「そうだったはずだね。そうでなかったならば---」に続く文として,「当時のスピーチコンテストで優勝者になれていただろう」と「いなかっただろう」の選択で, 文脈から後者のエが適切。

【3】1　①　イ　②　ア　③　オ　2　is it surprising that rates of organ donation vary　3　(解答例)　臓器提供の同意者の割合が, 1桁から10％台の国々と90％台の国々の2つのグループにきれいに分かれ, その間がないこと。　4　エ　5　(解答例)　オーストリアでは臓器提供に同意しない場合に申し出るかたちを取っているが, ドイツでは臓器提供に同意する場合に, 申し出るかたちを取っていること。
6　ウ　カ　(順不同)

〈解説〉1　①　空欄前に，筆者自身の言葉で疑問が書かれており「それが，研究が発表された直後に，私がコロンビア大の学生たちの教室で投げかけた質問である」とある。続いて，[実際に]どのように問いかけたのかが説明してあるので，「実際のところ」を意味する actually が適切。　②　文章を最小限に簡略化してみると，空欄前は Understanding the influence is important「影響力を理解することは重要だ」，空欄後は our beliefs affect all our explanations「私たちの思い込みは私たちの説明すべてに影響を与える」となっている。すなわち，「私たちの説明すべてに影響を与える[のだから]，影響力を理解しておくことは重要だ」となり，because があてはまる。　③　これも簡略化すると，空欄前が，all of us are willing to espouse our own theory of human choice「我々は皆，人間の選択についての自分自身の信念を守ることに熱心だ」，空欄後が，every argument of social consequence is an argument about why people make the choices they make 「社会的に重要な議論はすべて，なぜ人々が，彼らのする選択をするのかについての議論である」，とあり，後者は前者の強化および根拠づけの役割をはたしているので，「まさに，まったくのところ」を意味する indeed があてはまる。　2　It's not surprising that ---, nor ---. という文で，選択肢に that があるところから，「that 以下もまた surprising ではない」という文構造で，後半のSVも前半と同じとわかる。ただし，「～もまた---ない」の意味の neither，nor が文・節の先頭に置かれた場合倒置が起きるので，nor is it surprisingとなる。残った語で that節が形成され，rates of --- というかたちがつかめるので，that rates of organ donation vary (considerably) と続く。　3　段落冒頭の文で，such「そのような」とあり，直前の段落にその内容が書かれていると見て間違いない。直前の段落をさかのぼって見ると，前の段落最後の文に「2つのグループ」「ひと桁」「高めの90台」など「そのような大きな差」にあてはまるキーワードがあるのでそこをまとめる。　4　curveball は野球のカーブ，つまり変化球であり，「驚き」であるという意味でastonishment が適切。行動の差は国々の宗教観，医療体制，事故死率などの差から，あるいは臓器提供についての強制のあるなし，コミュニティ重視か個人尊重かの文化の違いなどから来ているのではないかとの学生の推測が第2段落に挙げられているが，これらの推測に反し，ドイツとオーストリアという，極めて文化・歴史の近い2国で異なる結果が出ていることを「驚きの変化球」と言ったのである。　5　臓器提供についての意志を表明するために人々がどういう行動をとることが必要か，が，下線を含む文の次の文 it's just the difference 以下に述べられており，具体的になぜ臓器提供を申し出る人の数に差が出たかの説明になっている。　6　第3段落に，学生たちが答えを出すことができなかったこと，そして彼らは何か彼らの知らない大きな違いが2国のあいだにあると推定したが，実際は実に簡単なことが原因だったことが述べられており，ウと内容一致する。また最後の段落冒頭に，「私たちが行う選択に対する，(選択の)初期設定による影響を理解することは重要である」とあり，「初期設定は私たちの選択に大きな役割を果たす」とするカと一致する。

【中学校】

【1】1　(解答例)　混み合った交差点を通過する際に，正面から来る車や左右から来る車，歩行者や信号などに同時に注意を払いながら，安全に交差点を通過することができるような能力。　2　where the goal is to bring about a change in　3　(解答例)　思考を言語へと置き換える際に，話者はメッセージが適切に理解されたかどうかについて，話し相手からのフィードバックを考慮に入れなければならないということ。　4　①　イ　②　ウ　③　ア　5　(1)　(解答例)　They are the situations where information critical to successful performance changes in unpredictable ways.　(2)　(解答例)　It needs to include both efficient processing and flexibility of attention control.　6　ウ

〈解説〉1　下線部を含む段落の最後，カッコ内に例として，「混み合った交差点を安全に通過する」とあるので，その際に必要な行動やそれを支える技術を考えて具体的に述べればよい。　2　選択肢からみて節となることがわかるので，先ず関係詞の where を置く。bring about

「もたらす」の目的語は a change で「〜の変化」とする in を後ろにとる。そうすると節の主語は the goal，動詞は is toしかない。「目標が，(ただでさえダイナミックな)環境に変化をもたらす原因となる」
3 下線部 This を受ける述部は requires the ability で「to以下の能力を要求する」であるから，それにあてはまる名詞をさかのぼって探すが，単語ではこれにあてはまるような事象を意味するものが見つからない。この場合は直前の文を受けたものを考えられるので，文全体を名詞節としてまとめる。 4 アの switching が③の task [switching]に，イの sustain「持続する」が①の[staying on] task に，ウの sharing が②のtask [sharing]に，それぞれ対応する。 5 (1) 冒頭の文の問題個所 *open* environmentsの直後に説明が補われているのでそこを引用し，文としてまとめる。 (2) 第2段落最後にL2 cognitive fluency needs --- で始まる文があるので，そこを解答として引用する。 6 最後の段落の始めに attention についての記述があり，ウと内容が一致する。アは to fight against successful performance とあるが，fight for でないと文主旨と一致しない。イは第2段落後半の In this sense 以下の文中の complementary to the automatic aspects of processing と矛盾する。エは Cohen らが「cognitive fluency につての重要な概括を提供している」としているが，文中では「attention とは何かについて重要な概括をしている」とあり，不一致。

【2】(解答例) 1 People grow through experience if they meet life honestly and courageously. This is how character is built. 2 I would use a systematic approach to encourage students to use all four skills. First, the teacher will prepare several stories for students to select one and read it. Then, they are to summarize the story so that they can go through the story once again to fully understand it and practice writing. The teacher should help students write their summary and revise it if necessary. Then each student is to find a partner who has not read the story he/she read and tell the summary to practice speaking. The partner could ask questions and both students can practice listening and speaking. (102 words)

〈解説〉1　解答例は Eleanor Roosevelt の有名な言葉であり英文に文句をつけるべくもないが，同じ表現を思いつかなければ，たとえば meet は face でもよく，character は personality としてもよいだろう。「勇気を持って」は日本語の感覚から with courage としても意味は通るが，英文にした場合，語尾 -ly で終わる副詞で揃えた方がすっきりするので，そのあたりの配慮には努めてほしい。　2　解答は一例であり，解答者によっていろいろな考えやアプローチがあってよいが，4技能を関連付けた指導方法でなければならないのは言うまでもない。「聞くこと」,「話すこと」,「読むこと」,「書くこと」の4技能の総合的な指導は今後も重視される方向であると思われるので，自分なりにいろいろな視点から指導法を練っておいてほしい。

【高等学校】

【1】1　most of which comes from L2 classroom contexts　2　①　エ　②　イ　③　ア　3 (解答例)　目的と目標という点で外国語で読むことが母国語で読むこととは異なってくる明らかな状況がある。

4　X　エ　Y　ウ　5　イ　オ　6 (解答例)　筆者は外国語で読むことは学術的知識よりも言語技能の習得に限定されると述べているが，授業で扱う教材には多様なものの見方や考え方を理解し，言語そのものや文化に対する関心を高められるようなものを選ぶべきである。

〈解説〉1　選択肢中関係詞の which に of が組み合わせられているので前に何かを加えるべきであることがわかる。most of which で，先行詞 L2 print につき「そのほとんどが」と叙述的に述べている。あとは述部で comes from の組み合わせに続き L2 classroom contexts を置けばよい。

2　①　hard-pressed は,「窮している，困っている」で,「問題を抱えて苦しんでいる」のエ。　②　automaticity は文脈から「母国語を処理するにあたっての自動的なアプローチ」という意味での「自動性」で,「母国語を本能的に，無意識に受け入れる」とするイ。　③　aspiration

は「願望，大志」で，同義のambitionでア。　3　in terms of ～ は「～に関して，～の点から，～の見地から」等の訳があてられる。目的と目標は，日本語ではあまり豊かな語彙がないが，英語では purpose, aim, object，(主として「目的」と訳される)，goal, target，objective (主として「目標」と訳される)その他非常に多く使用され，英訳の場合は文脈により適切な語を当てなければならない。本問の場合は和訳であるからその点は楽に訳せるだろう。　4　問題個所の直前の文に，「「外国語の授業で，読むことは学術的知識よりも言語技能の習得にしばしば限定されている」とあり，下線部はそれをまとめた文なので，「言語学習という課題を遂行する」のが「L2で読むことの目標」とするエがXにあてはまり，Yにはウが入って「学術的知識のベースをつくるということよりも」という文脈となっている。　5　第1段落に，L1 reader がその言語に触れる機会と L2 reader の機会との違いが述べられており，読む頻度，量の違いからいかにL1読者が自然に読み物を処理し理解できるようになるかが書かれており，イと主旨が一致する。第3段落冒頭の，「L2読者はしばしば非常に難しく，彼らの言語学的資源の上端に位置する素材を読むという世界的傾向がある」との文が，オと主旨が一致する。　6　指導要領第4款「各科目にわたる指導計画の作成と内容の取扱い」の2「内容の取扱いに当たっては，次の事項に配慮するものとする」以下に，「その外国語を日常使用している人々を中心とする世界の人々及び日本人の日常生活，風俗習慣，物語，地理，歴史，伝統文化や自然科学などに関するものの中から，生徒の発達の段階及び興味・関心に即して適切な題材を，変化をもたせて取り上げるものとし(以下略)」とあるので，その趣旨に沿った留意事項をまとめる。

【２】(解答例) 1　People grow through experience if they meet life honestly and courageously. This is how character is built.　　2　When students are to give presentations, teachers should keep in mind that the students should speak in their own words, not just reading Japanese-English translation. The important thing for students is to try to communicate in English, not to construct grammatically perfect sentences and read them. Teachers can help them by giving some easy-to-use sentences for presentation, such as "This morning I'm going to talk about ---," "First, I would like to give you an overview of ---," and so forth, if necessary. Teachers should also try not to check students' grammatical errors too severely so that students could speak confidently without fearing making mistakes. (106 words)

〈解説〉1　解答例は Eleanor Roosevelt の有名な言葉であり英文に文句をつけるべくもないが，同じ表現を思いつかなければ，たとえば meet は face でもよく，character は personality としてもよいだろう。「勇気を持って」は日本語の感覚から with courage としても意味は通るが，英文にした場合，語尾 -ly で終わる副詞で揃えた方がすっきりするので，そのあたりの配慮には努めてほしい。　2　自分の考えを記述する問題なので，自由にまとめてよい。解答例では，積極的にコミュニケーションをはかろうとする態度の育成および積極的な発表の姿勢を養うための留意事項が主に書かれているが，実際の授業を考えた場合，英語として理解不能の文で発表が行われても授業として成立しないという観点から，適度に文法的指導を行うべき，といった考えもあろう。解答としては自分の考えが理解しやすいかたちで伝えられており，誤りのない文章であることを第一に，簡潔にまとめる。

2013年度　実施問題

【中高共通】

【1】(放送による問題)　これはリスニング・テスト です。放送の指示に従って答えなさい。

ただいまから，リスニング・テストを行います。問題は1，2，3，4の四つです。聞いている間にメモを取っても構いません。

では，1の問題から始めます。問題はNo.1とNo.2の2問です。

これから読まれる英文に対する応答として最もふさわしいものを，続いて読まれる(a)，(b)，(c)の中から一つ選び，記号で答えなさい。なお，英文と応答は<u>1度しか</u>読まれません。

では，始めます。

No.1　Are you still keeping to your New Year's resolutions?

(a)　No. I haven't broken any yet.

(b)　Yes. So far, so good.

(c)　I wasn't sure what to say.

No.2　I'm really looking forward to the show. I've never seen her perform before.

(a)　I'm sure you'll be performing well.

(b)　I suppose she could probably say that.

(c)　She is great. You won't be disappointed.

次に2の問題に移ります。

問題はNo.1からNo.3までの3問です。

これから，短い対話文を読みます。そのあとでクエスチョンと言って質問します。その答えとして最もふさわしいものを，続いて読まれる(a)，(b)，(c)，(d)の中から一つ選び，記号で答えなさい。なお，対話文・質問・答えの選択肢は1度しか読まれません。

では，始めます。

No.1 M : Hi, Kumiko. What are you doing here in Sydney? You're the last person I expected to meet here.

W : I have a job here. I did my year abroad as a student and then was offered a job at the university as an interpreter in Japanese.

M : Do you sometimes go back to Japan?

W : Oh, yes. I visit my parents in my hometown every summer.

Question : What is Kumiko doing in Sydney?

(a) She is studying.

(b) She is working.

(c) She is offering a job to her friend.

(d) She is hoping to meet a man.

No.2 W : Tim, that was you that I saw in the flower shop near the station yesterday.

M : Me? In the flower shop? No, Kate. I think you must be mistaken.

W : Of course, it was you. You are hiding something, aren't you?

M : OK. I'll tell you the truth. I ordered a bouquet for Janet. Her birthday is coming up soon. I wanted it to be a surprise, so please keep it a secret.

Question : Did the man go to the flower shop yesterday?

(a) Yes. His birthday was coming up soon.

(b) No. The woman made a mistake.

(c) Yes. He wanted to order a birthday present.

(d) No. He had to keep it a secret.

No.3 M : Where is Ms.Sato? She knows our meeting starts at 9 : 30, doesn' t she?

W : Of course, she does. Don't worry. She will make it. Why do you feel so pressed?

M : Well, I must finish this meeting on time because I have another appointment at 12 : 30. I've already reserved a table at a restaurant.

W : I see. I'll call her if she doesn't show up by 9 : 15.

Question : What will the man do after the meeting?

(a) He will call Ms.Sato as soon as possible.

(b) He will reserve a table at a restaurant.

(c) He will show up at the meeting by 12 : 30.

(d) He will have lunch at a restaurant.

次に3の問題に移ります。問題はNo.1からNo.3までの3問です。

これから，あるまとまりのある英文を読みます。そのあとで，その英文について三つの質問をします。その答えとして最もふさわしいものを，質問に続いて読まれる(a)，(b)，(c)，(d)の中から一つ選び，記号で答えなさい。なお，英文・質問・答えの選択肢は，全体を通して2回読まれます。

では，始めます。

In your childhood, most of you were told that you must pay attention when others are speaking. As I watch young people these days, I realize that this etiquette no longer applies to their social interaction. It is often the case for them to engage in a face-to-face conversation while texting on their cell phones and checking Social Network Services on a computer. I heard that some professors say that they need to have a rule about the use of electronic devices in their college classes, such as "The use of electronic devices in the classroom is permitted only when it directly relates to class activities."

Perhaps, adults have stopped telling young people to put away their cell phones and pay attention because they themselves have become addicted to electronics. When I attended a large conference, I found that adults were doing the same thing, checking e-mail messages, going through the conference website on their smart-phones and tablet computers.

Changes in technology occurred rather quickly. Less than two decades ago, we didn't expect that everyone would have access to e-mail and check something on the Internet instead of visiting a library. Most students were born less than two decades ago. So they only know the life that is electronically connected all the time.

I understand the advantages of electronic devices, but I believe face-to-face conversation is still important for us. If they are looking down at their phones and computers, then they are not involved in interactions with others. I think that students should learn to articulate their thoughts effectively in a conversation and develop collaborative and leadership skills at school.

No.1　What does the speaker say about young people these days?

(a)　They have good manners of using electronic devices.

(b)　They are polite to the professors of their college.

(c)　They are addicted to computers and cell phones.

(d)　They use computers only for class activities.

No.2　Why have adults stopped telling the youth about the manners of using electronic devices?

(a)　Because their behavior is similar to young people's.

(b)　Because they can use computers better than young people.

(c)　Because education is very important for young generations.

(d)　Because electronic devices are useless in a conference.

No.3　What is the speaker's suggestion to students?

(a)　They should ignore rules to learn leadership skills at school.

(b)　They need to learn how to develop communication skills at school.

(c)　They should enjoy classes by using computers at school.

(d)　They need more electronic devices for interactions at school.

次に4の問題に移ります。問題はNo.1とNo.2の2問です。

これから，英語による対話文を読みます。(　　)のところに入る英語を聞き取り，書きなさい。対話文はそれぞれ2回読まれます。

では，始めます。

No.1　W : We have gotten new neighbors, Mr.and Mrs.Davis. Have you seen them yet?

M : No. I had a business trip and (I have been out of town all week).

No.2　M : Have you finished reading the book we were assigned?

W : Yes, but to tell the truth, (it took me quite a while to get through it).

これで，リスニング・テストを終わります。次の問題に移ってください。

(☆☆☆☆◎◎◎◎)

【2】次の英文や対話文の中の(　　)に最も適するものを，下のア～エからそれぞれ一つずつ選び，記号で答えなさい。

1　Put all (　　) in a bowl. Mix thoroughly by hand.

ア　recipes　　イ　equipments　　ウ　variables　　エ　ingredients

2　Mr.Young has been (　　) to the New York Branch.

ア　supervised　　イ　transferred　　ウ　fired　　エ　launched

3　When Jimmy and Lilly got married, they (　　) each other for about 10 years.

ア　were knowing　　イ have known　　ウ　had known

エ　had been knowing

4　My grandmother is (　　) one hundred.

ア　approached for　　イ　approached near　　ウ　approaching with

エ　approaching

5　Our dead father is watching (　　) us, don't you think?

ア　through　　イ　above　　ウ　over　　エ　below

6　It's no use worrying about the past. You should let (　　) of your past and move on.

ア　go　　イ　leave　　ウ　run　　エ　do

7　You must pay public (　　) bills without delay, or electricity, water and gas supply will be stopped.

ア　utility　　イ　component　　ウ　account　　エ　company

8　I won't get a driver's license unless it (　　) absolutely necessary.

ア　won't be　　イ　is　　ウ　has been　　エ　will have been

9　These tablets can make you feel (　　), so please be careful when you drive a car.

ア　drowsy　　イ　static　　ウ　twisted　　エ　embarrassed

10　At this supermarket potatoes are sold (　　).

ア　each pound　　イ　for the pound　　ウ　pound by pound

エ　by the pound

11　I often (　　) a good idea while I am in the bath.

ア　hit on　　イ　come over　　ウ　occur to　　エ　take on

12　A : When you have a lot of things to do, you should establish priorities.

B : I know, but it's (　　) said than done.

ア　better　　イ　more difficult　　ウ　easier　　エ　sooner

13　A : We've solved five questions and we have five to go.

B : Yes, we're just (　　) our homework.

ア　all the way from　　イ　halfway through　　ウ　on schedule

エ　in time for

14　A : Did you see the man who broke into the bank?

B : Yes. He (　　) in black and wore a pair of sunglasses.

ア　dresses　　イ　has dressed　　ウ　was dressed　　エ　has been dressed

15　A : I don't know how to do it.

B : You'll get (　　) of it soon.

ア　no chance　　イ　the hang　　ウ　the start　　エ　no idea

(☆☆☆◎◎◎)

【3】次の英文を読んで，あとの問いに答えなさい。

Everybody agrees that English is very difficult to learn. It's almost as difficult as Japanese! At first, Japanese students of English think they can understand the exact meaning of an English word, just by looking it up in a dictionary. The trouble is the same word can have many different meanings (①) how it is used. It depends on the context.

Let me give you an example. A Japanese friend of mine had a lot of trouble while he was trying to park his car along the Malibu waterfront near Los Angeles. He just couldn't find a parking place. At last he saw a big empty space. (②), there was a notice near it which read, "(1)<u>Fine</u> for Parking!" My friend wondered why there weren't any other cars parked there but he didn't worry. "If it's fine for parking, that's (2)<u>fine</u> for me too," he thought.

However, when he came back, he found a very tough-looking policeman waiting for him. He looked angry and had a notebook in his hand. My friend was rather worried. "Why are you parked here? Can't you read the notice?" shouted the policeman. My Japanese friend answered, "Well, of course I can read it. But the notice says it's fine, which means right, suitable or nice for parking, so that's why I parked here."

Luckily, the policeman seemed to have a good sense of humour, so after laughing a bit, he explained, "Fine in this sense means an amount of money you have to pay as a penalty. That's because you are not allowed to park here." Also, luckily, the policeman let him go with just a warning. But after that incident, my friend will always remember the two meanings of the word fine!

Once, (③) a misunderstanding, I was worried about my mother in Tokyo. She visited me once during a hot summer. So she wanted to buy a cool silk dress, but just couldn't find her size in a Tokyo department store. She was rather tired of hearing the sales girls' comments, "Even extra large is too small for you!" That was why I introduced her to a dressmaker.

So, one morning she went to the dressmaker while I went shopping. After I'd finished, I went along to the dressmaker but, not seeing my mother, I asked one of the assistants where she was. "Oh, (3)<u>she's having fits on the second floor</u>," was the reply. I was very worried. Why? Because having fits means going crazy, or mad, or being extremely angry. I rushed up to the second floor expecting my mother to be screaming or shouting about something.

(④), she was calm and smiling, evidently very happy about how her dress had turned out. Of course, the assistant should not have said having fits but having a fitting, or being fitted which means being measured for a suit or dress. Just a few letters can completely change the meaning.

Often Japanese students make mistakes in their English when speaking to foreigners because they're so nervous. In fact, (4)<u>sometimes they may be so nervous that they cannot say anything at all</u>. They may even give the wrong impression of rudeness or stupidity which foreigners sometimes don't understand.

I remember one time when I saw this actually happen in very difficult circumstances. Some time ago, my health insurance was handled by an American company. One morning, the manager called me and (5)<u>(a / I / him / favour / do / asked / could / if)</u>. He explained that the American president of the company, Mr.Starr had a house in Tokyo. Although he only stayed there for one week in a year, he kept it fully staffed with a cook, maids and gardeners.

Mr.Starr felt the son of his cook was very intelligent. He wanted him to be fluent in English, so the office manager asked me to give him English conversation lessons. Mr.Starr would be visiting Tokyo in three months' time and wanted to speak to the boy then... in English, of course.

The lessons went smoothly, as although the boy was very nervous at first, he was certainly very intelligent. I coached him in a model conversation that he might have with Mr.Starr.

[A]

[B]

[C]

[D]

Anyway, don't worry about making mistakes in your English. Sometimes it can be very amusing, and I really feel that humour is one of the best forms of international communication.

(Brian W.Powle, *My Humorous Japan Part 3*による。ただし，設問の都合で一部省略及び改変している)

1 本文中の空欄(①)～(④)に最もよくあてはまる語句を，それぞれ次のア～オの中から一つずつ選び，記号で答えなさい。ただし，文頭に来る語も小文字で示されています，また，同じ記号は二回以上使わないこと。

ア on the contrary イ in spite of ウ better yet

エ because of オ according to

2 下線部(1)，(2)はどのような意味で使われているか，それぞれの意味を，下線部(1)は11語で，下線部(2)は4語で，本来中からそのまま抜き出しなさい。

3 下締部(3)の表現を，筆者は「誰が，どのような行動をとっているという意味」に解釈したか，本文に即して日本語で答えなさい。

4 下線部(4)のような状況によって，筆者はどのようなことが生じると考えているか，日本語で答えなさい。

5 下線部(5)について，( )内の語を並べかえ，正しい英文を完成させなさい。

6 本文中の空欄A～Dに最もよくあてはまる英文を，次のア～エの中から一つずつ選び，その記号をA～Dの順番に並べかえなさい。

ア The only reply was silence as the boy looked down at his knees. Mr.Starr tried again, "Say, boy, you're playing sports, right? What sports do you like?" Mr.Starr's questions, though phrased in easy English, were difficult to understand because he spoke quickly. Unfortunately, silence greeted that question too and all the other questions Mr.Starr asked. Somehow, he couldn't sense the boy was just very nervous. Mr.Starr seemed to be very angry with my student and me.

イ　There was the great Mr.Starr sitting behind the desk. There's no doubt he was a very kindly and intelligent man but with his large body, red face and loud voice, he must have been very frightening for a young Japanese student. He spoke to the boy, "Well, how's it going, my boy? You're enjoying your English lessons?"

ウ　The interview was a disaster and naturally the lessons were not continued. However, I invited the boy and his father to my house. The father was happy to see his son speaking easy English to me quite confidently. I only wish that Mr.Starr could have been there to see that his money had not been wasted!

エ　At last Mr.Starr made his annual visit. My student and I went to the head office of the insurance company to meet the great man. We were first shown into an outer office from which we could hear Mr.Starr's booming voice from the inner sanctum. At last, a secretary opened the door and announced, "Mr.Starr will see you now."

(☆☆◎◎◎)

【中学校】

【1】次の英文を読んで，あとの問いに答えなさい。

Almost all English language teachers get students to study grammar and vocabulary, practise functional dialogues, take part in productive skill activities and try to become ①<u>competent</u> in listening and reading. Yet some of these same teachers make little attempt to teach pronunciation in any overt way and only give attention to it in passing. It is possible that they are nervous of dealing with sounds and intonation; perhaps they feel they have too much to do already and pronunciation teaching will only make things worse. (1)<u>They may claim that even without a formal pronunciation syllabus, and without specific pronunciation teaching, many students seem to acquire serviceable</u>

pronunciation in the course of their studies anyway.

However, the fact that some students are able to acquire reasonable pronunciation without overt pronunciation teaching should not blind us to the benefits of a focus on pronunciation in our lessons. Pronunciation teaching not only makes students aware of different sounds and sound features (and what these mean), but can also improve their speaking immeasurably. Concentrating on sounds, showing where they are made in the mouth, making students aware of where words should be stressed — all these things give them extra information about spoken English and help them achieve the goal of improved comprehension and intelligibility.

Three particular problems occur in much pronunciation teaching and learning.

・What students can hear : some students have great difficulty hearing pronunciation features which we want them to reproduce. Frequently, speakers of different first languages have problems with different sounds, especially where, as with / b / and / v / for Spanish speakers, their language does not have the same two sounds. If they cannot ②distinguish between them, they will find it almost impossible to produce the two different English phonemes.

There are two ways of dealing with this : in the first place, we can show students how sounds are made through demonstration, diagrams and explanation. But we can also draw the sounds to their attention every time they appear on a recording or in our own conversation. In this way we gradually train the students' ears. When they can hear correctly, they are on the way to being able to speak correctly.

・What students can say : all babies are born with the ability to make the whole range of sounds available to human beings. But as we grow and focus in on one or two languages, we lose the habit of making some of those sounds. Learning a foreign language often presents us with the problem of physical unfamiliarity. To counter this problem, we need to be able to show and explain exactly where sounds are produced.

・The intonation problem : for many teachers the most problematic area of pronunciation is intonation. Some of us find it extremely difficult to hear 'tunes' or to identify the different patterns of rising and falling tones. In such situations it would be foolish to try to teach them.

However, the fact that we may have difficulty recognising specific intonation tunes does not mean that we should ③abandon intonation teaching altogether. Most of us can hear when someone is surprised, enthusiastic or bored, or when they are really asking a question rather than just confirming something they already know. One of our tasks, then, is to give students opportunities to recognise such moods and intentions either on an audio track or through the way we ourselves model them. We can then get students to imitate the way moods are articulated, even though we may not (be able to) discuss the technicalities of the different intonation patterns themselves.

The key to successful pronunciation teaching, however, is not so much getting students to produce correct sounds or intonation tunes, but rather to have them listen and notice how English is spoken — either on audio or video or by their teachers themselves. (2)The more aware they are, the greater the chance that their own intelligibility levels will rise.

(Jeremy Harmer, *The Practice of English Language Teaching 4th Edition* による。ただし，設問の都合で一部省略及び改変している。)

1　下線部①～③の英語の定義として最もよくあてはまるものを，それぞれ次のア～エの中から一つずつ選び，記号で答えなさい。

①　ア　made of different parts or materials

　　イ　one of several parts of which something is made

　　ウ　including or dealing with all or nearly all elements or aspects of something

　　エ　having the necessary ability, knowledge, or skill to do something successfully

②　ア　to recognise the difference between two people or things

イ　to take someone's attention away from what they are trying to do

ウ　to make someone feel very annoyed or upset about something that is not acceptable

エ　to change the shape, appearance or sound of something so that it is strange or not clear

③　ア　to get something, especially by making an effort

イ　to officially end a law, a system or an institution

ウ　to give up completely a practice or a course of action

エ　to create or design something that has not existed before

2　下線部(1)の主張に対して，筆者は，発音に焦点をあてた指導を行うことに，どのような利点があると考えていますか。「音声的特徴」と「話す力」という言葉を使い，本文に即して日本語で答えなさい。

3　本文では，「自分の母語にない音声を聞き取れないとき」の発音指導の方法を，二つあげています。その二つの方法を，本文に即して日本語で説明しなさい。

4　下線部(2)を日本語に直しなさい。

5　本文の内容に即して，次の質問に英語で答えなさい。

(1)　In order to counter the problem of physical unfamiliarity, what do English teachers need to do?

(2)　What can teachers get students to imitate, even though they cannot explan different intonation patterns?

6　本文の内容に合うものを，次のア～カから二つ選び，記号で答えなさい。

ア　English teachers hesitate to teach sounds and intonation because they are too confident in their own pronunciation.

イ　Many students tend to blind themselves to the various benefits of overt pronunciation practice in English classes.

ウ　Some students have great difficulty hearing English pronunciation features which they are expected to reproduce.

エ　When students get older, they will realise the whole range of sounds available to human beings turns out to be wider.

オ　It is not so difficult for learners of English to hear ‘tunes’ or to identify the various patterns of rising and falling tones.

カ　What is important to successful pronunciation teaching is to have students listen and notice how English is spoken.

(☆☆☆◎◎◎)

【2】次の1，2について，指示に従って答えなさい。

1　次の日本語を英語に直しなさい。

子どもは親を愛することから始める。やがて，成長とともに親を評価するようになり，最終的には親を許すようになる。

2　「中学校学習指導要領」(平成20年3月告示)では，指導する語数が，改訂前の「900語程度までの語」から「1200語程度の語」に増加しています。この点について，授業を行う上でどのようなことに配慮しますか。あなたの考えを100語程度の英語で書きなさい。ただし，語数には，カンマやピリオド等の句読点，疑問符や引用符等の符号は含まないものとします。なお，解答の総語数を記入すること。

(☆☆☆☆◎◎◎◎)

【高等学校】

【1】次の英文を読んで，あとの問いに答えなさい。

(1)Theme-based instruction is not the same as content-based. In order to distinguish the two, let’s think of the former as a “weak” version of the latter. In the strong version (content-based), the primary purpose of a course is to instruct students in a subject-matter area, and language is of secondary and subordinate interest. For example, English for Specific Purposes (ESP) at the university level gathers engineering majors together in a course designed to teach terminology, concepts, and current issues in engineering. Because students are ESL students, they must of course learn this material in English, which the teacher is prepared to help them with.

A weak form of content-based teaching actually places an equal value on content and language objectives. While the curriculum, to be sure, is organized around subject-matter area, both students and teachers are fully aware that language skills don't occupy a subordinate role. Students have no doubt chosen to take a course or curriculum because their language skills need improvement, and they are now able to work toward that improvement without being battered with linguistically based topics. The ultimate ①payoff is that their language skills are indeed enhanced, but through focal attention to topic and peripheral attention to language.

This weak version is actually practical and effective in many instructional settings. It typically ②manifests itself in what has come to be called theme-based or topic-based teaching. Theme-based instruction provides an alternative to what would otherwise be traditional language classes by structuring a course around themes or topics. (2)Theme-based curricula can serve the multiple interests of students in a classroom and can offer a focus on content while still adhering to institutional needs for offering a language course per se. So, for example, an intensive English course for intermediate pre-university students might deal with topics of current interest such as public health, environmental awareness, world economics, etc. In the classroom students read articles or chapters, view video programs, discuss issues, propose solutions, and carry out writing assignments on a given theme.

Granted, there is a fuzzy line of distinction between theme-based instruction and "traditional" language instruction. You could easily argue that many existing reading and writing courses, for example, are theme-based in that they offer students substantial opportunities to ③grapple with topics of relevance and interest. I don't think it is important, or necessary, to dichotomize here. What is important is to view theme-based instruction as a context for the integration of skills.

Numerous current ESL textbooks, especially at the intermediate to advanced levels, offer theme-based courses of study. Challenging topics in these textbooks engage the curiosity and increase motivation of students as they tackle an array of real-life issues ranging from simple to complex and also improve their linguistic skills across all four domains of listening, sneaking, reading. and writing.

(H.Douglas Brown, *Teaching by Principles 3rd Edition* による。ただし，設問の都合で一部改変している。)

1　下線部①～③の英語の定義として最もよくあてはまるものを，それぞれ次のア～エの中から一つずつ選び，記号で答えなさい。

①　ア　an instance of turning or switching something off
　　イ　a point or level which is a designated limit of something
　　ウ　an advantage or a reward from something you have done
　　エ　a temporary or permanent discharge of a worker or workers
②　ア　to appear or become noticeable
　　イ　to tell someone that they must do a particular thing
　　ウ　to work skillfully with information to achieve the result that you want
　　エ　to campaign to arouse public concern about an issue in the hope of prompting action
③　ア　to complain about something in a bad-tempered way
　　イ　to struggle to deal with or overcome a difficulty or challenge
　　ウ　to cause someone to believe firmly in the truth of something
　　エ　to refuse to take notice of or acknowledge; disregard intentionally

2　下線部(1)はどのようなことか，「内容中心教授法」「テーマ中心教授法」「目的」という言葉を使い，本文に即して日本語で具体的に説明しなさい。

3　下線部(2)を日本語に直しなさい。

4　次は，本文中で述べられている筆者の主張の一部を，短くまとめたものです。(　X　)，(　Y　)に入る言葉を，それぞれ10字以内の日本語で書きなさい。ただし，句読点も字数に含めること。

テーマ中心教授法と伝統的言語教授法について，それらの違いを(　　X　　)かもしれないが，ここでは両者を(　　Y　　)ことは，重要ではなく，その必要はない。

5　本文の内容に即して，次の質問に英語で答えなさい。

(1)　What group of ESL students are used as an example of taking the course for English for Specific Purposes?

(2)　In the fourth paragraph, how should theme-based instruction be viewed?

6　本文の内容に合うものを，次のア～カから二つ選び，記号で答えなさい。

ア　Content-based instruction suggests an equal allotment of time for subject-matter and language teaching in class.

イ　In theme-based instruction, teachers and students usually focus more on linguistically based topics than on content.

ウ　The weak version deals with topics on current issues while integrating linguistic skills across all four domains.

エ　The strong version is less practical and effective than the weak one, especially when teaching advanced learners.

オ　The author argues that existing reading and writing courses are content-based as language is of secondary interest.

カ　In theme-based textbooks, real-life issues seem to attract students' curiosity and elevate their intrinsic motivation.

(☆☆☆☆◎◎◎)

【2】次の1，2について，指示に従って答えなさい。

1　次の日本語を英語に直しなさい。

子どもは親を愛することから始める。やがて，成長とともに親を評価するようになり，最終的には親を許すようになる。

2　「高等学校学習指導要領」(平成21年3月告示)では，「コミュニケーション英語Ⅰ」の学習内容として，生徒同士が英語で話し合ったり意見の交換をしたりする言語活動が示されています。この言語活動をより活発なものにするために，どのような工夫をしますか。あなたの考えを100語程度の英語で書きなさい。ただし，語数には，カンマやピリオド等の句読点，疑問符や引用符等の符号は含まないものとします。なお，解答の総語数も記入すること。

(☆☆☆◎◎◎)

解答・解説

【中高共通】

【1】1　No.1　b　　No.2　c　　2　No.1　b　　No.2　c　　No.3　d　3　No.1　c　　No.2　a　　No.3　b　　4　No.1　I have been out of town all week　　No.2　it took me quite a while to get through it

〈解説〉リスニングによる多肢選択問題である。リスニング問題は効率的に解答していくことが求められる。問題形式(放送は何回聞くことができるのか，メモは取ってよいのかなど)について把握しておく必要がある。本問題は事前に放送内容を予測することはできないが，問題文や質問文も全て提示されており，英文のレベル自体は易しい。普段からリスニングの練習を重ねていれば容易に正解にたどりつけるだろう。　1　会話での応答問題である。会話の状況や質問の応答の仕方を理解しているかが問われている。No.1はAre you～?で聞かれていることに着目するとcでは会話がなりたたない。New Year's resolutionは「新年の決意」。aではNoと後に続く内容が一致しない。よって正解はbである。　No.2はこの会話がショーを見に行く二人によって行われていることがわかれば，aとbは不適であることがわかる。cであれば会話が成立する。　2　短い対話文に続く質問に答える問題である。　No.1は男性がKumikoとシドニーで偶然出会った場面だと思われる。KumikoのI have a job here.の部分が聞こえていれば正解はbであることがわかる。 No.2は女性がTimに花屋で見かけたと言う場面である。TimはJanetの誕生日プレゼントを買うために花屋に行ったとあるので，正解はcである。 No.3はMs. Satoがなかなか会議に現れないために，男性が次のappointmentに間に合うかを心配している。… I have another appointment at 12:30. I've already reserved a table at a restaurant.とあるので，会議の後，レストランで食事をする約束があると考えるのが妥当であろう。よって正解はdである。 3 長い英文の後の質問文に答える問題である。放送される文章は長いが，2回放送されるので1回目を活用していこう。このSpeakerの言いたいことはスマートフォン等の電子機器の使用で，対面的なコミュニケーションがおろそかになったり，マナーが悪くなっているので，見直しや対策が必要であるということである。このように話の大枠がつかめれば，2回目はポイントを押さえて聞くことができるだろう。No.1はSpeakerが今日の若者に対してどのように述べているかという質問である。このSpeakerは若者がスマートフォンなどの電子機器などを使うことで，目の前で話している人や講義をしている人に対する注意が散漫になっていることに問題意識をもっている。よってcが正解である。 No.2はなぜ大人が若者に対して注意をしなくなったのかを聞いている。Perhaps, adults have stopped telling young people to put away their cell phones and pay attention because they themselves have become addicted to electronics. とある。このaddicted to electronicsは若者と共通しているので正解はaである。
No.3はSpeakerが提案していることを聞きとればよい。最後にI think that students should learn to articulate their thoughts effectively in a conversation and develop collaborative and leadership skills at school. とあるので正解はbである。 4 ディクテーションの問題である。日頃から練習を積み重ねて細かい部分まで聞き取れる練習をしておこう。

【2】1 エ 2 イ 3 ウ 4 エ 5 ウ 6 ア 7 ア 8 イ 9 ア 10 エ 11 ア 12 ウ 13 イ 14 ウ 15 イ

〈解説〉文法や語彙の選択問題である。　1は語彙の問題である。適切なのはエのingredients「成分，要素，原料」である。　2はBranchが「枝」という意味ではなく「支社」という派生的な意味で使われている。頻出単語なので覚えておこう。New York支社から察すると転勤になったと考えるのが妥当なので，イのtransferが正解である。　3　時制の問題である。JimmyとLillyが結婚したのは過去のことで知り合っていたのはその前であるから，過去完了形を用いるのが正しい。よって正解はウである。　4「100歳に近づいている」という意味なので，エが正解である。　5　watch over ～で「～を見守る」という意味になる。よって正解はウである。　6はlet go of ～で「～を手放す」という意味になる。過去にしがみついていないで前に進めということを述べているのである。正解はアである。　7はelectricityやwaterやgasなどの光熱費をどのようにいうかであるが，public utility billsとなる。よって正解はアである。　8はunlessなどの条件節のなかでは，たとえ未来の話であったとしても時制は現在形で表す。よってイが正解である。ちなみにif なども同様なので覚えておこう。　9はアのdrowsy「眠い，うとうとしている」をあてはめてみると，これらの薬を服用すると眠気が出ることがあるので車を運転する時はお気をつけください，となり意味が通る。他の選択肢は意味が通らないので不適となる。よって正解はアである。　10はpoundがポンドという重さの単位であることを知っていれば，単位をいうときの前置詞byを使うことがわかるだろう。よって正解はエである。　11はイディオムの問題である。hit onは「～を思いつく」，come overは「やってくる，ふらっと立ち寄る」などの意。occur toは「～を思いつく」，take onは「～に乗る」などの意味になる。意味からするとアかウに絞られるだろう。次にアとウは主語と目的語の取り方が違うことを考える。occur toはA good idea occurred to me.というように思いついたことを主語に取るので，この問題では不適となる。よってアが正解である。　12はウをあてはめれば，言うのは簡単だが行うのは難しいとなって意味が通る。あとは意味が不明瞭なので不適となる。　13は5問解いて5問残っているということから察するに

halfwayがふさわしいことがわかるだろう。正解はイである。　14は時制の問題である。break intoで「侵入する」という意味である。break into the bankは銀行強盗をすると解釈するのが妥当であろう。銀行強盗をBが目撃したのは過去のことであるのでウが正解である。　15はget the hang of ～で「～をどのようにするかを学ぶ」という意味となりこれが正解となる。

【3】1 ① オ　② ウ　③ エ　④ ア　2 (1) an amount of money you have to pay as a penalty　(2) right, suitable or nice
3 筆者の母親が二階で気が狂ったように，何かのことで叫んだり怒鳴ったりしているという意味。　4 緊張のあまり無言になると，ときには外国人に理解してもらえず，無作法であるとか，愚かであるという誤ったイメージさえ与えてしまうかもしれないこと。
5 asked if I could do him a favour　6 エ → イ → ア → ウ

〈解説〉1 ① カッコの前後の文脈の意味をとると「日本人英語学習者は初めはただ辞書を引くだけで正確な意味をとれると思っているが，実際は，語は複数の意味を持っており，文脈に依存する」という流れになる。したがって，カッコを含む文は「問題なのは同じ語でも，どの語がどのように使われているかによって，意味が変わってくることだ」という意味にしたいのでaccording toが妥当である。The trouble is (that) ～.「問題なのは～だ」　② 第2パラグラフは英語の多義語によって，日本人英語学習者が困った例を挙げている場面である。「ある日本人がLos Angeles近郊のMalibu waterfrontで駐車場が見つからず困っていたところ大きな空地を見つけた。さらに良いことにそこにはFine for Parking!という看板がありその日本人は (Fineの意味を間違えて) 駐車歓迎だと解釈した」となる。「空地を見つけ，さらに都合の良い看板があった」と良いことを追加しているのでBetter yetが妥当である。　③ 第5パラグラフからは，英語話者である筆者が英語の微妙な違いで困った日本での体験について書かれている。パラグラフ冒頭ではその話題の導入で「以前ある誤解のせいで困った」となる。したがって，because ofが妥当である。　④　カッコの直前で「2階で母がものすごく怒って叫んでいると予想した」とありカッコの直後では「母は落ち着いており微笑んでいた」とある。予想に反した展開になっているのでon the contraryが妥当である。　2　多義語fineの意味を知っていれば「都合がいい，すばらしい」と「罰金 (を課す) 」であると解答を予想して，該当箇所を素早く探すことができるが，知っていなくともmeans ～「～を意味する」と明示的に書かれているため，それぞれそれ以降をそのまま抜き出せばよい。　3　下線部の直後で筆者が困惑した理由が書かれている。having fitsという表現は「もの凄く怒った状態」を意味するので，筆者は2階へ駆け上がった。そして分詞構文で示されているexpecting my mother to be screaming or shouting about somethingの部分が解答の根拠になる。expect A to do「Aが～するだろうと思う」　4　下線部の直後の文が解答根拠となる。「日本人学習者はスピーキングの際に神経質になりすぎて何も言えないことが時々あり，その態度は外国人には無作法とか愚かといった間違った印象を与えかねない」と述べられている。　5　do A a favour = do a favour for Aで「Aのために尽くす，支援する」。さらにasked if ～「～かどうか尋ねる」。favourはイギリス英語の綴りが使われている。並べ替えであるためそのままの綴りを使用したい。　6　この並べ替えの部分は「神経質になりすぎて英語が話せずに誤解を与えてしまった」例を示している部分である。文の並べ替え問題は代名詞の照応関係をしっかり把握し，つなぎ言葉に注目すると素早く解答できる。まず選択肢エでは「Starr社長がいるオフィスを訪れ，社長がいる隣の部屋に通され，社長を待っていると，ついに秘書から中に入るよう言われる場面」が述べられている。選択肢イの冒頭で「Starr社長を初めて見た印象」が書かれているため，エとイがつながることがわかる。さらに選択肢イの最後でStarr社長が少年に質問している。その部分が選択肢アのThe only replyにつながるのでアが次に来ることがわかる。そして最後に「少年は神経質で沈黙してしまい，Starr社長は怒りレッスンが中止されてしまうが，その後筆者が少年とその父親を家に招き，少年が英語を話す姿を見て父が喜ぶ。そしてStarr社長もその場面にいたらなぁ」という状況が示された選択肢ウが来る。

【中学校】

【1】1 ① エ ② ア ③ ウ 2 発音指導によって生徒たちは異なる音声や音声的特徴について気づくだけでなく，彼らの話す力もまた，計り知れないほど向上するという利点。 3 音がどのようにして出されるのかを，教師が実際に発音してみせたり，図で示したり，説明したりして生徒に教えること。また教えようとする音が，録音された音声や自分たちの会話の中に出てくるたびに，生徒の注意をそれらの音に向けさせること。 4 生徒たちが意識すればするほど，彼ら自身の (発音の) 明瞭度が高まる可能性は，ますます大きくなる。
5 (1) They need to be able to show and explain exactly where sounds are produced. (2) They can get them to imitate the way moods are articulated. 6 ウ / カ (順不同)

〈解説〉1 ①～③ともに難しい語ではなく瞬時に解答したい問題である。単語を学ぶ際には語義だけでなく，同義語を一緒におさえるようにしたい。同義語を覚えることで，こういった定義の問題だけでなく，内容一致問題でパラフレーズされた選択肢に対応できたり，ライティングの問題で同じ表現を繰り返し使うことを避けられたりできる。
① competent「能力のある，有能な」 ② distinguish「区別する」 ③ abandon「あきらめる，放棄する」 2 下線部の発音指導を軽視する教師たちの主張に対して，次のパラグラフ冒頭Howeverからが筆者の主張。そして発音に焦点を当てた指導の利点はPronunciation teaching not only ～から始まる一文で述べられている。さらにこの後ろの文でも同じようなことが繰り返し述べられている。ただし「音声的特徴」と「話す力」にそれぞれ該当する英語はsound featureとtheir speakingであるため，前半の英文の内容をまとめれば十分である。
3 第3パラグラフから発音指導において困難となる点が3つまとめられており一つ目の・What students can hear: で「自分の母語にない音声

を聞き取れないとき」という内容が述べられている。そしてそれを克服するための発音指導が第4パラグラフのThere are two ways of dealing with this以降で2つ述べられているのでそれをまとめればよい。

4　ポイントはThe比較級 ～, the 比較級 ….「～すればするほどますます…だ」の構文とchanceが同格のthatをとっていることから「機会」ではなく「可能性，見込み」という日本語に直したい。またこの文ではriseの後ろにbe動詞が省略されていると考えることができる。つまり前半部分はthey are aware，後半部分はthe chance that their own intelligibility levels will rise is greatが比較級を伴って前へ出たと解釈すればよい。

5　(1)　・What students can say: の最後の部分が解答となる。本文ではweで述べられているが，質問はEnglish teachersが主語なのでTheyで解答しなければならないので注意したい。　(2)「生徒に何を模倣させるのか」説明している部分は最後から2つ目のパラグラフである。(1)同様解答の際，主語に注意したい。　6　アは第1パラグラフ3文目の内容と不一致。イは第2パラグラフの最初の文と不一致。エは第4パラグラフの What students can say: 以下の内容と不一致，オは The intonation problem: 以下の内容と不一致。

【2】1　(解答例)　Children begin by loving their parents. Then, as children grow older, they come to judge their parents and finally learn to forgive them.

2　(解答例)

I have two plans to successfully introduce these 1200 words.

Firstly, teachers should keep in mind the notion of passive vocabulary and active vocabulary. Especially, students will learn difficult words better as the passive vocabulary first, which means that if they can understand the meaning of the word, that's enough. Later, they can learn to use those words in their essay or speech as an active vocabulary.

Secondly, teachers should give students a chance to check the meaning of new words each other during the class. It will enhance their vocabulary acquisition, as well as the communication between the students. (100 words)

〈解説〉1　公式の模範解答では1文目はChildren begin by loving their parents.となっているが，これだと何を始めるのか分からないのでAt first, children love their parents. くらいが適当。2文目のjudgeも正しい・正しくないの判断のニュアンスがあるのでevaluateの方が適当であろう。また文意からするとthey come to judge their parentsのところはthey come to have likes and dislikes about their parents や they come to see their parents criticallyくらいの方がよい。このような抽象的な内容の日本語を英語にする場合には，まず日本語の真意を考えその内容を踏まえて「英語にしやすい日本語」に変換してから英語にするとよい。　2　語彙を効果的に覚える方法を2つほど述べられるとよい。解答例は受容語彙と発表語彙，また，相互に新出単語を授業内で確認することを挙げたが，これ以外にも単語リストを作って「帯活動」として毎時間授業内で時間を取って，単語の確認をするなどでもよい。対策としては単語の指導文法の指導長文読解の指導などをどのようにしたらよいか，自分ならどうするか考え，それを英語で書いてみる等がよいだろう。

【高等学校】

【1】1　①　ウ　　②　ア　　③　イ　　2　内容中心教授法では，教科内容の指導が主な目的で，言語の指導は副次的である。一方，テーマ中心教授法では，内容と言語の指導に等しく重点が置かれるため，二つの教授法が異なること。　3　テーマ中心のカリキュラムによって，教室では生徒たちの多様な関心を満たすことができ，また，語学の講座を設けることそのものに対する制度上の要求にしっかりと応えながら，内容に重点を置くことができる。　4　X　明確に区別できない　Y　二項対立的にとらえる　　5　(1)　Engineering majors are used as an example.　　(2)　It should be viewed as a context for the integration of skills.　　6　ウ，カ(順不同)

〈解説〉1　英単語の定義を答える問題。もし意味を知らなくても，前後の文脈から答えを絞り込むこともできるだろう。①　payoffは「報酬」

② manifest「明らかにする」　③ grapple with ～「(問題など)に取り組む」　2 内容中心教授法については1段落目の2～3文目を見ればよい。テーマ中心教授法の内容については2段落目の1文目に書かれている。本文では，テーマ中心教授法がweak version (form) of content-based teachingとも言われていることに注意する。　3 adhere「固守する」，per se「それ自体」。1文が長いので，andやwhileによる文のつながりを読み取ることが解答の鍵である。　4 4段落目に解答となる英文がある。Xにあてはまるのは，1文目の fuzzy line of distinction。Yにあてはまるのは3文目の dichotomize「二分する」である。
5 (1) 1段落目の4文目に，engineering majors「工学専攻」を例に挙げた説明がなされている。　(2) 4段落目の最後の文が答えとなる。
6 ウは，本文2段落目と4段落目に書かれている内容を正しくまとめているので正解。カは，最終段落の内容と一致しており，正しい。アは時間の配分について述べている点が不適。イは，テーマ中心教授法が内容よりも言語の指導に焦点をあてていると述べており，誤り。エは，本文は，the strong version(content-based) が，上級者を教える際に，weak one(theme-based)より現実的，効果的ではないとは言っていないので，不適。オは，本文は伝統的な教授法が内容中心であったとは述べていないので，不正解。

【2】1 (解答例) Children begin by loving their parents. Then, as children grow older, they come to judge their parents and finally learn to forgive them.
2 (解答例)

In order for the language activities to be effective, teachers should instruct students to pay attention to such phonetic features as rhythm and intonation, and the speed and loudness of connected speech when listening to or speaking in English.

For example, as for the loudness, it is not enough only to reach listeners. It is also needed to change the way of speaking according to the contents of utterance and emotions of speakers.

To improve students' communication competence, teachers should give them opportunities to use English in various language-use situations that are familiar to them. Through these lessons, students may become positive in using English. (105語)

〈解説〉1，2の両方の問いについて，解答例はあくまで参考にすべきものであり，様々な解答が考え得る。　1　公式の模範解答では1文目はChildren begin by loving their parents.となっているが，これだと何を始めるのか分からないのでAt first, children love their parents. くらいが適当。2文目のjudgeも正しい・正しくないの判断のニュアンスがあるのでevaluateの方が適当であろう。また文意からするとthey come to judge their parentsのところはthey come to have likes and dislikes about their parents や they come to see their parents criticallyくらいの方がよい。このような抽象的な内容の日本語を英語にする場合には，まず日本語の真意を考えその内容を踏まえて「英語にしやすい日本語」に変換してから英語にするとよい。　2　自分の意見を述べればよい所であり，様々な解答が考え得る。ただし，学習指導要領の内容をしっかりと踏まえたものを作成するように注意する。解答例は，1文目に学習指導要領に記載されている指導事項を引用し，それに続いて，その指導の具体例を述べている。

2012年度　実施問題

【中高共通】

【1】(放送による問題)これはリスニング・テストです。放送の指示に従って答えなさい。(スクリプト省略)

(☆☆☆◎◎◎◎◎)

【2】次の英文や対話文の中の(　　)に最も適するものを，下のア～エからそれぞれ一つずつ選び，記号で答えなさい。

1 How much is the taxi (　　) to the station?
　ア deal　イ fare　ウ ratio　エ debt

2 Professor Harris (　　) a lecture on current economic trends yesterday.
　ア gave　イ worked　ウ confessed　エ raised

3 My brother will (　　) this package to you on his way home.
　ア pour　イ bring　ウ have　エ fetch

4 Mike is very (　　) and always finishes his duties before five o'clock.
　ア evident　イ efficient　ウ continuous　エ consecutive

5 The new economic plan is both innovative and (　　).
　ア inconsistent　イ informed　ウ fearsome　エ feasible

6 For a 45-year-old man his behavior is quite (　　) and I cannot tolerate it.
　ア childish　イ childless　ウ childhood　エ childproof

7 It was very (　　) to hear Tom say such an unpleasant thing.
　ア dedicating　イ dedicated　ウ embarrassing
　エ embarrassed

8 Diesel engines produce pollutants, (　　) a serious environmental problem today.
　ア which results from　イ that results from　ウ which causes
　エ that causes

9 I would (　　) if you could help me.

ア appreciate イ appreciate it ウ be appreciated

エ have appreciated

10 No one remembers ( ) such a wonderful place in the small town.

ア there be イ there to be ウ there being

エ there is being

11 You had better rent a *kimono* ( ) it, if you want to save money.

ア than buy イ than to buy ウ than buying

エ rather than buy

12 My friends ( ) to the movie today instead of tomorrow.

ア insisted that they go イ insisted to go ウ insisted me to go

エ insisted to me going

13 A : How do you like your psychology class?

B : ( ) Dr. Adams is one of the most talented lecturers I've ever met.

ア I'm in the same boat. イ I'll hit the roof. ウ You bet.

エ It couldn't be better.

14 A : How did the man ( ) such a fortune?

B : He just worked very hard all through his life.

ア come by イ come down on ウ fall down on

エ fall behind

15 A : Why don't you ( ) the assignment and hit the sack?

B : You are quite right. I'm getting sleepy.

ア lie down イ get across ウ take apart エ wrap up

(☆☆☆◎◎◎◎◎)

【3】次の英文を読んで，あとの問いに答えなさい。

It seems like a reasonable enough proposition : you visit a particular chain of shops regularly, so you decide to sign up for their loyalty scheme. Each time you shop, you show your card, and accumulate points — which you can then redeem for vouchers or gifts. Fair enough. The shop gets your guaranteed custom, and you get rewarded for shopping with them. It seems like (1)<u>a win-</u>

win situation. That is, until you figure out what else the retailer might be getting from the deal.

(①) trying to get you to spend more money in their stores, loyalty programs are a way for retailers to collect information about their customers. Let's say you visit your local supermarket twice a week, handing over your loyalty card each time. Every single item you buy is recorded and the data is saved — perhaps for several years The UK's biggest loyalty scheme is the Nectar card, which claims to have some 13 million cardholders. When you look at their range of "sponsors" — Sainsbury's supermarkets, Debenhams department stores, BP, Vodafone, Threshers wine merchants, *to name but a few — the amount of information that's held about each cardholder is (2) "stunning," according to an industry source. It's estimated that in Britain, on average, loyalty card schemes hold more centralised information about their customers than the government does.

[A]

So what's the problem? Who cares if your supermarket knows a bit about you? After all, you're getting something out of it too, aren't you? The promoters of loyalty card schemes say they're just trying to offer a better service to their customers. But in the US, people have seen the potential in the huge reservoirs of information held by the card companies — and they're doing their best to get their hands on it.

The US-based Caspian group, which campaigns against loyalty card schemes, says that card data has already been used in American courts. In one case, a supermarket wanted to use register receipts to defend a personal injury action : the plaintiff claimed he fell on some spilt yogurt, the store proposed to prove he was an alcoholic by showing purchases of wine and spirits. And there are other, more sinister ways in which this data could be used against you.

[B]

Privacy advocates talk about the idea of (3) "function creep" —

information systems that have been set up for one reason can end up being used for other purposes. This is one of the biggest concerns about the introduction of Radio Frequency Identification (RFID) tags.

RFID is a tracking system that uses a tiny, transmitter chip joined to an antenna. The chip can "talk" to scanning devices within a certain range. So, *at its most benign, it would operate like a barcode, sending information to cashier machines. It would help track goods from manufacturer to warehouse to checkout. It would alert retailers if goods had been shelved in the wrong place, or if something was being stolen. Once our household appliances (②) the technology, the benefits could be the stuff of science fiction : a frozen chicken that tells the oven how it needs to be cooked, a *fridge that tells you when your milk has gone sour.

[C]

But there are other, more worrying uses for the technology. Stores might "notice" that you were wearing expensive clothes, and (4)<u>surreptitiously</u> raise their prices. And potentially, RFID would allow a particular person's movements and habits to be tracked at every moment of the day.

In Britain, experiments with RFID have been partly funded by *the Home Office. Tesco has trialled the tags in packs of razors, while Marks and Spencer announced that it would trial the tags by embedding them into packaging. The British government has announced that it will experiment with implanting RFID tags in car license plates and there are plans for all cars in Britain to be fitted with tracking devices. Mobile phone companies are already offering a service whereby you can register a phone number and then track the user. And in London, users of the Oyster smart travelcard have their every journey monitored. Each smart-card has a unique number linked to the owner's name, and that information is recorded (③) the card is swiped past a ticket gate. Transport for London says it plans to retain the information for "a number of years."

[D]

Even then, though, we need to ask ourselves if $_{(5)}$<u>the minor benefits</u> we get from loyalty schemes and smart-cards are worth the risks of being spied on. Contact retailers to let them know you're concerned about privacy, and demand more information about what they're doing to secure it. Don't be tempted by the offers of ten cents off dishwashing liquid and extra points with your cornflakes, and get rid of your loyalty cards. Maybe it is *paranoia, and maybe a lot of this technology will be implemented $_{(6)}$<u>(we / matter / it / what / about / do / no)</u>, but that doesn't mean we should just stand by and let businesses snoop into our shopping baskets − and our lives.

[　E　]

(注)　to name but a few：ほんの少し例を挙げてみても
at its most benign：最も無難な用途として　　fridge = refrigerator
the Home Office：内務省　　paranoia：過度の恐怖や不安

(Jessica Williams, *50 Facts That Should Change the World 2.0*による。ただし，設問の都合で一部省略及び改変している。)

1　下線部(1)とはどのような状況か，本文に即して日本語で説明しなさい。

2　空欄(　①　)～(　③　)について，最もよくあてはまる語句を，それぞれア～エの中から一つずつ選び，記号で答えなさい。

(　①　)：ア　As far as　　イ　As good as　　ウ　As long as　　エ　As well as

(　②　)：ア　catch up with　　イ　put up with　　ウ　stand up with　　エ　stay up with

(　③　)：ア　unless　　イ　until　　ウ　every time　　エ　over time

3　下線部(2)を別の語で言い換えたとき，最も近い意味の語をア～エの中から一つ選び，記号で答えなさい。

ア　astonishing　　イ　bursting　　ウ　escalating　　エ　demanding

4　次の段落を本文中に入れるとしたら，[　A　]～[　E　]のどの位置にいれるのが最も適当か。一つ選び，記号で答えなさい。

Businesses assure us that these methods of collecting information are not really about monitoring individuals. But all the same, controls need to be put in place to ensure that people are able to opt out of schemes they don't like — and that there is some degree of protection of the information that's collected. The British human rights group Liberty notes that the regulation of the information shouldn't be left up to companies. Privacy legislation needs an urgent overhaul if our information is to be given proper protection.

5　下線部(3)とはどのようなことか。40字以内の日本語で説明しなさい。ただし，句読点も字数に含める。

6　下線部(4)を別の語で言い換えたとき，最も近い意味の語をア～エの中から一つ選び，記号で答えなさい。

ア　considerately　　イ　reluctantly　　ウ　secretly　　エ　bravely

7　下線部(5)の具体例を，本文中から見つけ出し，日本語で二つあげなさい。

8　下線部(6)の各語が，正しい語順となるように並べ替え，その英語を書きなさい。

(☆☆☆☆◎◎◎◎)

【中学校】

【1】次の英文を読んで，あとの問いに答えなさい。

Types of Tasks

In communicative testing, students are required to work on a certain number of tasks given to them. (1)In designing a communicative test, the first thing for the designer to do is to choose the types of tasks which will reflect the students' actual communication situations in their everyday lives. Unfortunately, there are no guidelines offered by Japanese educators and researchers on the selection of appropriate communicative tasks. Indeed, we have to look to research findings from overseas.

There is a consensus among researchers that two types of tasks should be imposed for beginners : (2)*transactional* tasks (activities to get services or exchange things) and (3)*interpersonal* tasks (activities for maintaining personal relationships). It is argued that by setting tasks of these two types, a balanced coverage of language functions is maintained, thus freeing students from the possibility of biased assessment (Brown and Yule, 1983, pp.ll－16 ; Nunan, 1989, pp.113－115 ; Nunan, 1991, p.6). By imposing transactional tasks, we can test a number of essential functions, such as [X], etc., while interpersonal tasks will test functions like [Y], etc..

*In this connection, a survey of the functions which appear in current English textbooks for Japanese junior and senior high school students should also be made, as this is a prerequisite for fair evaluation. It is unfair and discouraging to include functions students might not have encountered in their lessons. A glance at several of the main English textbooks for junior high schools reveals that students will actually encounter a considerable number of functions during their three years of schooling. A similar survey should also be done on textbooks for senior high schools in order to obtain general information about the coverage and *distribution of the functions available to the communicative test designer.

Degree of Task Difficulty

Tasks in communicative tests should match students' proficiency levels. Tasks that are too demanding might discourage students from communicating in the foreign language, while those that are much too easy can bore students and fail to give them the incentive to communicate. Five factors which condition the difficulty of tasks have been cited by Nunan (1991, pp.24－28 ; pp. 47－49) : (a) vocabulary, (b) sentence structure, (c) topic, (d) number of items and persons, (e) type of relationship.

A brief explanation of the last factor might be needed. A relationship can be classified into (4)three categories ; static, dynamic, or abstract. A static relationship is represented by, for example, "describing *diagrams or patterns." Among dynamic relationships are included "describing a car crash," "*recounting how a piece of equipment works," and "retelling a narrative based on a *cartoon strip." Abstract relationships include "expressing one's opinion concerning a specific topic," and "justifying a certain action."

When we actually come to design a communicative task, it is advisable to have a table or *matrix with the above factors in it. Using this table for reference, we can then adjust the level of difficulty of the task we are designing. By so doing, it is also possible for the designer to set fair and representative tasks.

Evaluation Techniques

Techniques that have so far been exploited for evaluation can be grouped into two categories :

(A) The examiner evaluates the student's performance based on grade / level descriptions made beforehand.

(B) The student works on the graded tasks. Tasks successfully completed automatically represent the grade to be assigned.

The drawback of technique (A) is that the grade given tends to be subjective, and accordingly unreliable. Technique (B) has a similar drawback in that the grading of tasks is apt to be subjective and arbitrary. Developing reliable techniques is an absolutely essential requisite for the promotion and improvement of communicative testing.

(注) In this connection： このことに関連して
distribution：分布，分類　diagram： 図形，グラフ
recount： 話をする　cartoon strip： コマ割り漫画
matrix： いくつかの数などを長方形の表に並べたもの
(Masamichi Tanaka, *A History of Engiish Language Testing in Japan* による。ただし，設問の都合で一部省略及び改変している。)

1 次のア～ウによって定義される語を，それぞれ一語ずつ本文中からそのままの形で抜き出しなさい。なお，(　　)内にはそれぞれの語の最初と最後の文字だけ示してある。(例：定義される語が

wonderfulの場合は，(w...l)のように示してある。)

ア　an opinion that all members of a group agree with ＝(　c...s　)

イ　completely necessary ; extremely important in a particular situation or for a particular activity ＝ (e...1)

ウ　to change something slightly to make it more suitable for a new set of conditions or to make it work better ＝ (a...t)

2　下線部(1)を日本語に直しなさい。

3　下線部(2)及び下線部(3)の二種類のタスクを設定することによって，どのようなことが期待できるか。本文に即して日本語で説明しなさい。

4　空欄[　X　]と[　Y　]に入る機能として<u>適当でないもの</u>を，それぞれア～エから一つだけ選び，記号で答えなさい。

[　X　]：ア　asking　　イ　praising　　ウ　reporting
　　　　エ　requesting

[　Y　]：ア　attracting attention　　イ　greeting
　　　　ウ　introducing oneself / others　　エ　summarizing

5　下線部(4)について，次の①から③に示されたタスクの例はどの区分にあてはまるか。それぞれのタスクの例にあてはまる区分を(ア)static，(イ)dynamic，(ウ)abstractから一つずつ選び，記号で答えなさい。ただし，同じ記号を二回以上使わないこと。

①　A group of students explain with moving pictures the exciting episodes they experienced during their school trip.

②　In an oral interview test with an ALT, each student is asked to argue the pros and cons about their school uniforms.

③　A pair of students receive some national flags and then explain the shapes and colors that constitute each flag.

6　本文の内容に即して，次の質問に英語で答えなさい。

(1)　Has the original guideline to select appropriate communicative tasks been offered by Japanese researchers?

(2)　According to the author, what is necessary for the promotion and improvement of communicative testing?

7　本文の内容に合うものを，次のア～オから二つ選び，記号で答えなさい。

ア　Researchers agree that transactional and interpersonal tasks are the most effective for intermediate English learners.

イ　Unlike junior high school textbooks, a survey on functions in senior high school textbooks has not been conducted yet.

ウ　The application of Nunan's five factors can control the level of the tasks we design and can set fair and representative tasks.

エ　Subjective and arbitrary evaluation techniques as shown in (A) and (B) could help teachers save time when grading students.

オ　Junior and senior high school teachers have designed communicative tasks based on their own past experiences.

(☆☆☆◎◎◎◎)

【2】次の1，2について，指示に従って答えなさい。

1　次の日本語を英語に直しなさい。

読書の目的は，そのまま信じ込むためではなく，議論するためでもない。それは，あなたの人生を実りあるものにするためである。

2　小学校外国語活動の新設を受け，中学校第1学年の「聞くこと」「話すこと」の指導にあたってどのような点に配慮すべきだと思いますか。あなたの考えを，100語程度の英語で書きなさい。ただし，語数はカンマやピリオド等の句読点，疑問符や引用符等の符号は含まないものとする。なお，解答の総語数を記入すること。

(☆☆☆☆◎◎◎)

【高等学校】

【1】次の英文を読んで，あとの問いに答えなさい。

(1) <u>Classroom data from a number of studies offer support for the view that form-focused instruction and corrective feedback provided within the context</u>

<u>of communicative and content-based programmes are more effective in promoting second language learning than programmes that are limited to a virtually exclusive emphasis on comprehension, fluency, or accuracy alone</u>. Thus, we would argue that second language teachers can (and should) provide guided, form-focused instruction and corrective feedback in certain circumstances. For example, teachers should not hesitate to correct persistent errors that learners seem not to notice without focused attention. Teachers should also be especially aware of errors that the majority of learners in a class are making when they share the same first language background. They should not hesitate to point out how a particular structure in a learner's first language differs from the target language. Teachers might also try to become more aware of (①) that are just beginning to emerge in the second language development of their students and provide some guided instruction in the use of these forms. It can also be useful to encourage learners to take part in the process by creating activities that draw their attention to the forms they use in communicative activities, by developing contexts in which they can provide each other with feedback, and by encouraging them to ask questions about language.

Decisions about when and how to provide form focus must take into account differences in (②),of course. [X], say, trained linguists learning a fourth or fifth language, young children beginning their schooling in a second language environment, both younger and older immigrants who cannot read and write their own language, and adolescents studying a foreign language for a few hours a week at school.

Many teachers are aware of the need to balance form-focus and meaning-focus, and they may feel that recommendations based on research simply confirm their current classroom practice. Although this may be true to some extent, it is (③) the case that all teachers have a clear sense of how best to accomplish their goal. It is not always easy to step back from familiar practices and say, ‘I wonder if this is really the most effective way to go about this?' Furthermore, it can be difficult to try out classroom practices that go against the prevailing trends in their educational contexts. Many teachers still work in environments where there is (2) an emphasis on accuracy that virtually excludes spontaneous language use in the classroom. At the same time, the introduction of communicative language teaching methods has sometimes resulted in (3) a complete rejection of attention to form and error-correction in second language teaching. But it is not necessary to choose between form-based and meaning-based instruction. Rather, the challenge is to find the best balance of these two orientations.

Classroom-based research on second language learning and teaching has given us (④) answers to many questions. Through continuing research and experience, researchers and teachers will fill in more details, always recognizing that no single answer will be adequate for all learning environments. Among the questions we will continue to ask are these : How can classroom instruction provide the right balance of meaning-based and form-focused instruction? Which (①) will respond best to form-focused instruction, and which will be acquired without explicit focus if learners have adequate access to the language? Which learners will respond well to *metalinguistic information and which will require some other way of focusing attention on language form? When is it best to draw learners' attention to form — before, after, or during communicative practice? How should corrective feedback be offered and when should learners be allowed to focus their attention on the content of their utterances? Continued classroom-centered research, including the action research by teachers in their own classrooms, will provide further insights into these and other important issues in second language teaching and learning.

(注) metalinguistic：対象言語を説明するための言語や記号体系に関する

(Patsy M. Lightbown and Nina Spada, *How Languages Are Learned*による。ただし，設問の都合で一部改変している。)

1　次のア～ウによって定義される語を，それぞれ一語ずつ本文中からそのままの形で抜き出しなさい。なお，(　　)にはそれぞれの最初の文字が，[　　]にはその語が含まれる段落の番号が示されている。

ア　to start to exist ; to appear or become known ＝ (　e...　)[　1　]

イ　a new or difficult task that tests somebody's ability and skill ＝ (　c...　)[　3　]

ウ　said, done or shown in an open or direct way, so that you have no doubt about what is happening ＝ (　e...　)[　4　]

2　下線部(1)を日本語に直しなさい。

3　空欄(　①　)～(　④　)に入る最も適当な語句を，それぞれ次の語句群から一つずつ選び，記号で答えなさい。ただし，同じ記号を二回以上使わないこと。

語句群：ア　complete　　イ　partial
ウ　learner characteristics　　エ　teacher characteristics
オ　language features　　カ　language barriers
キ　hardly　　ク　often

4　空欄[　X　]に入る最も適当な表現を，次のア～エから一つ選び，記号で答えなさい。

ア　Quite different approaches would be confusing for

イ　Quite different approaches would be appropriate for

ウ　Quite similar approaches would be effective for

エ　Quite similar approaches would be instructive for

5　下線部(2)及び下線部(3)の特徴をもつ活動例を考え，それぞれ日本語で簡潔に書きなさい。

6　本文の内容に即して，次の質問に英語で答えなさい。

(1)　Should second language teachers avoid correcting persistent errors that escape from the learners' knowledge?

(2)　According to the author, what may many teachers feel simply confirms their current classroom practice?

7　本文の内容に合うものを，次のア～オから二つ選び，記号で答えなさい。

ア　Learners ignore the structural differences between their first language and the target language on purpose.

イ　It is useful to draw learners' attention to the forms whether or not they are used in communicative activities.

ウ　Teachers will ask how classroom instruction can provide the right balance between meaning-focus and form-focus.

エ　Research has revealed the best time to draw learners' attention to form － before, after, or during communicative practice.

オ　Action research in classrooms potentially provides understanding about important issues in second language studies.

(☆☆☆☆◎◎◎◎◎)

【2】次の1，2について，指示に従って答えなさい。

1　次の日本語を英語に直しなさい。

読書の目的は，そのまま信じ込むためではなく，議論するためでもない。それは，あなたの人生を実りあるものにするためである。

2　英語の授業において，コミュニケーション能力の育成に向け，ペアや小集団での学習活動を取り入れることにより期待される効果とその際の留意点について，あなたの考えを100語程度の英語で書きなさい。ただし，語数はカンマやピリオド等の句読点，疑問符や引用符等の符号は含まないものとする。なお，解答の総語数を記入すること。

(☆☆☆☆◎◎◎◎◎)

解答・解説

【中高共通】

【1】1　No. 1　(a)　　No.2　(b)　　2　No.1　(c)　　No.2　(a)
No.3　(b)　　3　No.1　(a)　　No.2　(d)　　No.3　(c)
4　No.1　Yes, but this time (I have been trying a healthier way).
No.2　I asked Kate to mail it to him. If he doesn't have the document, (we will send it again to his office right away).

〈解説〉放送される内容を聞いて，選択肢の中から一番適切だと思われる解答を選ぶ問題。放送が繰り返されるかどうかをしっかりと確認した上で，集中してリスニングに臨みたい。また，選択問題以外にもディクテーションや放送内容に関する質問に答える問題などが出題される可能性があるので，英語の発音の特徴(同化，脱落など)に日ごろから慣れ親しみ，また，正字法も確認しておきたい。

【2】1　イ　　2　ア　　3　イ　　4　イ　　5　エ　　6　ア　　7　ウ
8　ウ　　9　イ　　10　ウ　　11　エ　　12　ア　　13　エ　　14　ア
15　エ

〈解説〉1　タクシーの「運賃」にあたる選択肢を選べばよい。選択肢にはないが，料金にまつわる紛らわしい単語(tuition，fee，chargeなど)との語用の違いを確認しておきたい。　2　give a lectureで「講義をする」という意味になる。このように，日本語にすると「～する」という訳があてられるイディオムにはmake a speech「スピーチをする」などがある。動詞の主要な意味にとらわれすぎないことがポイント。
3　bring＋物＋to＋人で「人に物を持っていく」という意味になる。これと似た表現に，take＋人＋to＋場所「人を場所に連れていく」があるので，一緒に覚えておこう。　4　仕事をいつも5時前に終わらせる，マイクの性質を表す形容詞を選べばよい。efficientは物だけでなく人も修飾し，「有能な，敏腕な」という意味を持つ。よって，イが正解となる。それ以外の解答は，意味が合わない。　5　問題文の補語innovativeの前にbothがついていることから，andの後ろには前述の形容詞と同じ，比較的良い意味の形容詞が入ることが予想される。この条件に合う選択肢はエ「実行可能な」である。アとウはネガティブな意味であるから，除外される。イは，比較的良い意味だが文意に合わない。　6「子供っぽい」という意味の形容詞を選べばよい。よって，アが正解となる。他の選択肢の意味は，それぞれ，イ「子供がいない」，ウ「子供時代」，エ「子供にとって安全な」という意味である。
7　話し手が，トムの不愉快な発言を聞いて抱いた感情を，形容詞で表現している文である。正解はウ「気恥ずかしい，きまりが悪い」である。アとイは文意に合わないのですぐ除外できるが，エは意味が似ているので間違えやすい。現在分詞の主語は物，過去分詞の主語は人，と覚えておくとよいであろう。　8　非制限用法の関係代名詞whichと，原因・結果を表す動詞のどちらを選択するかがポイントとなる。先行詞の直後にカンマがついていることから，関係代名詞のwhich(非制限用法)が使われる。また，先行詞「汚染物質」は「深刻な環境問題」を「引き起こす」ものなので，動詞causeが選択される。よって，ウが正解となる。　9　動詞appreciateが「感謝する」という意味を持つのは，他動詞の働きをするときである。よって，目的語が必要となる。この条件を満たすのは，イのみである。　10　主節の動詞は現在形であるが，補部では過去の意味合いを持つ文である。よって，動名詞を持つウまたはエが正解となる。しかし，エは現在進行形の構造をとっており，それが存在there＋be動詞の構造と矛盾する。よって，正解はウとなる。　11　助動詞had betterに続く動詞は，原形になるはずである。アとエはともに動詞の原形を含んでいるが，アは比較接続詞のthanしか持たないので，誤りとなる。正解は，副詞ratherとthanが両方含まれるエである。　12　insistは自動詞としても他動詞としても使われるが，自動詞のときはon，他動詞のときはthat節をとることが多い(to＋人が入る場合もある)。よって，正解となり得るのはアしかない。また，theyとgoの間のshouldは省略されている。　13　Aの問いかけに対する

Bの返答から判断すると，Bは心理学の授業に対して好感を持っていると考えられる。好意的な感想を述べているのは，エ「最高だよ」である。他の選択肢の意味は，それぞれ，ア「私も同じ境遇にいます」，イ「ひどく腹をたてるでしょう」，ウ「まさにその通り！」である。
14　頻度の高い単語を使用したイディオムの意味を問う問題である。意味を推測しにくいので，日ごろから注意して学習しておきたい。意味は，それぞれ，ア「手に入れる，立ち寄る」，イ「～を攻撃する，罰する」，ウ「倒れる」，エ「遅れをとる」である。よって，一番文意に合うのはアである。　15　イディオムの問題である。Bの発言から，Bがこれ以上課題を続けるのが困難な状況にあることが読み取れる。よって，課題を「終わりにする，切り上げる」という意味になるエが正解となる。なお，問題文のイディオムhit the sackは「床に就く」という意味である。

【3】1　店は客からひいきにしてもらえることを約束され，客も買い物をすることによって店から見返りが得られるような，双方が恩恵を受けられる状況。　2　①　エ　　②　ア　　③　ウ　　3　ア
4　D　　5　ある目的で作られた情報システムが，結果的に他の目的に流用される可能性があること。(40字以内)　　6　ウ　　7　具体例1　食器用液体洗剤が10セント安く買えること。　具体例2　コーンフレークを買うとボーナス・ポイントが付くこと。　8　Maybe it is paranoia, and maybe a lot of this technology will be implemented (no matter what we do about it), …
〈解説〉1　直前の文の内容をまとめるとよい。ポイントは，店側も客側も利益を得る，ということが書かれているかどうかである。
2　①　tryingで始まる従属節は，後続する主節の主語loyalty programsが持つ特徴の1つである。主節の補語では別の特徴が述べられていることから，選択肢エ「Bだけでなく Aも」が一番適切な解答となる。それ以外の解答は，文意に合わない。　②　後続する文を解釈することが，正解への近道。科学技術が進展すれば，サイエンス・フィクショ

ン上の出来事が現実のものとなる，という文脈である。家庭用品が科学技術に「追い付けば」よいのだから，正解はアとなる。また，他の選択肢はそれぞれ，イ「我慢する」，ウ「付き添い役をする」という意味。　③　空欄に続く文の場面を思い浮かべることが大切である。カードが改札口を通る「度に毎回」，情報が記録されるのである。したがって，答えはウ。他の選択肢は，文意に合わないため，正しくない。　3　後続する文がヒントとなる。英国では，政府が持つ情報よりポイントカードを通して蓄積される情報の方がより整理されたものであると述べており，それは「驚くべきこと」であると判断できる。よって，最も近い意味の語はア「驚くべき，びっくりするような」となる。　4　1つのパラグラフを，本文中の適切な位置に挿入する問題。1回目の読みから，各選択肢の前後で繋がりに不自然な箇所がないかどうかを確かめておきたい。正解の空欄Dに至るまでに，ポイントカードや携帯電話の番号などによって得られた顧客情報が，各会社によって保存・利用されていることが説明されている。挿入文では，そういった情報流出問題に繋がるようなサービスに対して，何らかの規制がされるべきである，と述べられている。さらに，空欄Dの次の段落では，個人情報保護の観点からのまとめが述べられているので，Dが一番ふさわしい。　5　後続する文をまとめればよい。creepという動詞を用いることによって，情報システムのもともとの目的が少しずつ違う目的に逸れていく様子を表現している。　6　段落のはじめに，科学技術の利用においてより心配なことがあると述べている。店側が「秘かに」価格を上げれば，それは科学技術の悪用であり，我々の心配を誘うと言える。よって，正解はウ。なお，surreptitiouslyという単語の意味を知っていれば，文脈に頼ることなく正解を選ぶことが出来るので，日頃から低頻出語句にも強くなっておきたい。　7　同段落の3行目，Don'tから始まる部分をまとめればよい。訳して解答欄に書くときは，「～すること」という形にする。　8　譲歩を表すno matter whatの存在に気づけば，あとは残った単語を主語・動詞の順番に並べ替えればよい。ここでのitは，直前の内容「この種の科学技術が実行に移されること」を指す。

【中学校】

【1】1　ア　consensus　イ　essential　ウ　adjust　2　コミュニカティブなテストを設計するとき，先ず設計者がするべきことは，日常生活における生徒たちの実際のコミュニケーション場面を映し出すようなタスクを選ぶことだ。　3　言語機能がバランス良く継続的に扱われ，そのことによって生徒が偏った評価を受けずにすむこと。

4　X　イ　Y　エ　5　①　イ　②　ウ　③　ア

6　(1)　No, it hasn't.　(2)　Developing reliable techniques is (necessary for the promotion and improvement of communicative testing).

7　イ，ウ(順不同)

〈解説〉1　ア「グループのメンバー全員が同意する意見」と一致する単語は，本文の第2段落のはじめにも出てくる「consensus」である。イ「非常に必要であること，特定の状況または特定の活動において非常に重要であること」と一致するのは，本文第2段落の下から2行目に出てくる「essential」である。　ウ「新しい一連の状況によりふさわしいように，またはよりよい機能のために，何かをわずかに変えること」という意味に合う単語は，本文の第6段落に出てくるadjustである。　2　下線部の内容を和訳する問題。若干長めの文なので，主部と述部の関係をしっかりおさえておこう。the firstからisの手前までが主部で，to以下が補部となる。　3　第2段落の5行目以降の文をまとめればよい。thus以降は「言語機能がバランス良く継続的に扱われる」ことの結果である。　4　X　この空欄には，transactional tasksの機能が入る。「取引」に必要な要素は，アの「尋ねること」やウの「報告すること」，エの「要求すること」などであり，イの「称賛すること」は対象外である。　Y　この空欄には，interpersonal tasksの機能が入る。「人間関係」にまつわる機能には，アの「注意を引き付けること」やイの「挨拶すること」，ウの「紹介すること」などがある。エの「要約すること」は，人間関係において必須の機能とは言い難い。　5　①「修学旅行中に経験した，面白いエピソードを動く写真と一緒に説明する」タスクは，説明の対象が動的な性質を持っている。したがって，(イ)dynamicに分類される。　②「制服を着ることに賛成か反対かを尋ねられる」タスクは，説明の対象が抽象的なため，(ウ)abstractに分類される。　③「国旗の形や色を説明する」タスクは，説明の対象が静的な性質を持っている。よって，(ア)staticに分類される。

6 (1) 第1段落に，「残念ながら，適切なコミュニカティブ・タスクの選別に関するガイドラインは，日本人教育者や研究者によって提供されていない」とあり，さらに「海外の研究結果に注目しなければならない」とあるので，答えはNoとなる。　(2) 本文の最終段落，最後の文に注目すれば，問題文と一致する箇所が見つかる。問題文では「何が必要か」と問われているので，Developing reliable techniques is (necessary …)とまとめるとよい。　7 選択肢の中から，本文の内容に合うものを選ぶ問題である。第3段落の5行目以降に英語の教科書の調査が行われたとあるが，中学校向けのものだけで，高等学校向けのものに関してはこれからなされるべきであると説明している。よって，選択肢イは正解となる。また，第4段落と第6段落の記述を見るとNunan(1991)からの引用で，5つの要素がタスクの難易度を調整するとある。さらに，それらの要素を利用することにより，公平かつ代表的なタスクを設定することが可能であると説明している。したがって，ウも正解となる。他の選択肢が不適切なのは，以下の理由による。

ア：第2段落のはじめに「2つのタスクは初心者に課されるべきである」とあり，問題文と矛盾する。エ：「主観的・恣意的な評価技術は，生徒の成績をつける際に教師の時間の節約となる」わけではない。よって，エは不正解。オ：問題文に関する記述は，本文では述べられていない。したがって，オも不正解である。

【2】1 (例) The purpose of reading is neither to blindly believe nor to argue about what you have read. Instead, it is to make your life fruitful.

2 (例) Junior high school English teachers should grasp the kinds of

language activities that their first-year students have experienced in elementary school. Then, teachers should take into account the following key points: First, it is important that students compare the sounds of such spoken English as "How are you?" with the way it looks when expressed in written English. Second, students should know the appropriate contexts and contents for listening and speaking; for example, the introductions of students' everyday lives and of their favorite things. Third, during lessons, teachers should pay more attention to students' linguistic accuracy than in elementary school. (総語数：100語)

〈解説〉1　和文英作問題。問題文自体が翻訳調なので，英語に直しやすい印象を受けるのではないだろうか。作文のポイントとして，S is to 不定詞という構造を使うことやneither A nor B という表現のnorに気をつけることが挙げられる。副詞(blindly)をtoと動詞(believe)の間にはさむ表現法は現在広く認められているが，フォーマルなライティングでは避けるべきと考える人もいる。　2　小学校英語活動からの接続を受けて，中学校の英語科で留意すべきことを英語で記述する問題。模範解答では小学校での活動内容を把握することが前提として書かれており，その上で，①音声と文字の対比，②文脈・内容を意識したリスニング活動，③正確さへの配慮の3点を挙げている。まず，小学校での活動内容を把握することはとても重要である。活動内容について正確かつ詳細な情報を得るためには，小学校との情報共有が急務になってくるであろう。複数の小学校を卒業した児童が入学する場合には，出身小学校によって，生徒の力に差が存在する可能性もあるので，授業内容を組み立てるときに注意が必要となる。例示された3点は生徒たちの戸惑いを減らすために重要である。①については「読むこと」とも大きく関連している。音声のみで提示されていた言語を文字として見たときには，ローマ字つづりとの違いから，音声と文字を結びつけることに困難が生じると予想される。活動から教科への変化によって今まで英語に親しんでいた生徒が，苦手意識をもってしまわないように特段の配慮が必要であることを理解しておきたい。

【高等学校】

【1】1　ア　emerge　イ　challenge　ウ　explicit　2　教室で得られたデータによって，コミュニカティブで内容中心のプログラム内で与えられる，形式重視の指導や修正フィードバックの方が，力点のほとんどが知識理解，流暢さ，あるいは正確さだけに限定されるプログラムよりも，第二言語学習をより効果的に促進するという考え方が，多くの研究で立証されている。　3　①　オ　②　ウ　③　キ　④　イ　4　イ　5　下線部(2)　(例)　(言語表現の場面を欠き，言語活動の正確さのみをねらい,）教師に続いて機械的な発話を繰り返す活動。　下線部(3)　(例)　(言語形式や誤りを修正することを全く意識せず，)ペアで週末の出来事について語り合うだけの活動。

6　(1)　No, they shouldn't.　(2)　They may feel that recommendations based on research do.　7　ウ・オ(順不同)

〈解説〉1　ア　to start to existから「現われる」の意味を想起したい。イ　a new or difficult taskthat tests sb's ability and skillから「手ごたえのある仕事，問題」の意味を想起し，それを手がかりにchallengeにたどりつきたい。普通は「挑戦」を想起するが，基本語についてはこのような別の意味もおさえておきたい。　ウ　said, done or shown in an open or direct way, so that you do not doubt what is happeningの，特にin an open or directwayから，「明示的」explicitを導き出したい。これは英語の論文などでもよく目にする単語で，反意語のimplicitも合わせて覚えておきたい。また，常日頃から英英辞典で基本的な単語の表現法を確認しておくことも大切である。　2　CLT(Communicative Language Teaching)の指導法として注目されているFocus on Formに基づいた指導法についてのテクストである。普段から様々な英語教授法についてアンテナを高くし，従来の伝統的な教授法との違いを整理し明らかにしておくと，イメージしやすい。「主語と動詞を変えない」「分からない語は前後から推測する」などのポイントを考慮し，自然な日本語訳にしたい。　3　それぞれ正解とそれに対応する錯乱肢があるので，それも参考にしながら話の流れに沿うものを選択する。　4　空欄の後では，様々な立場の学習者のことが述べられているので，ウとエは冒頭のsimilarが不適格。また，違ったアプローチがよいという文脈なので，アはconfusingが不可。　5　(2)は言語使用が全くない状況，(3)は逆に文型や文法の指導が全くない状況を述べているので，その両極を強調した活動について考える。　6　内容を覚えていない場合には，本文中から同じ表現を見つける。(1)は本文5行目にpersistent errorがあり，(2)は最後の段落と同じ内容である。　7　ア　第1段落7行目にThey should not hesitate to point out「指摘すべきだ」とはあるが，ignore「無視している」とはない。よって不正解。　イ　第1段落11行目に，～ they use in communicative activities,「コミュニケーション活動で使用する際に」と限定しているが，選択文はwhether or not they are used in communicative activities.「コミュニケーション活動で使用してもしなくても」とあるので不正解。　ウ　第4段落3～4行目に同じ意味内容を表す英文があるので正解。　エ　選択文は「formに注目させる最もよい時期はコミュニカティブ活動のプラクティス前・後・最中である」と断言しているが，第4段落7行目の「注目させる時期はいつが最もよいか」という問いには，同段落でこれから解明される旨が述べられているので不正解。　オ　第4段落最後の文が同じ意味内容を表しているので正解。

【2】1　(例) The purpose of reading is neither to blindly believe nor to argue about what you have read. Instead, it is to make your life fruitful.

2　(例) Students will benefit from pair work and small-group activities. The relatively small size of pairs and groups enables students to receive more specific and collaborative instructions than the general instructions for the whole class. Group work also allows teachers to pay careful attention towards their students' individual differences in competence and aptitude. In order to make the most of these benefits, teachers should practice the following two points: First, teachers should create genuinely communicative situations which students actually encounter in their daily experiences. Second, teachers should provide their students with as many opportunities to use English as possible in class. (総語数：100語)

〈解説〉1 和文英訳問題である。「AでもなければBでもない」は「neither A nor B」,「そのまま信じ込む」は「blindly believe」,「実りの多い」は「fruitful」で表現すれば良い。believeとargue aboutの目的語となるものを補って書くこと。 2 解答例での効果と留意点は以下の通り。[効果]：学習者がより具体的で協同的な指導を受けられる。教員が生徒個々の能力と適性に応じて指導できる。[留意点]：学習者が実際の生活場面で遭遇しそうな言語活動を設定する。教員は学習者が英語を使用する機会をできる限り多く与える。100語程度(7～8行)の制限があるので，普段からテーマに沿った構成を考えてエッセイを書く練習をしておくことが大切である。

●書籍内容の訂正等について

弊社では教員採用試験対策シリーズ（参考書，過去問，全国まるごと過去問題集），公務員試験対策シリーズ，公立幼稚園・保育士試験対策シリーズ，会社別就職試験対策シリーズについて，正誤表をホームページ（https://www.kyodo-s.jp）に掲載いたします。内容に訂正等，疑問点がございましたら，まずホームページをご確認ください。もし，正誤表に掲載されていない訂正等，疑問点がございましたら，下記項目をご記入の上，以下の送付先までお送りいただくようお願いいたします。

① **書籍名，都道府県（学校）名，年度**
（例：教員採用試験過去問シリーズ　小学校教諭 過去問　2025年度版）
② **ページ数**（書籍に記載されているページ数をご記入ください。）
③ **訂正等，疑問点**（内容は具体的にご記入ください。）
（例：問題文では“ア～オの中から選べ”とあるが，選択肢はエまでしかない）

〔ご注意〕
○ 電話での質問や相談等につきましては，受付けておりません。ご注意ください。
○ 正誤表の更新は適宜行います。
○ いただいた疑問点につきましては，当社編集制作部で検討の上，正誤表への反映を決定させていただきます（個別回答は，原則行いませんのであしからずご了承ください）。

●情報提供のお願い

協同教育研究会では，これから教員採用試験を受験される方々に，より正確な問題を，より多くご提供できるよう情報の収集を行っております。つきましては，教員採用試験に関する次の項目の情報を，以下の送付先までお送りいただけますと幸いでございます。お送りいただきました方には謝礼を差し上げます。
（情報量があまりに少ない場合は，謝礼をご用意できかねる場合があります）。
◆あなたの受験された面接試験，論作文試験の実施方法や質問内容
◆教員採用試験の受験体験記

送付先
○電子メール：edit@kyodo-s.jp
○FAX：03-3233-1233（協同出版株式会社　編集制作部 行）
○郵送：〒101-0054　東京都千代田区神田錦町2-5
協同出版株式会社　編集制作部 行
○HP：https://kyodo-s.jp/provision（右記のQRコードからもアクセスできます）

※謝礼をお送りする関係から，いずれの方法でお送りいただく際にも，「お名前」「ご住所」は，必ず明記いただきますよう，よろしくお願い申し上げます。

教員採用試験「過去問」シリーズ

山形県の
英語科 過去問

編　集	© 協同教育研究会
発　行	令和6年1月25日
発行者	小貫　輝雄
発行所	協同出版株式会社
	〒101-0054　東京都千代田区神田錦町2 - 5
	電話　03－3295－1341
	振替　東京00190－4－94061
印刷所	協同出版・POD工場

落丁・乱丁はお取り替えいたします。